DATE			

ROBERTSONIAN ECONOMICS

ROBERTSONIAN ECONOMICS

An Examination of the Work of Sir D. H. Robertson on Industrial Fluctuation

John R. Presley

HM

HOLMES AND MEIER PUBLISHERS, INC.
New York

First published in the United States of America 1979 by
HOLMES & MEIER PUBLISHERS, INC.
30 Irving Place, New York, N.Y. 10003

Library of Congress Cataloging in Publication Data

Presley, John R
    Robertsonian economics.

        Bibliography: p.
        Includes index.
        1. Business cycles. 2. Robertson, Dennis Holme,
Sir, 1890-1963. I. Title.
HB3711.P79   338.5'42   78-25958

ISBN 0-8419-0471-5

Printed in Great Britain

Especially for Barbara, but also for Catherine and Joanne

Contents

Preface

I have such a vast number of acknowledgements to make that I hardly know where to begin. This study has taken five years to complete and has involved my being in contact with a wide variety of economists, not only over the length and breadth of the United Kingdom, but on both sides of the Atlantic.

My greatest debt is to Professor S. R. Dennison, who has allowed me access to the private papers and correspondence of Sir Dennis Holme Robertson, and has guided and advised me throughout this period. I have enjoyed immensely my visits to Hull University and am very thankful for the energy he has devoted to my work during a period when his time has been a very precious commodity.

The initial encouragement to undertake this work came from three people in particular — Professor R. D. C. Black, Professor D. P. O'Brien and Professor D. Swann. I am very grateful to them. Professor D. P. O'Brien has continued to provide copious and constructive comments upon my drafts throughout. Professor D. Swann has remained my Head of Department and has succeeded in giving me all the assistance possible at Loughborough University. I also wish to thank Dr. T. Weyman-Jones of Loughborough University for his valuable help in giving me a different perspective of certain parts of the work, M. Danes, a fellow student of 'Robertsonian Economics' for freely expressing his views and providing much assistance and Professor E. G. Davis of Carleton University for giving me an insight into R. G. Hawtrey's work.

My gratitude goes to all those who have talked and corresponded with me on this project, in particular to A. Bevan, Professor A. W. Coats, P. Coffey, A. Dick, Professor M. Friedman, Sir J. R. Hicks, Professor D. Patinkin, Lord Robbins, S. Shenoy, Professor O. Steinger, Dr. E. Owen Smith, Professor B. Tew, Professor T. Wilson, and Professor J. N. Wolfe. Many people have allowed me to utilise and to quote from correspondence. In this respect I am grateful to Sir J. R. Hicks, Professor D. Patinkin, Professor T. Wilson and Sir Geoffrey Keynes.

Extracts from this book were presented at seminars in various places. I particularly benefitted from seminars given at the History of Economic Thought Conference at Durham University in 1975, at the Department of Economics, Lancaster University in March 1977, and from a staff seminar at Loughborough University in March 1977. My thanks go to all the members of these seminars. My undergraduate days were spent at Lancaster University; I was put through my paces by the late Professor P. W. S. Andrews, Professor A. Macbean, J. Taylor, J. Rhodes, D. Pearce, A. Airth and G. McGregor-Reid. I will always remain in their debt for the encouragement they gave me, and the enthusiasm they showed economics. I could not have wished for a better baptism to the subject.

I have been fortunate to receive financial assistance during my study of Robertson's work. The Wincott Foundation put me on my feet, and the Social Science Research Council kept me there over the last two years. This enabled me to gain access to a large volume of research material which I would otherwise have been unable to obtain. It also meant that I could travel around the United Kingdom in search of information. Without this help the study would have been substantially weakened, and I therefore thank my benefactors for their generosity.

A study of this kind invariably puts many strains upon library staff. It never ceases to amaze me how librarians can remain so patient when faced with a borrower who cannot remember, or does not have, the full reference for a book or an article. I have received great patience and help from a number of libraries; in particular I wish to thank the library staffs of Loughborough University, the Marshall Library and King's College Library, Cambridge, Newcastle University, Hull University, Sheffield University and the London School of Economics. My special thanks goes to Nottingham University Library which was perhaps burdened more than most by my enquiries. The Department of Economics at Nottingham University also put up with my presence during my period of sabbatical from Loughborough University in 1976. I am very grateful to both Professor J. R. Parkinson and Professor B. Tew for allowing me all the facilities of their department during my stay with them and for making me so welcome.

This work has yielded much satisfaction but its preparation has taken a great amount of time, effort and energy. The sacrifices that have been made, however, are not exclusively the author's alone. My wife and two daughters have suffered my absence of body and mind during the working out of 'Robertsonian Economics'. I am therefore deeply grateful to them — to Barbara for being so understanding and supportive, especially during periods of mental agony (!) — to Joanne and Catherine for the happiness they offer to all around them.

Finally I wish to thank Mrs. J. Tuson who has struggled with my illegible handwriting over the years and helped to make this book presentable. My thanks also go to Mr. J. Kelly, currently an undergraduate at Loughborough University, who has assisted me in the preparation of footnotes.

The errors which still persist are my responsibility alone. I hope they are few!

John R. Presley, 1977

Introduction

This book is not intended as a full biography of Sir Dennis
Holme Robertson.[1] It is an examination of the most important
aspect of his work as an economist — his theory of industrial
fluctuation; but before this examination is undertaken it is necessary
to survey the background against which Robertson put forward
his views on economics. This task can only be accomplished by
providing a brief biography.

SIR DENNIS HOLME ROBERTSON — IN AND OUT
OF CAMBRIDGE

It is now 62 years since Robertson's first book was published.[2]
This contained the skeleton of his theory of industrial fluctuation,
a theory which he held throughout his lifetime, and which was
suitably covered with flesh in the multitude of publications which
followed to his death in 1963.

He was born in 1890, the youngest of six children and the
son of the Headmaster of Haileybury School. The Robertsons
originated from Scotland and had for generations been principally
clergymen or schoolmasters. In the year Dennis Robertson was
born, his father resigned from his post at Haileybury and became
a country parson at Whittlesford in Cambridgeshire. In many
ways Dennis Robertson benefitted from this move, for his father
was able to devote himself to his childrens' education. In 1902,

already well educated in the classics, he went to Eton; here he excelled, making many friends and eventually becoming captain of the school.[3]

From Eton he gained a classical scholarship to Cambridge in 1908. He continued to prosper both academically and socially, gaining a I-i in the first part of the classical tripos in 1910 whilst enjoying himself thoroughly in Cambridge. He took an active part in amateur dramatics and continued to develop his musical interest.[4] He won, for three successive years, the Chancellor's Prize for English Verse.

Fortunately for the economics profession he was not to stay a classical scholar. In 1910 he turned to the economics tripos gaining a first in Part II of the tripos in 1912; this was achieved despite his many and varied non-academic interests in Cambridge, amongst which were numbered his activities as President of both the Liberal Society and the Union.

Cambridge economics and Marshallian economics were synonymous at that time. Although Robertson was not taught by A. Marshall, who had retired in 1908, the *Principles of Economics* remained the recommended textbook. A. C. Pigou and J. M. Keynes, both former pupils of Marshall, continued to uphold the Marshallian tradition during Robertson's undergraduate studies. It was J. M. Keynes who became Robertson's Director of Studies; this was the beginning of a very long and productive partnership which flourished especially in the 1920s, but which was to suffer as a result of the 'Keynesian Revolution' in the late 1930s.[5]

After graduation Robertson remained as a research student in Cambridge. In 1914 his research thesis won for him a Trinity Fellowship (in the previous year the thesis had gained the Cobden Prize); it also became his first book in 1915. But the war interrupted his academic work; he joined the army and after service in England he was posted to Egypt and Palestine.[6] He did not return to the Trinity Fellowship until 1919.

This heralded the beginning of his most productive period as a monetary economist. His most widely read book, *Money*, was published in 1922 as a Cambridge Economic Handbook. This was a textbook for undergraduates, but it quickly established Robertson's reputation as a monetary expert. It remained in the forefront as a textbook on monetary theory until the 1950s and appeared in a new edition as late as 1948. M. Friedman has seen fit to remark that it: 'is a masterpiece of exposition as well as of content'.[7] But *Money* was only the first of a number of writings in the inter-war period which attempted to analyse the role of monetary factors in the trade cycle. *A Study of Industrial Fluctuation* (hereafter referred to as the *Study*) had presented a *real* theory of industrial fluctuation. It was a purpose of later writings to examine the behaviour of money, the rate of interest, and saving and investment in the cycle, and from this to establish the most appropriate types of counter-cyclical policies.

The collaboration between Keynes and Robertson in the 1920s resulted in several major works, though none were published under joint authorship. These works included not only *Money*, but also the *Tract on Monetary Reform*,[8] *Banking Policy and the Price Level* (hereafter referred to as *Banking*) and the *Treatise on Money*.[9] The 1930s witnessed less of a combined effort. Each went their separate ways, Robertson developing the theory of fluctuation he had expounded in 1915, whilst Keynes worked on *The General Theory of Employment, Interest and Money* (hereafter referred to as the *General Theory*). After 1936 they became involved in a debate over the validity of Keynes' theory. This partnership was significant in the development of both Robertsonian and Keynesian economics; for this reason a later chapter explores their relationship in the inter-war period in more detail.[10]

Robertson also continued to be actively interested in liberal policy, again to some extent working alongside J. M. Keynes. He had been brought up in a Cambridge which had little respect for state control, but which did tolerate some interference with the free enterprise economy.[11] He was not a socialist; he, for example, regarded Cole's suggestion for the establishment of co-operatives as belonging to the realm of 'Cloud-Cuckoo Land'.[12] Yet at the same time he was not a staunch defender of capitalism. In fact in Mr. Ernest Benn's fourfold classification of economists according to their degree of support for capitalism, Robertson remarked, 'I knew that I should come out, if not in the lowest class yet not very far away'.[13] Robertson never had serious political ambitions; his involvement went as far as contributing to Liberal Party Summer Schools, and to policy documents, but no further.

With the exception of eight months spent travelling in the Far East in 1926–7, and four months spent in India (1933–4) working on a statistical enquiry with A. L. Bowley, Robertson remained in Cambridge until 1938. Then he was invited to become a member of the Appointment Board for the Chair in Banking at the London

School of Economics. He declined this invitation instead preferring to be considered as a candidate for the post. He was duly elected to the Chair and so was able to escape from the ferment of the Keynesian Revolution taking place in Cambridge at that time. He taught at the London School of Economics for one year only before the outbreak of the second world war.

During the war he worked as an economic adviser to Sir F. Phillips who was the Third Secretary in the Treasury with particular responsibility for overseas finance. This work took Robertson to Washington in 1943, where he assisted in the preparations for the Bretton Woods Conference. Here again he was to work with Keynes as a member of the British delegation. On Pigou's retirement he was able to return to Cambridge as Professor of Economics. He occupied this post until his retirement in 1957.[14] Much of his energy was devoted in this post-war period to his lectures in Cambridge (which were published in three volumes),[15] and to general policy issues. After Keynes' death, he did not apply the same vigour to the theoretical debate surrounding the Keynesian revolution, but he still remained its strongest critic.

He gave evidence to the Committee on Finance and Industry in May 1930,[16] and to the Canadian Royal Commission on Banking and Finance in 1962.[17] He was a leading member of the Royal Commission on Equal Pay (1944–6), and the only economist amongst the 'three wise men' of the Cohen Council on Prices, Productivity and Incomes, (1957–8). Honorary degrees were given to him by several British Universities as well as those he received with great pride from Louvain, Columbia, Amsterdam and Harvard. He had been a Fellow of the British Academy from 1932, and was knighted in 1953.

He wrote nine books covering almost every aspect of economics[18], and had ninety-one articles published between September 1912 and September 1962, of which no fewer than thirty appeared in the *Economic Journal*. Many articles were collected to form six further books over the period 1931–66, the final collection being edited by Sir John R. Hicks.[19]

WHY STUDY ROBERTSON'S WORK?

From this brief biography one can begin to ascertain the importance of Sir D. H. Robertson in the development of economics; yet since his death in 1963 only one major article has appeared on Robertson; this was a critical obituary article written by P. Samuelson.[20]

Robertson's work is of crucial importance to economists and economic policy makers for two main reasons.

i) His publications provide a *major* contribution to the study of cyclical movements in the economy. Commenting upon the subject matter of fluctuations, money, credit and employment, Robertson himself states: 'this has always been to me the most interesting part of economics — the only part to which I can hope to be remembered as having made any personal contribution'.[21] The importance of this contribution has to some extent already been appreciated by economists. Fellner wrote in 1952: 'after so many years a surprisingly small part of Robertson's early contribution is outmoded in the sense that a problem with which it is concerned seems to have lost the significance, or in the sense that a statement is clearly less adequate than later statements of other authors on the same subject'.[22] One purpose of this book is to show that this statement is still valid in 1977.

ii) We have already seen that Robertson worked with, and was influenced by, J. M. Keynes in the inter-war period. Referring to the development of Keynes' work Lord Robbins argues: 'no-one with even a speck of justice in his make-up could deny to Sir Dennis a very appreciable share of the credit'.[23] The publication of the *Collected Writings of John Maynard Keynes*[24] enables not only a closer examination to be undertaken of the contribution by Robertson to the development of Keynes' thought, but also an assessment of the strength of Keynes' influence upon 'Robertsonian economics' to be made.

The book chooses as its focus the theory of industrial fluctuation, since this is where the majority of Robertson's writings were concentrated, where he made the greatest impact upon the study of economics and where much of the debate between Robertson and Keynes took place. The discussion is restricted to the case of a *closed* economy and therefore there is no examination of those aspects of Robertsonian theory which relate to the operations of international trade, the international monetary system or the gold standard. Likewise there is no exploration into the field of micro-economics, where Robertson can claim to have contributed in particular to the development of the theory of competition and utility analysis.[25]

The three parts into which this book is divided reflect differences in subject matter. But they also to a large degree indicate three stages in the development of Robertsonian ideas. Part I examines the Robertsonian theory of industrial fluctuation. It concentrates upon the *real* theory to be found in the *Study* and isolates the origins and major influences upon Robertson's work. It also seeks to establish the relationship between Robertsonian theory and the alternative theories of fluctuation existing in 1915.

Part II examines the role of saving and investment and the operation of monetary forces in the trade cycle. The inter-war period saw a disposition amongst economists to discuss the trade cycle, and policy aimed at regulating it, in terms of the relationship between saving and investment. Robertson was anxious after the *Study* to determine the influence of monetary forces upon the cycle and to investigate the relationship between real and monetary forces. The attention devoted to saving and investment in this period gave Robertson a framework in which to do this. The period came to an end with the debate surrounding the *General Theory*. This again centred upon the relationship between saving and investment and the determining forces in the trade cycle; for this reason a large proportion of this part of the book is given to a consideration of the main arguments of the debate and Robertson's contribution to them.

The final part of this work is, by way of a conclusion, a survey of Robertson's proposals for regulating the trade cycle. Attention is directed particularly to the problems of unemployment and inflation. Robertson began by propounding a *real* theory of fluctuation; monetary forces were then integrated into this real theory in his work in the inter-war period; even after 1945 Robertson remained faithful to this theoretical analysis despite the intervening Keynesian revolution. After 1945 he sought primarily to stress the policy implications of his theoretical approach and to contrast and compare them with the Keynesian policy recommendations. It is therefore fitting that the final part of this work should similarly consider the policy aspects of Robertsonian analysis.

Part I

The Theory of Industrial Fluctuation

1 Background to A Study of Industrial Fluctuation in 1915

INTRODUCTION

The overall aim of this book is to examine the work of Sir Dennis Holme Robertson on the trade cycle. It must begin, however, in very much the same way that the study by Robertson began. The main influences upon his early work are to be found in the theories of the trade cycle which had been expounded before 1915. This chapter provides a classification of these theories, such that they can be later examined in relation to the Robertsonian theory of industrial fluctuation.

Robertson was aware, from the very beginning, where his labours should be concentrated. Economists had accumulated many, and varied, views on the subject of the trade cycle by 1915. Robertson saw his task to be: 'in the direction of developing and synthesising the various and often conflicting opinions which have already been expressed'.[1] His first approach to the study of industrial fluctuation had in fact been to summarise a number of theories and to test these against empirical evidence. He was diverted from this course by A. C. Pigou, who wrote: 'You have collected an astonishing amount of material and have made comment on it in such a way that I feel sure you will eventually make something very good indeed. But, of course, at present, the thing is mainly a great mass of raw material. Marshall used to instruct one that the *bones* of a piece of work, which was really one's own production, grew gradually and then the whole thing came together round them. You haven't yet got the bones; you haven't thought through the material. The next stage is to sit and stew on all these facts and partial explanations until some coherent unity grows up and the separate facts fall into their proper place'.[2] Whether or not this advice did provide the direction for his future work is difficult to determine in retrospect; there may have been other, unknown influences; but the approach adopted by Robertson does bear a striking resemblance to this counsel. Robertson was recommended to take a *positive* rather than a critical line in his study. In particular, and this is very significant, Pigou instructed, though with some reservation: 'You ought more consistently and thoroughly to dig down behind money appearances to real facts' ... and to 'distinguish more between causes of a *general* kind affecting industry as a whole and special causes affecting particular industries'.[3]

By 1915 Robertson's Trinity Fellowship dissertation had become *A Study of Industrial Fluctuation*, providing economists with what T. S. Ashton describes as a 'Novum Organum.'[4] The following pages will yield witness to the extent to which the Pigovian trail was followed in this major contribution to trade cycle theory.

THE EVOLUTION OF TRADE CYCLE THEORY

Recognition of the cyclical movements in western economies grew out of the concern of political economists, particularly in the latter part of the 18th century, with what were called 'commercial crises'. Such crises had many descriptions ranging from a state of 'melancholy decay of credit' to a state of 'sinking of trade',[5] and represented what is now considered to be one particular phase of the cycle. Having established that crises occurred at fairly regular intervals, economists naturally ventured to explain what happened between periods of crisis. Hence the birth of the now voluminous literature on the trade cycle.

It has been customary to place much of the credit of original thinking on the trade cycle with Clement Juglar.[6] He put forward in 1860 the idea that the trade cycle had three phases, a period of prosperity, followed by crisis, followed by a period of liquidation, culminating once more in prosperity. Recognition of cyclical movements in economic activity had however taken place long before 1860. Willard Phillips had observed wavelike movements in business in the American economy in 1828,[7] declaring that: 'business will have its floods and ebbs'. In England, John Wade, a journalist, wrote on the 'commercial cycle' and the 'periods of prosperity and depression';[8] later in 1837 Lord Overstone described the cycle in the following manner: 'the history of what we are in the habit of calling "state of trade" is an instructive lesson. We find it subject to various conditions which are periodically returning; it revolves apparently in an established cycle. First we find it in a state of quiescence — next improvement, — drawing confidence, — prosperity, — excitement, — overtrading, — convulsion, — pressure, — stagnation, — distress, — ending again in quiescence'.[9]

Spiethoff, despite referring to Juglar as the originator of 'the new study of crises as phenomena of economic organisation',[10] regards the main original contribution on the trade cycle as coming from T. Tooke (1774–1858). Tooke not only described commercial expansion, crisis and depression, but also pointed out that they exhibited cyclical characteristics.[11] Whoever deserves the credit for recognising the trade cycle, it is evident that by the middle of the last century, economists were aware of its existence, and were beginning to devote more attention to studying it.

THE MEANING OF THE TRADE CYCLE

As a preliminary to discussing the theories of the trade cycle, it is important to determine what in fact economists meant by the business or trade cycle before 1915. The first problem is to decide which particular cycle merits attention. Is it a price cycle, a credit cycle, a cycle in general economic activity, or a cycle in output and employment?

There is a tendency, particularly amongst Keynesians, to place early trade cycle theory within classical economic thinking, and, in doing so, to suggest that its major concern before 1936 was with fluctuations in prices not output, nor employment. This is a gross misrepresentation of the situation; not only is it incorrect to imply that classical economists were solely interested in prices and money income, but, even allowing for this, it is incorrect to incorporate early work on the trade cycle within the body of classical economic thought. As Wesley Mitchell has so rightly asserted: 'It was not the orthodox economist however who gave the problem of crises and depressions its place in economics, but sceptics who had profited by and then reacted against their teachings'.[12]

Robertson was aware of this Keynesian misconception and was at pains to emphasise, and quite rightly so, in the new introduction to his *Study*, that the focus of his work was upon fluctuations in real national income.[13] Other trade cycle theorists were similarly disposed to study fluctuations in business or commercial activity, and not purely a price cycle. The aforementioned Wesley Mitchell defines business cycles as: 'a species of fluctuations in the economic activity of organised communities. The adjective "business" restricts the concept of fluctuations to activities which are systematically conducted on a commercial basis. The noun "cycles" bars out fluctuations which do not recur with a measure of regularity'.[14] Later sections will show that even the earlier economists had shown this disposition to concentrate upon fluctuations in economic activity, emphasising fluctuations in both output and employment.[15] The latter quotation also brings out a further characteristic of the cycle which had been investigated before the turn of the century; this is its regularity. The cycle was seen to have a number of phases, each phase logically following on from another in every cycle. In 1860, for example, Juglar observed that crisis always followed prosperity, prosperity followed liquidation, and liquidation followed crisis. Furthermore, the period of the cycle was observed to be regular in length. Juglar found it to be of approximately 10 years duration. Earlier John Wade had witnessed a commercial cycle of depression and prosperity of an average length of between 5 and 7 years. But, as Schumpeter remarks, the idea of the 10 year cycle seemed to gain popular support in the mid 19th century.[16] It was with an examination of this cycle that Robertson was occupied. He did not study microeconomic cycles, nor the Long cycle in business activity, recognised after 1915 by Kondratrieff as being an international cycle of between 48 and 60 years duration.[17]

By 1850 therefore the various phases of the business or trade cycle, and its periodicity, had already been the subject of discussion of many major works in economics. However it would appear that the impetus for the development of modern business cycle theories came with Juglar's work.[18] It was only after this had penetrated economic analysis that economists began to pay considerable attention to the study of the full cycle, rather than purely to commercial crises.[19]

THEORIES OF THE TRADE CYCLE

A complete theory of the trade cycle must possess two specific features. It must be able to explain why both the upswing and downswing of the cycle occur; that is how one phase of the cycle is transformed into the next. A considerable number of theorists had, by 1915, put forward their own explanation of the trade cycle. It is not true to say that: 'it was widely taken for granted that short-term fluctuations in the economy reflected changes in the quantity of money, or in the terms of and conditions under which credit was available'.[20] This again shows the error of labelling everything pre-*General Theory* as belonging to classical economic thought. Many economists had challenged Say's law.[21] Supply was not seen to create its own demand, nor did all theories propose that there was a natural tendency to full employment in a free enterprise economy. Trade cycle theory grew out of this discontent with the basic premises in classical economics. The ideas of Lauderdale, Malthus and Sismondi on the trade cycle resulted from their challenge to Say's law; from 1890 onwards this challenge was accelerated in the works of Aftalion, Tugan-Baranowski, Spiethoff, Robertson and others.

In the 1880s no fewer than 180 separate causes of crises and depressions were submitted to the committee of Congress, and in 1895 M. Bergmann accounted for 230 different opinions on the causes of the business cycle.[22] Such a multiplicity of thought on the cycle makes it impossible to develop any sane approach to their elucidation without some form of classification.

The classification of theories itself raises numerous problems. It is extremely difficult to decide the appropriate basis on which to classify theories. W. Persons struggled with this difficulty in 1927.[23] He argued that: 'Helpful classifications of theories of business fluctuations might be made on the basis of various criteria; such as the nature of fluctuation, periodic or non-periodic, the origin (that is, the beginning) of the fluctuation, the cause assigned to the lapse from prosperity to depression, the remedies offered, or the element in the author's explanation which he emphasises most in his discussion of the causes'.[24] Persons finally decided the best classification was to divide theories into two groups — those which put the cause of the cycle on institutional factors (for example the theories of J. A. Hobson and A. Spiethoff) and those which emphasise non-institutional factors (for example the agricultural theories of W. S. and H. S. Jevons). Adopting this approach it would still be necessary to subdivide the two categories of theories, and hence the need for further criteria. Cassel supported a classification based upon the type of economy to which the theory relates, distinguishing between theories which are applied to agricultural economies and those which seek to explain cyclical movements in modern capitalist economies.[25] The former theories were apparently considered unworthy of discussion since a study: 'which is to be valid for the whole of Western Europe, cannot, in general, go back further than the beginning of the (18)70s.'[26] This implies that the disappearance of the agricultural economy, and the appearance of large amounts of fixed capital, can be dated to the 1870s. Others have similarly made a distinction on these grounds. Wesley Mitchell argues that: 'It is not until the use of money has reached an advanced stage in a country that its economic vicissitudes take on the character of business cycles'.[27] The suggestion here is that the advent of the business cycle came alongside the development of modern capitalist production. This kind of distinction has led in the past only to a denial of the importance of agricultural theories of the cycle.

A further possibility is to classify theories according to the methodology of the theory. Three basic approaches to a theory of the trade cycle are discernable: the philosophical approach based entirely upon casual observation, the empirical or factual approach, as in the case of the studies of Clement Juglar and Tugan-Baranowski, where a theory is the end product of a thorough statistical examination of past trends in the economic system and the econometric or mathematical approach as in the case of so many modern theories, perhaps of which the best known is that of J. R. Hicks.[28] Although this may suffice for a modern classification of theories, the principal limitation for pre-1915 classification is the non-existence of theories which would suitably fit into the third category — that of econometric studies. Likewise a distinction between theories which are endogenous and those which are exogenous becomes meaningless because endogenous theories have developed mainly within the mathematical approach to the trade cycle.[29] Classification must proceed therefore, not on the basis of the type of economy to which the theories relate, nor according to the approach of the theory, but according to how the theory explains the cause of the cycle.

This is not to say that classification now becomes straightforward.

Explanations of the trade cycle rarely lay blame upon one cause alone. It is also necessary to establish which cause the theorist is emphasising above all others. The difference between theories is often a difference in emphasis rather than a difference in absolute and indisputable terms. A further problem is to make a clear distinction between cause and effect, that is to decide which factors are active in creating the cycle and which factors are merely reacting themselves to the cause, and perhaps aiding or allowing the cyclical movement. In any classification there must therefore be a certain element of danger. This must follow where classification is based upon a subjective assessment of what each theorist is emphasising above all else; it is all the more difficult since an attempt is being made to fit each theory into a rigid, well-defined, compartment.

The ultimate problem is the choice of compartments into which theories can be placed. Tugan-Baranowski visualised three groupings, theories of production, theories of exchange, credit and monetary circulation, and theories of the distribution of income.[30] Wesley Mitchell similarly divided theories into three compartments, those which trace business cycles to physical processes, those tracing them to a more emotional process and finally those tracing business cycles to institutional processes.[31] Each compartment contains separate smaller compartments.

In the following chapters seven major compartments are discernable:

1) includes the 'agricultural' and 'physical' theories of the cycle, comprising the works of W. S. Jevons, H. S. Jevons, H. L. Moore and W. Sombart. This type of theory seeks a connection between periodic agricultural cycles and periodic industrial cycles, or, in the work of W. Sombart, between the output of organic and inorganic materials and the industrial cycle.

2) contains theories which put the cause of the downswing of the cycle upon over-investment, or the nature of the modern capitalist production process; in this category one can include numerous writers of the 1890–1915 period, in particular Aftalion, Bickerdike, Tugan-Baranowski, Spiethoff, Cassel, Schumpeter and G. H. Hull. The common core of these theories is that during the prosperity phase each argues that over-production takes place in the capital good industries relative to

the consumer good industries. This brings the downturn of
the cycle. Despite this common core there is a great deal
of variety amongst this particular group. It is important to
realise that by 1915 there had been no development of the
monetary over-investment theories which are associated with
F. A. Hayek and L. Robbins amongst others. The major
writings of Hayek did not appear until the beginning of the
1930s.[32] These had a definite influence upon Robertson's later
works, and although not included in this chapter will provide
essential reference in later chapters. Although not within the
over-investment group of theories, it is important to remember
that Karl Marx had already written of the ultimate downfall
of market economies based upon private investment decisions,
and had studied, in particular, the influence of the longevity
of capital goods upon economic activity.[33]

3)   is occupied by the under-consumption theories of Malthus
     and Sismondi and later J. A. Hobson. There is a wide variety
     of theories within this group depending upon the nature of
     under-consumption in each theory. Foster and Catchings later
     developed an under-consumption theory[34] and in so doing
     they drew comment from Robertson.[35]

4)   The psychological theories drew accelerated support after 1915
     with the publications of A. C. Pigou and J. M. Keynes'
     emphasis on the role of expectations. During the period in
     question they are to be seen in the works of John Stuart
     Mill and John Mills.

5)   includes the monetary theory of R. G. Hawtrey, which gained
     considerable support during the first part of this century.
     The cause of the cycle is placed entirely upon the functions
     of money and credit in the economic system.

6)   contains those theories which concentrate upon the role of
     profits, wages and costs in the creation of the cycle. The
     most notable contribution in this field came from W. Mitchell
     and J. Lescure.[36]

7)   includes a number of 'all embracing' and 'accident' theories
     where no one cause of the cycle is emphasised, but multifarious
     causes are suggested. Here the works of W. Roscher and
     T. Veblen dominate.

Finally, and not within the general classification, this part of
the book will briefly discuss the neo-classical views on the trade

cycle. Robertson must undoubtedly have been influenced by these since he was brought up within the neo-classical Cambridge tradition. Discussion will centre, wherever possible, upon those works which were known to Robertson at the time of writing his *Study*. These were the agricultural theories of W. S. and H. S. Jevons, the over-investment theories of Tugan-Baranowski, A. Aftalion[37] and G. H. Hull,[38] the monetary theory of R. G. Hawtrey,[39] and the work of Labordère.[40]

2 The Nature of the Industrial Fluctuation and the Robertsonian Methodological Approach

As a further prerequisite to the study of Robertsonian theory, it is essential to enquire more deeply into the nature of the industrial fluctuation which Robertson sought to explain, and to examine the manner in which he set about explaining it.

THE NATURE OF INDUSTRIAL FLUCTUATION

From the beginning, Robertson was fully occupied with explaining the causes of industrial fluctuation. Such fluctuation, he accepted, exhibited a cyclical nature, with the trade cycle in European countries lasting on average between 7 to 10 years; the American counterpart he observed may last as little as 2 to 3 years.[1] He did not devote any consideration at all to Kondratieff's long cycle, and declared: 'we had better wait a few centuries, until there are more of these objects under the microscope, before making up our minds whether there is anything "cyclical" about them'.[2] His *Study* is an attempt therefore to explain both the downturn and upturn of the business cycle, and as such constitutes a complete theory of fluctuation.

The trade cycle was more than a cycle in prices or credit in Robertsonian literature. Indeed it is the fluctuation in output and employment which is stressed above all else in the early works.[3] The clearest description of fluctuation that one finds in published material is contained in his *Banking*. The cycle is: 'a quasi-rhythmical movement in the level of prices, in the level of money profits, and the level of employment'.[4] He continues by arguing that such movements imply the existence of corresponding movements in the volume of production and consumption. Although all capitalist countries were subjected to this trade cycle, the phases of the cycle were not synchronised from country to country, nor did each country suffer the same degree of fluctuation in each phase of the cycle.[5]

Robertson was critical of work which did not place sufficient emphasis upon output and employment. In his review of Tugan-Baranowski[6] he complained of its preoccupation with the circulation of credit, and its neglect of fluctuations in output and consumption. Later, in 1926, he accused Sir Ernest Benn of failing to take account of the problem of general unemployment.[7] The general over-concentration on price fluctuations Robertson thought was excusable to some extent, since price indices were much more reliable, and available, than indices of employment.[8] The major concern of his *Study* in 1915, however, was with fluctuations in real national income; but, as he pointed out in 1948,[9] although he considered this to be a main innovation, he claimed no great originality for it, citing the work of A. C. Pigou.[10]

Not only did Robertson regard the trade cycle as being different between countries, he also observed that the characteristics of the trade cycle within each country would vary from one cycle to the next. Hence later he agreed with Rostow that: 'the combinations of forces within the moving economy are, like those in political life, in an important sense always new and fresh. No year is quite like another year'.[11] He felt that not all depressions would be characterised by a decline in real income;[12] nor, for example, that wages need necessarily always lag behind prices in a period of prosperity.[13] The trade cycle was impossible to define precisely, hence it was not surprising that by 1915 a 'consistent and comprehensive explanation' of it had not been given.[14]

All of the major works of Robertson on fluctuation also recognised that cycles may differ between kinds of production.[15] More pronounced cycles will take place in construction good industries with consumer good industries being less affected; Robertson suggested in his early writings that consumer good production may not decline in a depression.[16] It is the fluctuation in capital good production which is significant in the derivation of Robertsonian theory; it is from this that the *inevitability* of the cycle, portrayed by Robertson,[17] stems.

Finally, with this view of the nature of fluctuation, one needs
to enquire as to the reason why Robertson placed so much emphasis
on the study of variations in real income. The answer is to be
found in his approach to the study of economics.[18] He believed
that the ultimate subject matter of economics is economic welfare.
The best indicator that exists of economic welfare is the level
of aggregate real income. Therefore, the study of economics can
be mainly directed to an examination of the determination of
real income; consequently it is extremely important to isolate the
causes of the fluctuations in real income. Robertson was aware
that he needed to explain *both* turning points of the cycle, but
he did not regard boom and depression as equal and opposite
evils. Although the boom contained: 'a not negligible amount
of overwork and overstrain, an intensification of industrial strife,
a burgeoning of cupidity and fraud' and 'the increase in real
enjoyable income is less than it seems to be, and to many individuals
a negative quantity',[19] such features were not as detrimental to
total welfare as the state of depression.

METHODOLOGY

In *Lectures on Economic Principles* Robertson writes of the tools of
inductive and deductive reasoning which are available to the
economist.[20] The inductive method, that of collecting and observing
facts, of deriving theories on the basis of these facts, and of testing
these theories, was the method religiously followed by himself 40 years
earlier in his *Study*.

It is apparent that in his preparation of the Cobden Essay
(which later became the *Study*) he did not carry the inductive
method far enough. In 1913 he was deeply engrossed in a large
mass of statistics relating in particular to the construction, transport
and agricultural sectors of the economy.[21] His intention at this
stage was to comment upon existing theory in the light of the
facts he had accumulated. This approach had been stimulated
by his critical view of those theories which had not at that time
appealed to the facts; in particular this criticism was directed
at the work of R. G. Hawtrey for neglecting statistics completely,
at Tugan-Baranowski for looking only at monetary statistics, and
at G. Hull for not looking comprehensively at the statistics he
was supposed to be examining.[22] It was Pigou who encouraged

Robertson to go beyond this negative approach, to the second stage of the inductive process and to formalise his own theory of fluctuation.[23] Robertson remained faithful to the use of statistical enquiry in economics throughout his writings. His review in 1929 of the work undertaken by Wedgwood on the distribution of wealth clearly shows his great respect for thorough statistical enquiry.[24] Although he had less respect for the questionnaire approach as a means of appealing to the facts in economics.[25]

The first edition of the *Study* brought with it the final Robertsonian step into inductive reasoning, such that it was not only a synthesis of existing theories of fluctuation, but a positive contribution to trade cycle theory.[26] It was also indicative of a very important Robertsonian belief which will recur over and over again in the following chapters. All theories have some validity; different theories may be relevant at different times. Not all trade cycles are identical, not all trade cycles are therefore to be explained in an identical fashion.[27] The danger with most theories is that they tend to over-estimate their own importance.[28] The economist cannot be 'masquerading as a man of science in a universe not of cells and atoms but of passions and volitions'.[29] Economics is a study of human responses. Responses might differ over time, such that the explanation of economic events will vary. Looking back in 1948 on his *Study*, Robertson felt that he had allowed his own enthusiasm to overcome him, such that he had resolved to force every statistic 'to tell a story'.[30] A story on occasions which was incorrect, or, if correct, did not remain so indefinitely.

This belief goes a long way to explaining his distrust of the mathematical approach to theorising, of which he never made significant use.[31] Although the economist should utilise statistics,[32] he should exercise care in his use of mathematics. In particular Robertson directed this warning against the use of mathematical models of the trade cycle, a usage which grew stronger over the years. Such models, although probably useful, over-simplified the explanation of the trade cycle and tended to create a neglect of those forces acting upon the cycle which were either exogenous to that particular model or were difficult to fit into the model in a mathematical form. Consequently the forces endogenous to that particular model received an emphasis in the explanation of the cycle. The degree to which cycles are self-generating became over-estimated. In this respect the role of innovation in the trade cycle, and the lumpiness and discontinuity of the investment process, which Robertson chose to emphasise in explaining the cycle, had been excluded from the popular models of the cycle.[33]

The use of such limited mathematical models tended in turn to over-simplify the remedies available for economic ills.[34] In addition Robertson remained sceptical that econometric methods could be used to complement the mathematical model; this scepticism stemmed from a doubting of the continued stability of the parameters of mathematical models over time, and was sufficient for Robertson to conclude that there is a probability that 'more truth will . . . be wrung from the interpretive studies of the crude data' as in his *Study*.[35]

Two other features of Robertsonian theorising must be emphasised at the outset. Firstly, from the 1915 *Study* onwards, Robertson always felt that he could examine the micro-economy and gain from this analysis explanations of the cycle in aggregate economic activity. He adopted what could be called a 'structural approach' to the cycle, arguing through the effects of various sectors of the economy upon the aggregate.[36] In this manner he avoided the criticism which he had raised against R. G. Hawtrey, that it grossly underestimated: 'The effects of a dislocation in one trade upon the volume of production in other trades'.[37] Secondly, and no less important, he always used in theorising a *dynamic* and not static approach; this is most evident in the period analysis of *Banking*[38] and in his criticism of Keynes' *General Theory*.[39]

3 The Robertsonian Theory of Industrial Fluctuation — An Outline

INTRODUCTION

In this chapter the skeleton of the Robertsonian theory of fluctuation is examined. Subsequent chapters will concentrate more fully upon important aspects of this theory, and trace the origins and influences upon it, putting the flesh upon the bones.

The direction which the views of Robertson on industrial fluctuation were to take is evident from his early work undertaken in the course of his preparations for the *Study*. In a paper read to the Royal Statistical Society, he chose to examine evidence relating to the gestation period of investment, and the length of life of investment.[1] He did not at this stage formalise his theory. A review of *Good and Bad Trade*[2] again gives some indication of his early views. He accused new work on commercial crises of having a: 'determination to burrow below mere monetary phenomena followed by the same relapse into monetary terms at all critical stages of the argument'.[3] Hawtrey's work was, in his view, no exception to this generalisation.

Robertson by contrast was already committed to emphasising the importance of over-investment in the cycle. He complained of: 'that recurrent tendency of the business community to an over-investment of its resources in fixed capital which . . . common observation suggests is the dominant characteristic of modern fluctuations'.[4] The same comment was repeated word for word in a review of the work of M. Tugan-Baranowski and A. Aftalion;[5]

Tugan-Baranowski was regarded as placing too much emphasis on monetary factors; but Robertson was much less critical of the work of Aftalion, and interesting comparisons can be made of their theories,[6] particularly in relation to the role of investment. It is not surprising therefore that, when his first book appeared, strengthened by Pigou's encouragement to 'dig down to real facts',[7] Robertson was to emphasise *real* as opposed to *monetary* causes of the cycle, and to present a 'real' theory of fluctuation dominated by the inherent features of a capitalist economy with a heavy dependence upon the investment process. As such it was the first theory of its kind in British literature.

THE MOVEMENT FROM DEPRESSION TO RECOVERY

The theory of industrial fluctuation builds upon a micro-economic analysis of the causes of fluctuation in output in particular industries.[8] This is not meant to imply that the fluctuation of a particular industry will necessarily cause a significant movement in aggregate output; but Robertson did acknowledge the interdependence of industries believing that fluctuation could be transmitted from one sector of the economy to the next, in particular from the agricultural to the industrial sector.[9]

An expansion of aggregate industrial output out of the depression will occur when either the supply of productive effort offered by the labour force is increased, or the average productivity of each unit of effort is increased. Significant changes in either are invariably to be found where the cause of an expansion in a particular industry can be more generally applied to other industries at the same time. The cause most emphasised in Robertsonian literature is the occurrence of an invention which raises the average productivity gained from each unit of effort supplied. In 1915 Robertson also stressed the influence of an increase in agricultural production, caused by changing weather conditions, which brings a fall in the exchange value of agricultural relative to industrial produce. This change in relative prices would create an increase in the amount of aggregate effort supplied by the labour force, and hence increase industrial production.[10] This is indicative of how changes in one sector of the economy are regarded as potentially exerting a significant influence upon aggregate production. Robertson also argued that agricultural abundance may raise business confidence, increasing the expected returns from investment, and boosting the production of capital goods.[11]

In addition, the expectation of an increased productivity of construction goods[12] may be sufficient to generate a general recovery. Here the increased attractiveness of investment is anticipated by a revision in the marginal utility of capital goods relative to that of consumer goods. This revision is normally undertaken as a result of any one of three events, either because of the wearing out of a large proportion of the existing stock of capital goods, or the discovery of new territories and consequently new areas for the application of capital goods, or the occurrence of a legal or physical invention.

The above causes of the upturn of the cycle demonstrate four important general features of Robertsonian theory:

1) the *real* nature of the causes of the upturn. Monetary forces, in particular the extension of credit, are not the cause of the upturn. Banks may respond to an increased demand for credit during expansion, but this is a *symptom* of the cycle and not a force instigating the cycle.

2) the emphasis placed upon the fluctuations that occur in capital good production through the cycle. It is the marginal utility of capital goods which varies; the marginal utility of consumer goods is relatively stable. Hence the cycle is primarily one in the demand for capital goods and in turn the production of such goods.[13] Later Robertson did acknowledge that a variation in the demand for consumer goods may set off the recovery.[14]

3) the fluctuations in output are in response to movements in prices. Each of the potential causes of expansion acts firstly upon the level of prices of some goods relative to those of others, especially the prices of capital goods relative to those of consumer goods; it is this change in prices, bringing in turn a change in the margin between price and cost, which leads to the response of industry to expand output. The change in prices is not however the cause of fluctuation but the means of *transmitting* the original cause to the volume of production. In other words producers react to price signals which reflect the underlying cause of fluctuation.

4) The ability of changes within particular sectors of the economy to have substantial repercussions upon the aggregate level of economic activity, sufficient in fact to cause the existence of a trade cycle exhibiting large swings in employment, prices and production.

THE CAUSES OF THE DOWNTURN

The theory of fluctuation put forward by Robertson is normally classified as a non-monetary, over-investment theory.[15] This is a justifiable classification on the grounds that the crisis is seen to be caused by over-investment, and the factors generating this are non-monetary in nature, and associated with inherent characteristics of the capitalist system of production.

In the same way that the upturn is stimulated by an increase in the marginal utility of capital goods relative to that of consumer goods, so the downturn is brought about by a downwards revision in the marginal utility of capital goods, bringing a contraction in the production of capital goods. This downward revision is an effect of the over-investment occurring during the expansion. The characteristics of the upturn therefore guarantee the inevitability of the downturn. The increased marginal utility of capital goods at the trough of the depression stimulates investment and brings recovery; but this investment will be excessive for a number of reasons.

An increase in the price of a commodity during a period of recovery provides an inducement to investment. The length of time necessary for investment to be realised, that is its gestation period,[16] maintains high prices by delaying the additional supply of consumer goods that will be forthcoming. As a consequence all producers are tempted to react to the high prices. The general ignorance as to the amount of investment other producers are undertaking leads to over-investment; but eventually producers must realise that an excessive increase in the production of consumer goods must result from the over-investment. Prices fall and recession must follow: 'the longer therefore this period of gestation, the longer will the period of high prices continue, the greater will be the over-investment and the more severe the subsequent depression'.[17] But recession can occur before the increased production of consumer goods caused by investment reaches the market. The realisation that the close of the gestation period will yield an excessive additional supply of consumer goods leads to a collapse in the demand for capital goods before this additional supply is forthcoming. Producers expect that further investment will involve a sacrifice of present enjoyment disproportionate to the enjoyment which will be afforded by the new consumer goods which it is proposed to create.[18] Over-investment is no more than a failure of the economy to maintain the ideal distribution of production between consumer and capital goods.[19]

During the boom the average productivity of a unit of effort will decline. There will be a growth of real costs of production as producers resort to less efficient methods of production and organisation,[20] and to employing 'incompetent and over-tired'[21] labour and more expensive sources of supply of raw materials. Profit margins diminish and output contracts.

Depressions are seen to be aggravated by what Robertson calls the 'imperfect divisibility and intractability of the instrument'.[22] The scale of production and the large size of the unit of investment act so as to tempt the producer to enlarge his capacity to a greater extent than would be required to meet demand. Similarly the intractability of investment, by which is meant the inability to withdraw previous investment (because of the period of time required to close down and then reopen, and the consequent costs involved) would aggravate the depression. The proposition that the length of the life of an instrument of production might affect the duration of the cycle also commanded some support from Robertson. Investment might exhibit lumpiness caused by its life-span and the need for replacement. An initial burst of investment would lead to periodic lumps of replacement investment determined by the life-span of the capital good.

Although agricultural abundance is seen as a possible cause of the upturn, agricultural shortage, and the consequent alteration of relative prices of agricultural and industrial production, does not merit the same role in explaining the downturn of the cycle. Small agricultural crops will be damaging to the boom, but are only of secondary importance as the cause of collapse to those forces causing over-investment.[23] In later writings, even less emphasis is placed upon the possible impact of agricultural change upon the cycle; this is possibly a reflection of the diminishing contribution of agricultural production to aggregate output in most western economies.

The major cause of collapse therefore is the diminishing attractiveness of investment during the boom; but in 1915 Robertson had some sympathy with the thesis that investment might be excessive in relation to the amount of saving available.[24] The stock of consumer goods during the boom might not be sufficient to allow the investment intentions of producers to materialise. This stock represents the *real* saving available for investment, the finance which allows the investment to be undertaken until a further expansion in consumer goods output results at the end of the gestation period. If the availability of consumer goods is inadequate for the community to live upon whilst a greater proportion of resources is devoted to capital good production, investment has to be postponed or abandoned and capital good industries are plunged into depression. Robertson had no sympathy in 1915 with those over-investment theories which lay the blame of the downturn upon the failure of the commercial banks to supply the loanable funds needed to match the investment, that is upon the failure of *monetary* saving to meet investment demand.[25] A shortage of *real* saving is a possible cause of the crisis, but the crisis will occur anyway whether or not such a shortage exists when the marginal utility of capital goods is devalued relative to that of consumer goods.

THE INEVITABILITY OF THE CYCLE AND THE ROLE OF MONETARY AND PSYCHOLOGICAL FACTORS

Under a capitalist system there is bound to be an inevitable discontinuity in achieving economic progress. A steady rate of economic progress requires continuity in the rate of growth of capital equipment, but this continuity is made difficult by the indivisibility and durability of fixed capital. The final comment of Robertson in his *Study* is to this effect: 'out of the welter of industrial dislocation the great permanent riches of the future are generated'.[26] This view is also emphasised in later publications.[27] Looking back on *Banking* in 1949, Robertson comments that he was anxious at that time to differ from the orthodox view which he saw as wanting stability in output, achieved through price stability, which in turn could be brought about through banking policy.

Output and price stability are not always compatible and fluctuation in output is sometimes desirable: 'under certain conditions an exceptionally rapid expansion of output, and under others a contraction of output — the former associated with a rise and the latter with a fall in the general price-level — must be regarded, on a balance of considerations, as economically desirable'.[28] He acknowledged that this later emphasis had been prompted by the work of both Wicksell and Cassel.[29] In evidence to the Macmillan Committee he is similarly disposed to argue that: 'a feature of modern industrial progress, partly aggravated by avoidable causes but partly inevitable, is that it proceeds discontinuously — in lumps and by jumps'.[30] The remedy for such fluctuations may be more damaging than the disease. If a capitalist system is to be maintained cyclical movements in economic activity are an unavoidable consequence of the features of the investment process and are in fact desirable if the economy is to progress.[31] Fluctuation can therefore be regarded as *appropriate* or *inappropriate*.

It is in relation to the generation of inappropriate fluctuations in output that one encounters monetary and psychological forces acting in Robertsonian theory. He was aware in 1915, and more so in his later publications (especially in the 1920s), that two theories of fluctuation were gaining most support from British economists; these were the so-called monetary and psychological theories.[32] Robertson was not convinced by either theory. The role of both monetary and psychological factors was to *exaggerate* cyclical movements set in motion by the *real* forces acting upon economic activity. Monetary expansion or contraction could neither send recovery on its way, nor end the boom; similarly the absence of errors of optimism or pessimism on the part of businessmen would not eliminate the trade cycle. However Robertson felt that monetary expansion could take the price level beyond the point required to bring about appropriate changes in aggregate output, and hence facilitate unwarranted expansion which inevitably resulted in depression. Conversely monetary restriction might depress the price level below its appropriate level in the downturn.[33] Psychological factors could equally enlarge the boom, or the depression; optimism generates further over-investment in the boom, pessimism damages investment in the depression. These forces therefore were additional to those creating over-investment in the previous section, leading to inappropriate fluctuations in output.[34]

SOME PRELIMINARY CONCLUSIONS

Several important features of the Robertsonian theory of fluctuation emerge from the last two chapters and will be emphasised in the analysis of the following chapters:

a) Robertson is the *first* British economist to stress the role of *real* factors and not monetary factors in the trade cycle.

b) Even before the publication of the *General Theory*, he is very much concerned with the problem of unemployment, and with fluctuations in output and investment. He is not solely concerned with the price/credit cycle in his early publications.

c) He favours an *empirical* approach to the study of industrial fluctuation. He believes that the activity of individual sectors has repercussions throughout the economy. These repercussions are transmitted through price movements.

d) He distrusts the model building approach to cycle theory, believing that such models oversimplify the true situation.

e) The causes of recovery are more important in Robertsonian theory than the explanation of the downturn, since the boom is believed to breed its own destruction. Recovery is caused by the increased attractiveness of investment. This is the result of one of the following:
    i) exceptionally good crops in the agricultural sector,
    ii) an increase in the need to replace instruments of production in some important trade or groups of trades,
    and above all else,
    iii) the occurrence of an invention in some important trade or group of trades.

f) Recovery does not require an initial increase in the demand for consumer goods. The marginal utility of consumer goods remains relatively constant. Robertson observed that, in general, consumption fell during a revival. He did not lay much stress on the accelerator in 1915, but in later writings he did acknowledge that recovery can begin in the consumption trades.[35]

g) The downturn of the cycle results from over-investment. Robertson put forward a non-monetary, over-investment theory of the cycle. The temptation to over-invest results mainly from the repercussions on the volume of investment of its gestation period.

h) Depressions are aggravated by the 'imperfect divisibility and intractability of the instrument' and the longevity of the instrument. But these features of investment also mean that fluctuation in output and employment is to some extent desirable or appropriate.

i) Monetary and psychological factors might be responsible for *undesirable* changes in output. They cannot instigate the trade cycle on their own, but need the prior impact of *real* forces to set the cycle on its way.

j) Over-investment leads to over-production relative to particular demands. This brings depression. The 'temporary gluttability of large groups of particular human wants'[36] is seen as a leading cause of the depression. The decline in the marginal utility of capital goods causes the downturn, bringing a decline in the demand for capital goods. It was in this respect that investment may be excessive. It may not be excessive in relation to the availability of real or monetary saving during the boom, as other theories held.

In the following chapters a more detailed examination is given of these crucial aspects of Robertsonian theory. In Chapter 4 the role of the price mechanism in the cycle will be observed and the links between micro and macro economic activity explored in a more rigorous analysis of the causes of expansion. Chapter 5 will delve more deeply into the theory of the crisis. Chapter 6 will look at the implications of fluctuation in agricultural production for the industrial cycle; Chapter 7 will examine the role of psychological and monetary forces in the cycle and extend the analysis to consider Robertson's views on the acceleration principle, on the under-consumption theories, and give a preliminary indication of the links between Robertsonian and Marshallian theories. The operation of saving in the cycle became the focus of discussion in the economic analysis of the inter-war period. This will be the subject of Part II of this book.

4 The Causes of the Upturn

Robertson began his study of industrial fluctuation in 1915 by considering the forces which instigate variability in output within particular industries. This was proceeded by an investigation as to whether fluctuation in one industry could be transmitted to other industries such that a cycle in aggregate output is exhibited. The negative answer he found to this question prompted him to enquire as to whether the *cause* of fluctuation in a particular industry may be simultaneously causing fluctuation in other industries in the economy. Bearing this approach in mind, this chapter begins by examining the Robertsonian explanation of fluctuation in particular industries and shows the role of price movements in linking the initial cause to the change in output it creates. It then outlines the causes of fluctuation which are regarded as potentially having a significant impact upon several industries at any one time. A closer examination is also undertaken of the theoretical framework utilised by Robertson.[1]

THE CAUSES OF FLUCTUATION WITHIN PARTICULAR INDUSTRIES

There are two possible causes of changes in output within a particular industry, the first and less important here, is a fluctuation in supply attributed largely to the nature of fixed capital within that industry. This will be discussed in relation to the causes of the downturn of the cycle.[2] However, it is relevant here to enquire as to the influence of cost changes upon the volume of production. The second is a fluctuation in the demand for the product of that industry which brings a variation in its price; either fluctuation, whether it be supply or demand, by changing costs or prices, will be responsible for yielding a change in the profit margin.[3] This, in turn, will act as an incentive to either expand or contract output. This approach was not new in 1915, being within the Marshallian tradition.[4]

FLUCTUATIONS IN COSTS

In the *Study* the relationship between costs and desired output within an industry is treated as an empirical question. Changes in cost, and corresponding changes in output, are examined in both consumer and construction good industries.[5] The theoretical relation which was expected to be found, and which is postulated more clearly in *Banking*,[6] is that an increase in costs will tend to diminish output by shrinking profit margins; a fall in costs will raise profit margins and provide an incentive to produce more. Concentrating upon the period 1890–1910, Robertson finds that for the cotton, jute and woollen industries, three industries depending upon an annual harvest of the raw material, prosperity and depression fluctuate in accordance with the cost of the raw material.[7] Similarly, in the construction good industries, which include coal, shipbuilding and iron and steel production, it is found that increasing cost brings depression[8] (and vice versa); but Robertson is not convinced by the thesis put forward by G. Hull and J. Lescure[9] that fluctuations in costs are invariably responsible for cyclical movements in the construction good industries. Empirically this is disputed because little correlation is obtained between falling raw material costs and the level of investment undertaken; high costs do not appear to prevent investment taking place.[10] The conclusion is reached that cost fluctuations on the majority of occasions in construction good industries do not have a profound influence upon the output cycle in these industries but merely create 'tentative oscillations and false starts';[11] only in one respect are cost fluctuations significant.[12] This is where, in the case of the upturn, the lowering of costs has been caused by the occurrence of invention. The application of invention to the production process in an industry may not immediately stimulate prosperity, but on most occasions Robertson believed that it did act so as to raise the receipts of the industry and boost investment.

In invention therefore we have the primary cause of a fluctuation in costs in the construction good industries, which yields variability in investment and output within these industries; this is our first clue as to the cause of the upturn in macroeconomic activity in Robertsonian theory.

FLUCTUATIONS IN DEMAND

Robertson gave two further reasons why an industry might be encouraged to alter its scale of operation because of forces on the demand rather than the supply side.[13] Firstly, if an industry revises its demand for the products which it can receive in exchange for its own production, then this will lead to an alteration in its own level of output. Again the emphasis is upon the importance of this within the capital good and durable consumer good industries. The desire for such goods is likely to vary depending upon the existing stock of goods in the hands of consumers or producers; a war or an earthquake, or some extreme happening which destroys this stock, will stimulate an increased desire for these goods;[14] but more especially, demand, as well as supply, will be influenced by the occurrence of invention[15] which raises the desire for capital goods. Robertson cites the impact in this respect of inventions relating to railways, electrical power, diesel power, and iron and steel manufacture.[16]

Secondly, the output of an industry may increase in response to a rise in the exchange value of its product, that is a rise in its real demand price,[17] the number of units of other products that can be gained in exchange for one unit of its own production.[18] In this respect fluctuations in agricultural production which are 'due to a variation in the bounty of nature' are very important.[19] Whether the output of an industrial group is expanded as a result of a good harvest depends upon the demand elasticity of that industrial group for agricultural produce;[20] but agricultural change is not the only possible cause of an alteration in the exchange value of an industrial product. A reduction in the operating costs of other industries may increase the real demand price; here again the forces of invention and innovation may be at work;[21] in addition, the change in taste for the product of an industrial group may impose some change in the exchange value of that product.

It is apparent from this discussion that it will be essential to explore in more detail the connection between a change in exchange value (relative prices) and its effect upon output; but first we need to extend this micro-analysis to a consideration of the possible causes of an expansion in aggregate output.

FROM DEPRESSION TO RECOVERY

The foregoing microeconomic analysis provided Robertson with the means to explain the upturn in aggregate economic activity. The stimulation of output in one industry cannot bring a general revival in output; but the forces creating an expansion in one industry may be acting simultaneously in a like fashion upon other industries. This is particularly true of two such forces, the occurrence of invention and the advent of a bountiful harvest. The latter is reflected in an increase in the exchange value of all industrial groups, and generally results, according to Robertson, in an extension of industrial output.[22] The former merits more attention at this point.

THE ROLE OF INVENTION

An invention which is widely applicable to industry will not only lower the real operating costs of production, bringing a 'general rise in the productivity of effort',[23] but also increase the demand for capital goods,[24] and alter the relative prices of products; this causes industrial output to change. Invention may lead to an extension of transport facilities, as the product stimulated by it may require mobility from the location of production to its markets. It may also require the assistance of the iron and steel trades in its application to industry and therefore boost output in that important sector of the economy. During the final stages of depression there is usually a decline in production costs as the productivity of labour increases and production techniques are improved.[25] The possibility of applying an invention during the depression acts so as to increase the marginal utility of capital goods relative to that of consumer goods. The invention stimulates an increase in the *expected* productivity of capital goods and boosts the demand for such goods. The consequence is a significant change in the output of the capital good industries, with no necessary change at the beginning of recovery in consumer good output. But this is only a temporary rise in the marginal utility of capital goods. Once the invention has been fully exploited, given the durability of capital equipment, then the demand for capital goods must fall. Hence the offspring of the boom is a depression. The most relevant feature of the cycle therefore is the volatility of the output of the capital good industries relative to that of the consumer good industries.[26] The conviction of the *Study* is that fluctuations in the marginal utility of construction goods 'furnish the key to the most important aspects of modern industrial fluctuations'.[27]

This theoretical view of the upturn has strong support in the statistical enquiry in the *Study*. This is found in the booms which occur as a result of inventions in the electrical industry (1902–7), railways (1872), and in the steel industry (1882). Later, in 1926, Robertson is able to add the innovations relating to oil power which are seen as being responsible for recovery in 1912.[28]

However, not all inventions will bring recovery. It is important to distinguish between two possible implications of invention. Firstly, invention may be such that it can be applied in a group of industries simultaneously, or within the majority of firms within a large industry. This would be the case, for example, where a new source of power can be applied throughout industry, or a new means of transport utilised. Secondly, innovation in one industry may have repercussions upon other industries where that innovation *cannot* also be applied. For example, it may increase demands placed upon the transport sector, or upon raw material suppliers. It was Robertson's belief that, for an invention to successfully generate a recovery, it must be such that it could be introduced in a large group of trades; it would be unlikely for the repercussions of an invention within one industry to be sufficient to create a *general revival*.[29]

Emphasis must also be placed upon the point that invention in *a particular sector* of the economy can bring a general revival. The stimulation of output in one sector is not necessarily at the expense of a diminution of output in other sectors; most industries can, and do, prosper at the same time, yielding a net expansion of output rather than a redistribution of the total product between industries.[30]

This belief in the importance of the role of invention and innovation in the cycle continues right through to *Lectures on Economic Principles* (see bibliography for details: hereafter referred to as *Lectures*) in the 1950s. The application of a new invention, or the new-found application of an old invention, is still regarded as the cause of most upturns in the 19th century.[31] The only notable shift in the Robertsonian argument first appeared in the late 1930s.[32] This is indicated by a greater support for the argument that the accelerator is operative in most cycles, and that expansion need not necessarily start in the capital good industries but may originate in the consumer good industries (as the marginal utility of consumer goods increases relative to that of capital goods). This new-found faith in the accelerator persists again into the 1950s, and in his Cambridge Lectures.[33]

THE ROLE OF INVENTION — THE INFLUENCES UPON ROBERTSONIAN ANALYSIS

It is apparent from the publications and correspondence of Robertson that there were no positive influences from other economists upon him in his emphasis upon invention in promoting economic revival. His Cambridge contemporaries had not in 1915 acknowledged the importance of real factors in the cycle. Pigou was in fact criticised by Robertson for underestimating the importance of inventions in his *Wealth and Welfare*.[34] Later Pigou complimented Robertson on his discovery of the importance of invention; commenting on the *Study*, he wrote to Robertson: 'the part played by inventions are very good and important; this strikes me — the stress laid on that and its working out — as the most important original contribution in this book'.[35] Despite this, Pigou did not himself stress inventions in his later work, suggesting, in 1929, that real causes of the cycle could be disregarded, except where 'large inventions' and harvest variations occurred.[36] Hawtrey had provided a negative influence in that Robertson was critical of what he regards as his over-emphasis upon monetary factors within the cycle.[37] Keynes' first venture into trade cycle theory was prompted by an early draft of the *Study*, and therefore was not significant in influencing the working out of the Robertsonian thesis.[38]

Equally the continental literature, which closely resembled the content of the *Study*, had not penetrated Cambridge before 1915. In retrospect Robertson wrote: 'I think that in 1914, blissfully ignorant of a great mass of continental literature, I felt quite brave in awarding the prize apple for trouble making to the twin goddesses of investment/invention and innovation, or at any rate splitting it between them and the god of weather'.[39] This is also indicative of how far Robertson felt he was being contrary to British and American literature on the trade cycle at that time.

But he was not totally ignorant of continental literature. As noted previously he had reviewed the works of both Tugan-Baranowski and A. Aftalion before writing the *Study*.[40] Both had put forward over-investment theories of the trade cycle, but Robertson had offered the same criticism of the work of Tugan-Baranowski as that which he raised against R. G. Hawtrey. Tugan-Baranowski sought to explain the volatility of expenditure on capital goods[41] in terms of the relationship between free and real capital. In a depression the accumulation of free capital eventually brings, through a lowering of its price, an increased demand for real capital (for funds to be invested in capital goods).[42] This causes the upturn. Aftalion had similarly put the blame of the cycle upon the capitalist system of production.[43] Fluctuations in the output of fixed capital were responsible for cyclical movements. These fluctuations were to be explained by changes in the level of consumer demand, small changes bringing relatively large changes in the demand for capital goods. But here it is the marginal utility of consumer goods which initially increases, and which is responsible for the movement out of depression, a thesis not supported in 1915 by Robertson. So neither Tugan-Baranowski, nor Aftalion, stressed the role of invention in the cycle; nevertheless the work of both authors must have given Robertson some encouragement to support an over-investment theory of fluctuation, and to delve more deeply into the causes of fluctuation in the capital good industries.

The only major inspiration of the Robertsonian approach appears therefore to be found in the wealth of statistics which he accumulated for his *Study* and which he managed to decipher sufficiently to offer invention and innovation the worship he thought they deserved.

SIMILARITIES WITH CONTINENTAL LITERATURE

The work of three continental economists in particular has also laid stress upon invention, innovation or both in causing the trade cycle. These are A. Spiethoff,[44] G. Cassel[45] and J. Schumpeter.[46] Although Robertson was aware in 1914 that Spiethoff was also working on business cycles he had no knowledge of his views other than that he proposed a shortage of *real* saving theory of crisis.[47] The work of Cassel exerted a strong influence upon Robertson during the preparation of *Banking*,[48] but not before. Schumpeterian theory contains the closest resemblance to the role of innovation found in the *Study*, but this was not known to Robertson until 1927.[49]

Spiethoff regards the cycle as an unavoidable feature of capitalism.[50] As with Robertsonian theory, it is the fluctuation in investment which is held as the prime mover in industrial fluctuations. The change in investment creates a response in consumption through its effects upon income and output. Spiethoff was not convinced by the thesis supported by Tugan-Baranowski[51] that the accumulation of loanable funds during the depression phase would be sufficient in time to stimulate the outburst of investment that is characteristic of the outset of prosperity. The main factor creating this outburst is, not the pressure from the supply of loanable funds, but the advent of new profitable investment opportunities and outlets. These are a consequence of either new inventions or the opening up of new territories. Prosperity once under way becomes self-sustaining. Investment increases income, output and purchasing power bringing increased demand for consumer goods (the multiplier process). Prices rise stimulating further investment; so the process continues in a cumulative fashion. Eventually the supply of loanable funds is diminished, blocking further expansion; alternatively or simultaneously, the investment outlets are exhausted and investment falls due to a need merely to replace worn out capital equipment rather than to make net additions to it, the outcome being recession. If new inventions and new territorial discoveries occur in a regular, evenly distributed manner, the resulting investment outlets would not be concentrated at the bottom of the depression. The assumption of this theory therefore is that such inventions and discoveries are unevenly distributed over time, since without this the cycle would not be generated.[52]

The same basic ideas contained in the work of both Tugan-Bar-

anowski and Spiethoff on the cycle are repeated in the early
work of G. Cassel.[53] In later life, however, his theory moved
more towards being a monetary theory of the cycle, along the
same lines as that of R. G. Hawtrey.[54] The most interesting
original contribution of his work rests with his interpretation of
the influence of the rate of interest on the cycle; because of
this his theory differs slightly from that of Spiethoff. During the
prosperity phase the rate of interest rises as a result of the shortage
of loan capital which develops through over-investment. The rise
in the rate of interest dampens the level of investment since it
reduces the *value* of capital goods.[55] The analysis then runs parallel
to that of J. M. Keynes and K. Wicksell, investment being taken
to be sensitive to interest rate changes. The fall in the rate of
interest during the depression increases the 'value of capital goods'
and stimulates the recovery of investment. The importance of the
rate of interest is thus in its effect on the profitability of investment,
and therefore the volume of investment that takes place in any
given period.[56]

Finally, but of most importance, is the work of Joseph Schumpeter. To him the business cycle is a normal feature of the process
of economic development.[57] The underlying assumption that inventions and discoveries are unevenly distributed over time, which
the theory of Spiethoff rested upon, was challenged by Schumpeter,
who emphasises the role of innovation in the cycle. Innovation
takes the form of either changes in production or transportation
methods, changes in the organisation of industry, the opening
up of new markets, or new sources of raw materials, or the
introduction of a new product.[58] It therefore involves investment.
The boom consists of a burst of innovation; the downturn is
characterised by its absence. Although invention may proceed at
a steady rate over time, its application to industry is likely to
be lumpy. Thus, during depression, invention may occur but there
is a failure to apply it. Innovation requires a positive decision
to invest by entrepreneurs which will not be forthcoming during
depression. The movement into prosperity is facilitated when a
few entrepreneurs decide to innovate. Their success acts as an
example to other entrepreneurs and produces a 'herd like' movement
of innovation, and the required burst of investment for prosperity.[59]
A pre-condition for this is a ready supply of bank credit. The
upper turning point must follow as 'depression is nothing more
than the economic system's reaction to the boom or the adaptation

to the situation into which the boom brings the system'.[60] Prosperity must come to an end when the new investment brought about by innovation has passed through its gestation period, and ultimately swells the flow of consumer goods. Consumer good prices must fall, reducing profitability, and leading the marginal firms into liquidation. Secondly, as prosperity proceeds, the opportunities for further investment decline, particularly as the increased flow of consumer goods comes on to the market. Both these reasons are active in providing the downturn of the cycle.

Robertsonian theory is most similar to this Schumpeterian analysis. Both make a sharp distinction between invention and innovation. It is not the occurrence of invention which is of significance in the timing of the cycle, but its application to production techniques. Innovation takes place on a relatively grand scale at the end of the depression, even though invention may be distributed evenly over the cycle. Robertson also, though not with the strong emphasis contained in Schumpeter's work, portrays businessmen as sheep, who will follow the initial investment undertaken by the braver entrepreneurs.[61] Thus the trickle of innovation at the end of depression may soon be turned into a torrent bringing the volume of investment required for recovery. This kind of business behaviour is not totally irrational. Firstly, since some entrepreneurs are prepared to innovate, this is taken as indicative of improved business conditions. Secondly, it may be that the sheep amongst the entrepreneurs feel that unless they also invest quickly, the initial burst of investment demand may bring increased costs in the capital good industries and make delayed investment unprofitable.[62]

THE THEORETICAL FRAMEWORK — THE ELASTICITY OF DEMAND FOR INCOME IN TERMS OF EFFORT

Each of the potential causes of the upturn of the cycle isolated in the last section have their initial impact upon either the agricultural or capital good industries. The essential theoretical analysis required is to explain how the change brought about in one sector of the economy can be transmitted to aggregate production. Robertson has to show that an expansion in output in one sector would not necessarily be at the expense of output in other sectors, that is that the potential causes of the upturn does not merely redistribute existing resources between sectors rather than enlarge total output. Unfortunately his exposition is confined to footnotes, and the resultant brevity does not aid a total clarification of his arguments.[63]

It is convenient to divide the economy into three sectors, A, B and C, their products being *a*, *b* and *c*, to assume that there is an absence of money, and that production in each industry is performed by a 'group of equal co-partners'.[64] This represents a simple barter economy. What will happen given either increased agricultural production, or the occurrence of innovation within a particular sector or at least in a number of industries within a sector? (Both changes are the most important sources of revival).

Let us first consider agricultural abundance. In a barter economy, if sector A is the agricultural sector, the rate of exchange between A, B and C will alter. More units of agricultural produce will be obtainable for each unit of the products of B and C. The crucial question is whether or not this situation gives rise to more or less output in B and C. This depends upon the *elasticity of demand for income in terms of effort* in both B and C, that is the responsiveness of income to changes in the effort price of acquiring that income.[65] Concentrating upon the relationship between sectors A and B, a diminution in the price of *a* in terms of *b* yields a decline in units of effort which need to be expended by sector B in order to acquire a unit of income (measured in terms of *a*). If the demand for income in terms of effort is elastic, then the fall in the price of *a* in terms of *b* will lead to an increase in the aggregate effort expended on production in sector B. If it is inelastic then the decline in effort price will result in a decline in aggregate effort in sector B. This is shown diagrammatically in Fig. 1.

Let the price of a unit of income of *a* (the effort resources necessary to achieve a unit of *a*) fall to E_1; with an elastic demand for income in terms of effort curve $(d_1 d_1)$, the aggregate effort expended by sector B to undertake purchases from Sector A is given by the area $OY_1 TE_1$, which exceeds $OY_0 XE_0$. If the demand for income curve is inelastic over the relevant range $(d_2 d_2)$, the change in effort price results in a decline in the aggregate effort in sector B going on purchases from A $(OY_2 ZE_1)$. In a similar fashion we could explore the impact of the agricultural abundance upon the aggregate effort devoted to acquiring *a* in sector C.

It still remains to determine the change in the aggregate effort

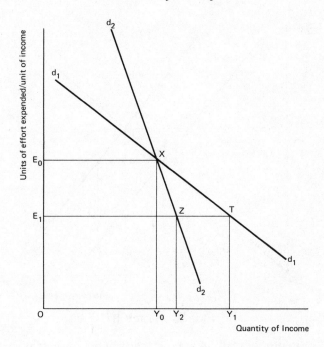

FIG. 1. Demand for income in Sector B in terms of effort price

which sector B will devote to the purchase of the products of sector C (and vice versa). This is shown in Figure 2 which is a modification of the Robertsonian analysis in the *Study*.[66] This diagram relates to the amount of effort expended in sector B as a result of agricultural abundance. The vertical axis measures the marginal utility of effort in terms of b or c $\left(\dfrac{dU}{dE_b}\right)$, $\left(\dfrac{dU}{dE_c}\right)$, and the horizontal axis measures the aggregate effort used in producing b. MU_b^0 shows the marginal utility of effort gained from producing b; MU_c shows the marginal utility of effort to be gained from producing c at each level of effort expended in sector B. Hence the greater the aggregate effort expended in sector B, the less effort there is available to expend in sector C, (this does not preclude the possibility that aggregate effort in *all* sectors can increase as a result of the agricultural abundance), and the higher is MU_c. If B's effort demand for income is elastic then the amount of effort expended on a, as a result of a fall in its effort price, may move from OA to OA_1. This leads to MU_b^0 being displaced

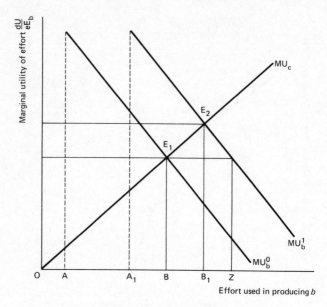

FIG. 2. Sector B

to MU_b^1. Equilibrium will now be reached at E_2 where the marginal utilities are equated ($MU_c = MU_b^1$); before, equilibrium existed at E_1. The amount of aggregate effort now utilised by B to purchase from sector C has fallen from AB to A_1B_1 or by B_1Z. Nevertheless, the aggregate effort expended by sector B has increased from OB to OB_1, as a result of the agricultural abundance. The steeper is MU_c, and the flatter is MU_b^0, the smaller will be the change in aggregate effort in sector B, given the initial assumption of an elastic effort demand for income in that sector.

The ultimate conclusion is that, given an elastic effort demand for income, agricultural abundance must stimulate aggregate effort in the economy, and consequently aggregate output, bringing a general revival. But the extent of this revival depends upon: 1) the elasticity of the effort demand for income in each sector, 2) the proportion of total effort devoted to purchasing from sector A; if the agricultural sector is small then OA and AA_1 will be relatively small and BB_1 will be diminished, 3) the rate of increase/decrease in the marginal utility of effort in the various sectors.

The impact of the other main cause of a general revival, innovation, can be examined in a like manner. Innovation within one sector of the economy, or a group of industries within one sector, may yield a reduction in real costs in those industries which, in turn, may result in a diminution of barter prices and therefore a reduction in effort prices for other sectors. Whether or not this stimulates output in other sectors again depends upon the elasticity of the effort demand for income. The fact that innovation has taken place itself reflects a change in the intensity of desire for capital goods in the innovating industries, and a revision in their demand for income (in terms of effort) curves.[67] This represents a fall in the effort price faced by capital good industries and may (again depending upon demand elasticity) result in an extension of aggregate effort and hence output on their part.

By virtue of this kind of analysis Robertson concludes: 'increased prosperity arising from this cause (invention, innovation) in any single group of trades is not necessarily secured at the expense of any other group, and so may legitimately, if the field over which it extends be sufficiently wide, be regarded as an explanation of a constructional and a general revival'.[68]

The argument of this section can be construed in terms of *price* elasticities of demand. We have a situation where the elasticity of demand for agricultural produce is greater than unity. Hence a fall in price will bring an increase in total expenditure upon agricultural produce. What Robertson is suggesting is that the increase in total spending on agricultural produce is *not* undertaken at the expense of expenditure in other directions. The desire to spend more on agricultural produce is met by an extension in productive effort, and consequently a net expansion in output and income. If the price elasticity of demand for agricultural produce is less than unity, a fall in price will reduce expenditure in this direction and lead to a diminution in the supply of effort forthcoming.

The above analysis of industrial fluctuation does appear to be confined to the work of Robertson. The use of effort elasticities of demand for income was however also utilised by Dalton to discover the impact of taxation upon aggregate effort.[69] It was later employed by A. C. Pigou in his working out of the repercussions of changes in one industry upon others during the course of the cycle.[70] This represented a sophistication of his earlier work which had reached the same conclusion as that of Robertson on the repercussions of agricultural change upon other industries.[71]

The major criticism of this theoretical framework[72] is Keynesian in nature and arises where the barter economy is replaced by a monetary economy. Unless there is an increase in total monetary demand there will be no change in aggregate output; for example, an increase in monetary expenditure on agricultural produce must be at the expense of expenditure on other produce. Whether this criticism is valid depends upon the constancy of total monetary demand in the above circumstances. Clearly Robertson would argue that the change in relative prices signalling the revival must result in an extension of the aggregate effort supplied by the labour force in a money economy. The extra produce yielded by this additional effort will constitute an addition to total monetary demand. In the face of a static money supply, the price level will adjust to accommodate the increased volume of purchases taking place.[73]

In this section the upturn has been viewed in terms of an increase in the marginal utility of effort. It must be borne in mind in the following chapter, on the causes of the downturn, that the downturn also can be analysed by employing this framework and in terms of a diminished marginal utility of effort.[74]

5 The Theory of Crisis — From Boom to Recession

There were three types of over-investment theories of crisis known to Robertson during the course of his preparation of the *Study*. Tugan-Baranowski[1] argued that the investment during the boom became excessive in relation to the supply of credit available to finance it, and consequently the capital good industries suffered. Labordère and Spiethoff[2] proposed that over-investment occurred relative to the available stock of consumer goods required to accommodate this investment. (This stock represented a stock of *real* as opposed to monetary saving). Aftalion[3] believed that over-investment resulted, not because of a shortage of saving to finance it, but because the *demand* for capital (instrumental) goods fell below the available supply.[4] This was a consequence of a decline in the marginal utility to be gained from capital goods relative to that of consumer goods. It was Aftalion's theory that commanded most support from Robertson,[5] although he did have some sympathy for the *real* saving thesis.[6] In this chapter the reasons for over-investment taking place are explored in more detail. It is not necessary to date Robertsonian theory in this context since he remained faithful to the views expressed here throughout his later writings.

THE GESTATION PERIOD OF INVESTMENT

Even before the *Study* Robertson had provided several hints at what he thought was most responsible for over-investment. These hints appeared as comment on, and development of, the work of Aftalion.[7] In his review of Aftalion's work[8] he supports the manifest importance of the gestation period of investment, which yields too much investment.[9] In a paper to the Royal Statistical Society[10] he chooses to extend the statistical enquiry of Aftalion's work on the gestation period to several English industries and considers their implications for the industrial cycle.

In his *Study*, the fact that investment does not instantaneously materialise in the form of fixed capital equipment means that the boom must inevitably give rise to its own destruction. The gestation period brings this about in the following manner. An increase in the prices of commodities during a period of recovery provides an inducement to investment. The length of time necessary for investment to be realised maintains high prices because of the lag in the supply of additional commodity output. As a consequence all producers are tempted to react to the high prices. The general ignorance as to the amount of investment other producers are undertaking leads to producers over-investing, such that eventually a large increase in the production of commodities will result. Prices fall and recession follows. What is more 'the longer therefore this period of gestation, the longer will the period of high prices continue, the greater will be the over-investment and the more severe the subsequent depression'.[11] This particular thesis appeared in the *Study* despite the objection of Keynes who failed to appreciate that more investment could occur than was profitable,[12] and is supported by empirical evidence relating to the production of coal, pig-iron, ships, cotton and coffee.[13] This evidence yields the conclusion that the period of gestation is important in determining the intensity and duration of the phases of several past fluctuations in output. In relation to shipbuilding Robertson concludes 'it should be observed that owing to the length of the period of gestation the impact of several successive independent ripples of demand frequently exercises an effect upon the output of new ships which resembles that of a continuous and concentrated breaker'.[14] The period of gestation varies from one product to the next and over the course of the cycle for each product. Particular attention is focused in the *Study* on the role of the transport sector. Robertson appreciates the influence of the transport system on the gestation period, that is the need for transport to bring capital equipment to its place of usage. This often prolongs the period of installation of equipment.

The gestation period however is not only responsible for too much investment in the above context. It also aggravates the running down of stocks of consumer goods which are needed to meet consumer demand whilst resources are being diverted to cater for investment. The longer the period of gestation, the heavier the demands upon the stocks of existing consumer goods.[15]

It is relevant at this stage to indicate the influence that Aftalion had upon Robertson's work. This influence was undoubtedly significant since, whilst working on the *Study*, Robertson had written that Aftalion's work was the most constructive contribution to the trade cycle theory ever made with the possible exception of Jevons' work.[16] In relation to the downturn Aftalion argued that 'the chief responsibility for cyclical fluctuation should be assigned to one of the characteristics of modern industrial technique, namely the long period required for the production of fixed capital'.[17] The length of the time period in the production of fixed capital disguises the amount of investment that is taking place as a result of the increase in consumer wants. The businessman is unaware of the extent of investment being undertaken by his fellow businessmen, and is therefore unable to adjust his volume of investment according to this. The danger which can arise occurs when businessmen over-react to an increase in consumer demand by over-investing in capital goods.[18] The occurrence of over-investment during the period of prosperity and the increase in output of consumer goods that it eventually yields, culminates in a saturation of consumer demand. The natural reaction to this saturation is for businessmen to curtail any further expenditure on capital goods, demands upon capital good industries fall and recession sets in.

From this it can be seen that there is much in Aftalion's thesis which Robertson utilised in his *Study*. In the next section it will be demonstrated that Robertson was also convinced by Aftalion's emphasis upon the influence of the durability or longevity of capital equipment in prolonging the depression. However, he was not convinced in 1915 by his explanation of the upturn of the cycle in terms of the acceleration principle.[19]

THE DURABILITY, IMPERFECT DIVISIBILITY AND INTRACTABILITY OF CAPITAL EQUIPMENT

Karl Marx[20] appears to have provided the main inspiration for Robertson to enquire into the relation between the length of life of capital and the trade cycle. Marx had argued that the occurrence of crises at ten yearly intervals could be explained by the fact that the average life of capital was ten years. As a consequence it was suggested that investment will proceed in a discontinuous fashion, with periodic bursts of investment every ten years followed by years of inactivity.

This thesis commanded some support from Robertson. His early statistical enquiry confirmed an average life of capital of ten years in railways and cotton spinning though not in the case of shipbuilding or other industries.[21] He observed that investment was not distributed evenly over time but was clustered, and that such periodic outbursts of investment must give rise to periodic lumps of replacement investment determined by the lifespan of the capital equipment. But, if the average life of capital varied from industry to industry, there could be no inevitability in the cycle as a consequence of the Marxian theory that a burst of replacement investment would occur in all industries simultaneously. Nevertheless, Robertson sought to enquire whether past peaks in investment activity had been characterised by replacement or net investment. He found that the evidence did tend to support Marx; in the case of railways, cotton, wool and shipbuilding investment activity appeared to coincide with the lifespan of the machinery employed. The length of life of capital was therefore another possible cause of the wide fluctuations in activity in the capital good industries which were a feature of the trade cycle.

The imperfect divisibility of capital equipment and its intractability were also forces tending to aggravate the depression, and to add to the over-investment taking place during the upswing.[22] Capital equipment is not often employable in small units hence the investment decision necessitates a choice between buying an excessively large-sized unit of investment or none at all. As a consequence, if investment takes place, the additional output which it may eventually generate could exceed the additional demand for which it was undertaken. This type of occurrence was regarded as most severe in the public utility services.[23] Such industries, the notable examples being the railway and electricity industries, require heavy expenditure on capital equipment in order to create a large continuous network of such equipment.[24]

The reverse argument also holds true. Because of its indivisibility, investment is intractable. It is impossible in some industries to close down, or lie idle, capital equipment as a result of a shortfall in demand. Robertson gives a comparison of the coal and pig iron industries. Intractability is more extensive in the coal industry where the lying idle of capital equipment would be unwise in two respects. The closing down of collieries is costly, particularly if provision has to be made also for their possible re-use, and it may represent a danger to the work force. The closing down of a blast furnace is a decision which, although still costly and perhaps inconvenient, can more lightly be undertaken; even so, this is also a good example of the indivisibility of capital equipment. The failure to keep in use one furnace may herald a significant drop in the total output of the iron producer.[25]

CONCLUSION

In this chapter the strength of the *real* forces responsible for the crisis has been witnessed. These real forces are represented primarily by the gestation period of investment, but also by its durability, its imperfect divisibility, and allied with this, its intractability. Working together during the upswing, these features of investment lead to an excessive outlay upon capital equipment which ultimately depresses the marginal utility of these goods relative to that of consumer goods. The inevitable result is a downturn in the capital good industries and the onset of depression.

6 Agricultural Forces in the Trade Cycle

Many of the continental over-investment theories had developed as a critical response to agricultural theories of the cycle.[1] In contrast to this, in this section, we find Robertson extending considerable importance to agricultural forces, particularly in generating a recovery. Approximately one third of his *Study* is devoted to an examination of the relation between crop production and industrial activity. This, despite the position held by economists in 1914, that: 'to exhibit any leaning towards celestial or crop theories was indeed, to invite the suggestion that one ought to go to see a doctor'.[2]

TWO BRANCHES OF AGRICULTURAL THEORIES

Two variants of agricultural theories were already well established prior to 1915. Robertson was well aware of both of these.[3] The first, and more extreme, gained only limited support in the *Study*. This was associated with W. S. and H. S. Jevons in the U.K., and with H. Moore in the United States.[4] It hypothesised a connection between climatic conditions and a cycle in agricultural production, the agricultural cycle in turn causing the industrial cycle.

On the basis of statistical observation, W. S. and H. S. Jevons proposed that the cycle in spots on the sun created cyclical weather conditions, bringing a cycle in crop production. W. S. Jevons' theory was a result of a comprehensive study of the records of

English trade from 1721 to 1878; in this he estimated that the average time lapse between commercial crises was 10.44 years. Evidence on the occurrence of sun spots gave the sun spot interval to be 10.45 years. From this he proposed that: 'it seems probable that commercial crises are connected with a periodic variation of weather affecting all parts of the earth, and probably arising from increased waves of heat received from the sun', and concluded: 'judging this close coincidence of results, according to the theory of probabilities, it becomes highly probable that two periodic phenomena, varying so nearly in the same mean period, are connected as cause and effect'.[5] This precise theory was to perish not on the misuse of statistical methods, in that correlation does not *necessarily* imply causation, but upon the revision of the observed length of the sunspot cycle.

This revision of the sunspot cycle stimulated H. S. Jevons to revise his father's theory in 1909,[6] still maintaining the causal link between crop cycles and business cycles. Using meteorological evidence which put the period of solar radiation at three and a half years, H. S. Jevons attempted to show empirically the existence of a three and a half year periodicity in crop yields. As the trade cycle is of seven to ten and a half years average duration, he concluded that it takes more than one period of good crops to initiate a boom period.[7] Thus a single trade cycle was no longer seen to be revolving on the basis of a single crop cycle.

The theory of H. Moore was based upon substantial statistical evidence, and benefited from the availability of newfound statistical techniques (correlation and regression analysis). The evidence presented related to rainfall data in the crop-producing areas of Ohio and Illinois. Moore found that: 'the weather conditions represented by the rainfall in the central part of the United States, and probably in other continental areas, passed through cycles of approximately thirty-three and eight years duration, causing like cycles in the yield per acre of the crops'.[8] This established the duration of the crop cycle somewhere between that of W. S. Jevons and that of H. S. Jevons. This he later confirmed by investigating crop cycles in England and France.[9] A high correlation was shown to exist between crop yields and certain business activity indicators such as the price level of pig iron production. As with W. S. Jevons, he took correlation to imply causation.[10] However, in later work he was ready to accept that this natural cause of the cycle may be partially or totally offset by the effects of other causes, natural or social, regular or fortuitous.[11]

All of the theories outlined here not only have in common the idea that the crop cycle causes the business cycle but each regards an increase in crop yields as having a beneficial effect on business activity, and a decrease in crop yield as having a depressing effect on industrial output.

The second variant of agricultural theories is typified by the work of Piatt Andrew before 1915.[12] It is important here since Robertson explores in his *Study* some of the links suggested by Piatt Andrew between agricultural and business activity. This approach seeks only to establish that changes in agricultural output can exert an influence upon industrial production. There is no disposition to argue that an agricultural cycle exists at all. Piatt Andrew concentrated his empirical investigations into five important channels through which a change in agricultural production may be able to influence business activity. These were to establish the impact of such a change upon the consumption of non-agricultural produce, upon the incomes of farmers and the related trades, upon the balance of trade and bank reserves, upon the demand for transport services, and upon those manufacturing trades which use an agricultural product as a raw material. He was led to the conclusion that all the expansions in America between 1872 and 1905 were initiated by agricultural abundance, and most of the downturns preceded by agricultural depression.

It is against this background and these conclusions that Robertson set about his own statistical enquiry into the role of agriculture in promoting industrial fluctuation.

AGRICULTURAL INFLUENCES UPON INDUSTRIAL FLUCTUATION — THE ROBERTSONIAN THEORY

The Robertsonian approach to analysing the effects of changing crop volume and value upon economic activity has both a micro and macro aspect. The first line of enquiry is to ascertain the influences of agricultural variation upon particular industries, an approach not dissimilar from that of Piatt Andrew. From this there are clues as to the role to be dispensed by Robertson to agriculture in bringing aggregate industrial fluctuations.

The most significant argument investigated is that changes in crop volumes will alter incomes in the agricultural sector which, in turn, will have repercussions upon the demand for capital equipment.[13] The initial argument is self-evident. The income of farmers depends upon the annual crop volume. If this volume increases, farm incomes will rise (if the demand for the crop(s) is elastic). Less straightforward are the consequences of increased farm incomes for the demand for capital equipment. There is strong support for the proposition that the increased purchasing power of farmers must raise the demand for capital equipment, either directly, if farmers buy more agricultural machinery and improve production techniques, or indirectly in that, even if increased farm incomes are used to pay off mortgages, or to extend cultivated land acreage, those receiving additional farm expenditures will themselves have more income to spend on capital equipment.[14] But there may be exceptions to this general rule. Clearly the capital-intensive farmer (e.g. the wheat producer) will have greater scope for expenditure on new machinery; the labour-intensive producer (e.g. rice farmer), with a lack of substitutability of factors, cannot enlarge his purchases of capital equipment despite increased receipts. In addition, looking beyond the agricultural sector, the net effect upon the demand for capital goods must depend upon the type of redistribution of income that has taken place. If aggregate income is fixed, a wealthier farming community implies a decline in the real income in other sectors. This in turn may signal a decline in the demand for consumer goods which may have a depressing effect upon the demand for capital goods. In a monetary economy one might also find credit being concentrated in the prosperous agricultural sector at the expense of the other sectors. Robertson sought to resolve these opposing arguments by considering the experiences of both the United States and Britain. Invariably he found that the evidence connected increased farm incomes with an upsurge in the demand for capital goods, the only major exception being the building industry in Britain which in the period examined (1869 to 1913) was depressed during periods of agricultural prosperity.

However, the enlargement of the demand for capital goods is not solely dependent upon the increase in crop values. Following again the analysis of Piatt Andrew, Robertson also investigated the effects of increased crop volume upon the demand for transport services, both land and sea transport. Increased crop volume puts pressure on transport facilities such that more rolling stock, engines, railways, and shipping has to be provided to cope with demand. This increase in demand will heighten, in turn, the demand for the products of the iron and steel industry.[15]

The effect of increased crop values upon the consumer good industries is more complex. A redistribution of income in favour of agricultural producers must increase the demand for certain types of consumer goods, but the overall effect on the consumption trades is uncertain. The fortunes of the consumption trades in the period 1880 to 1913 are seen to have been dictated by the condition of the purchasing power of the population in India, and by the income of the British working classes. The former varied with the state of the rice harvest in India. A low price of rice gave the Indian population more purchasing power to buy British exports, particularly cotton goods. This export trade was so significant[16] that it dictated the course of consumer good output.[17] In this case therefore, agricultural change in another country is seen to have an impact upon British output through its effect upon the demand for exports. The change in the purchasing power of the working class in Britain, through agricultural abundance, can be either positive or negative. If the abundance is a result primarily of a heavy wheat crop, consumption may expand due to an inelastic demand for wheat which lowers total expenditure on wheat and raises the purchasing power of the working class, lowering that of wheat producers.[18]

THE IMPACT UPON AGGREGATE OUTPUT OF AGRICULTURAL FLUCTUATION

The opposition to agricultural explanations of the cycle was already well established by 1915. The validity of the sunspot theory had been questioned on scientific grounds; the sunspot cycle could not be firmly established and as a consequence neither could the cycle in agricultural production.[19] But this did not condemn agricultural fluctuation to a passive role in the cycle. Robertson believed that agricultural change, not necessarily regular in nature, may be one of the main forces causing the upturn; it is an exogenous force with the same possible consequences as invention and innovation; as such it need not be the determining force behind every industrial cycle.

There are two main criticisms of this thesis which Robertson had to overcome. Many argued that agricultural change merely redistributed a fixed aggregate income between, in particular, the agricultural sector and the working classes. There would be no increase in the aggregate purchasing power within the community,[20] and therefore no stimulation afforded to aggregate output by increasing crop volumes. It is in answering this criticism where the concept of *effort* elasticity of demand becomes relevant.[21] A change in the rate of exchange between agricultural and industrial products can bring a net increase in aggregate output. Whether it does or not depends upon whether the effort elasticity of demand for agricultural produce is greater or less than unity. If it is greater than unity, agricultural abundance will lead to an expansion of effort by industrial producers and consequently to an increase in industrial output bartered in exchange for agricultural produce. If effort elasticity falls below unity then industrial output will decline. Nevertheless the change in the rate of exchange imposed by agricultural variation cannot only redistribute income, but also raise or diminish the aggregate level of income.[22] Hence Robertson concludes: 'in certain circumstances the total volume of industrial activity may be diminished by an increase in the volume of crops, but that it is not likely in any case to be diminished much, and is more likely on the whole to be increased'.[23]

The second major criticism is that agricultural fluctuation is so small that it cannot be responsible for the more extensive changes in industrial output in the cycle.[24] In most Western economies by 1915 the agricultural sector contributed a much smaller proportion of national product than it did sixty years earlier. This fact weighed heavily against the agricultural theories; but this did not automatically preclude the fluctuations in crop volume and value remaining from having a substantial repercussion on industrial output. The important statistical exercise undertaken by Robertson was therefore to ascertain the extent of agricultural fluctuation. Inter-temporal compensation, the storing of crops in years of glut and their release in years of dearth, did iron out some of the alteration in the ratio of exchange which would have otherwise taken place.[25] But nevertheless considerable alteration in the ratio of exchange still occurred. Inter-local compensation[26] did not gain statistical support. A diminution in the supply of a crop from one source was not offset by an increase in supply from other sources. Indeed Robertson took the commonality of weather conditions experienced by most suppliers as indicative of some justification for the sunspot theory.[27] Neither was it found that variation in crop yields was minimised by the increased diversity of crops planted by farmers. Again, the dearth of one crop was not counteracted by the glut in another. The overriding conclusion was that agricultural fluctuation was not negligible, and could still influence industrial fluctuation in 1915.

Therefore in his *Study* it is apparent that considerable weight is given to the possibility of changing weather conditions bringing industrial revival; the emphasis upon it bringing a collapse is not as great. In general, agricultural abundance will stimulate production overall, and agricultural shortages would have a depressive effect.[28] In later work, however, the role of agriculture did not gain the same attention. In *Banking* Robertson concludes that agricultural periods: 'do not furnish a complete explanation of the periodicity of industrial output', but that movements in the volume of agricultural output strongly influence both the times at which various stages of the cycle occur, and the magnitude which cycles attain.[29] Even in his Cambridge lectures he remains faithful to the influences of the soil upon a revival. But in *Lectures* he excludes any reference to the effort demand analysis of his *Study* and concentrates instead upon applying the microeconomic argument of early writings (particularly the influence of changing farm incomes upon investment) at the macro level,[30] an approach which Keynes had utilised in the *General Theory*.[31]

It is not surprising therefore, with this kind of emphasis upon the role of agricultural fluctuation in the cycle, that Robertson took exception to the comment by W. Beveridge that primary producers, and consumers of their products had been a neglected aspect of trade cycle theory.[32]

7 Robertson and the Alternative Theories of Industrial Fluctuation

As a final aid to achieving a clearer perspective of the Robertsonian theory of fluctuation, it is worthwhile to survey its relation with alternative theories; in particular to survey here the Robertsonian standpoint on the operation of the accelerator in the cycle, to examine the role of psychological and monetary forces in the cycle, to witness the reaction of Robertson to the under-consumption school, and to clarify the extent to which Marshallian economics influenced the theory of fluctuation.[1]

THE ACCELERATION PRINCIPLE AND THE CYCLE

Aftalion's work is the source of Robertson's knowledge of the acceleration principle in 1915.[2] He had argued that a small change in consumer demand during the depression would be sufficient to create a much greater change in the demand for capital goods. The level of investment in any period is determined by the rate of change in consumer demand.[3] Modern macroeconomic textbooks are now littered with numerical examples of this principle which show the initial magnification of capital good production as a result of a small change in consumer demand; this is followed, because of the durability of capital equipment, by a sharp diminution in the demand for these goods.[4] All go to prove the point which Aftalion was anxious to make, namely that the volatility in the cycle is to be found principally in the capital good industries

59

and not in the consumption trades. Hence Aftalion asserts that the existence of the capitalist system of production: 'has caused the appearance and repetition of economic cycles'.[5]

Robertson, in the *Study*, does acknowledge that there is a possible link between changes in the demand for consumer goods and the amount of investment subsequently taking place. At the micro level an increase in demand will raise prices, and hence the margin between prices and costs; this margin in turn will help determine the producer's investment decision.[6] The essential point here is that the transmission mechanism from the change in consumer demand to investment is through price changes; this contrasts with the usual statement of the accelerator where prices are constant. The general impression gained from the *Study* is of its scepticism of the importance of the acceleration principle in causing macro-industrial revival.[7] This is borne out of the contention that the marginal utility of consumer goods remains fairly stable over the cycle.[8] (Although it would not necessarily follow that this stability creates a *stable* demand for consumer goods over the cycle. If, for example, income is changing through the cycle so too might be consumer demand even if the marginal utility of consumer goods is constant).[9] It is the marginal utility of capital (construction) goods which fluctuates, and which is responsible for the cycle. This fluctuation is primarily brought about by other sources than that of changing consumer demand, principally by invention and innovation affecting costs of production. This is supported by empirical observation which suggests that the period of revival in construction good industries is frequently characterised by a fall in consumption, not an expansion.[10]

The scepticism over the importance of the accelerator disappears from Robertsonian literature by the end of the 1930s. It becomes one of the main weapons which Robertson uses against Keynesian multiplier analysis.[11] In 1937 Robertson agrees with the importance which Harrod attaches to the accelerator in the upswing,[12] arguing that 'the principle of acceleration deserves pride of place in any analysis of the trade cycle';[13] but at the same time he recognises other determinants of investment, and highlights the interference to the smooth working of the accelerator imposed by invention. The same year, in a radio broadcast,[14] Robertson built a theory of fluctuation around the accelerator declaring it to be 'at the root of the whole trouble'. He did however point out the limitations of the principle. If idle capacity exists, an increase in consumer demand need not lead to an expansion in the demand for capital goods, but merely to the reutilisation of idle capacity. The rate of interest, and invention, and 'all sorts of things' would also influence the level of investment again disturbing the precision of the acceleration principle. This support for the principle continues in the post-war period, particularly in *Lectures*,[15] but Robertson consistently emphasises that the accelerator alone is not responsible for determining investment. Indeed he finds some consolation in the Hicksian role for autonomous investment in the cycle, preferring this role, however, to be slightly deflated,[16] but not totally nullified. He declares in *Lectures*, contrary to his opinion in the *Study*, that the accelerator has always for him taken pride of place in the cycle,[17] even though it has its limitations.[18]

In the *Study* recovery begins in the 'instrumental trades'[19] and is eventually passed on to the consumer good industries. *Lectures* is less definite than this; the expansion can begin in either capital or consumer good industries; wherever it begins it will be transmitted from one to the other.[20] This ultimate faith in the acceleration principle marks perhaps the most significant shift in Robertson's views on the cycle over his lifetime.

THE UNDER-CONSUMPTION SCHOOL — ROBERTSONIAN COMMENT

As with the over-investment school of industrial fluctuation, the under-consumption school comprises multifarious theories. All theories, from the early work of Malthus and Sismondi[21] to the more developed under-consumptionist stance of J. Hobson[22] and W. F. Foster and W. Catchings[23] are not complete theories of the cycle. Each concentrates upon explaining the downturn without reference to the revival.

The works of Hobson and Foster and Catchings drew most attention from Robertson.[24] In common with other theories the blame for the crisis is placed upon an inadequacy of consumer spending. This under-consumption in turn reflects over-saving by the community. But in what sense is there over-saving? There is an increase in saving at the end of recovery, parallel with a diminution in the level of consumer spending (because income saved cannot also be spent). This increased saving will flow into the capital good industries; that is, there will be an increase in investment financed by the additional saving. This investment will ultimately bring an increase in the output of consumer goods at a time when consumer demand is deficient (because of the over-saving taking place). This leads to the Hobsonian proposition that there will be an *optimum* rate of saving[25] which will prevent the inadequacy in consumer demand arising during the recovery. The major cause of under-consumption is the maldistribution of income. During the upswing too great a proportion of total income is in the hands of the higher income groups, those with a high propensity to save. The remedy therefore is seen to be the raising of wage levels and consequently a greater equalisation of incomes between the various income recipients, such that those who desire to consume also have the purchasing power to do so.

Part II will provide a more complete picture of the Robertsonian comment upon the under-consumption theory. The following brief observations will be sufficient at this stage:[26]

1) In contrast to the under-consumption school, Robertson emphasises the importance of investment, not consumption, as the leading force in the crisis. It is not the gap between consumer demand and output which brings the downturn, but the deficiency of demand for capital goods in relation to capital good production (caused by a downward revision in the marginal utility of these goods relative to consumption goods). Again it must be emphasised that in the *Study* Robertson regarded the volatility of the consumption trades as relatively negligible during the upswing. The crisis is characterised by an over-production in the capital good industries, not in the consumption trades, nor in both together. Robertson found that capital good production tended to decline towards the end of the upturn before consumer good production. This also supported his thesis and worked against the under-consumption school.[27]

There are passages in the *Study* which do suggest, as Robertson admits,[28] that his theory is 'quasi-Hobsonian' in character.[29] He believes his theory merits this description because the downturn in the instrumental trades must eventually have repercussions upon the consumption trades.

2) The alternative theory of crisis which gains limited support from Robertson in the *Study*[30] bears an even greater dissimilarity

with the under-consumptionist view. The cause of the crisis, which may operate before the more conventional Robertsonian over-investment mechanism begins to function, is the shortage of saving needed to accommodate the investment intentions of producers. Under-saving, not over-saving, is the cause of the crisis. Saving here is defined as the stock of consumer goods, accumulated during the depression, which the community can live upon during the recovery, whilst a greater proportion of resources flow into the capital good industries away from consumer good production. If this stock of *real* saving is inadequate to meet the investment demand, investment intentions have to be abandoned, and capital projects left unfinished. The inevitable consequence is a depression beginning in the capital good industries. The under-consumptionist adopts a totally contrasting approach. During recovery, investment takes place whilst the supply of consumer goods is deficient. Eventually the capital equipment generated by investment must be completed, and will result in an expansion in the supply of consumer goods; at this stage the demand for consumer goods becomes deficient in relation to its supply. There is no anchor put on the advance of investment by a shortage of saving.

3) Less important a feature of the later work of the under-consumptionist, in that it is not essential to the explanation of the crisis, is the proposition that all saving need not necessarily flow into investment. This is more in keeping with the Robertsonian theory of interest.[31] Robertson too upholds this proposition, arguing that saving can be hoarded, or used to buy titles which do not necessarily generate new investments. It does not however merit any special consideration in the crisis, since the upturn must be characterised by an excess of investment over saving and not vice-versa.

4) Finally, the means of preventing the crisis through a redistribution of incomes, advocated by the under-consumptionist, did not find favour with Robertson. It would not be in the interests of economic progress to instigate such a redistribution. If the capitalist system of production was to be retained, because of the features of investment, economic progress would not be steady. Cyclical fluctuation is inevitable and to some extent a justifiable feature of a capitalist system seeking to enlarge its productive capacity. In the short run, the wage earner might suffer due to the ups-and-downs of industry, but in the long run he must benefit[32] from the increase in the standard of living promoted by cyclical variations.

THE ROLE OF PSYCHOLOGICAL AND MONETARY FORCES IN THE CYCLE

The grouping together of psychological and monetary forces is justified principally by the common role which Robertson attaches to each in the cycle. This is a passive role in which, although not guilty of causing the underlying economic instability in the cycle, monetary and psychological forces are regarded as potential villains exacerbating this instability. This grouping is also justifiable in the sense that the psychological and monetary theories of fluctuation were together the most popular theories during the most productive years of the working out of the Robertsonian thesis (1913–1930).

Most modern economists are familiar with the psychological theory of the cycle put forward by A. C. Pigou.[33] In this errors of optimism and pessimism on the part of businessmen are responsible for the cycle.[34] Similarly, Keynes too was to lay some stress upon uncertainty and expectations and their repercussions upon business activity, particularly investment.[35]

By 1915 several economists had already emphasised psychological factors in the cycle. Many of the previous theories mentioned also acknowledged a role for psychological factors in the cycle, without accepting this role as being the cause of the cycle. Aftalion recognised that the gestation period of investment, because of the uncertainty it created in relation to the investment decision, may lead to errors in business operations. Schumpeter also felt that the herd-like movement of businessmen during prosperity may be exaggerated by errors of optimism. However, three economists above all others in the pre-1915 period had very definite views that psychological factors were of utmost relevance in any discussion of the cause of the cycle. These were: John Stuart Mill, John Mills and W. H. Beveridge.

In 1848 John Stuart Mill wrote of prosperity being established on a wave of speculation and overconfidence, bringing price rises and over-commitment by merchants.[36] The bubble bursts with speculative selling, prices fall, and the ensuing panic leads to depression. Thus the cause of the crisis is the excessive speculation which cannot be maintained, inevitably leading to collapse.

John Mills was of the opinion that a cyclical movement in the minds of businessmen created the cycle in trade.[37] Out of a period of increasing trade is bred a feeling of optimism. This in turn breeds recklessness and over-excited trade, culminating in stagnation. Recovery can only take place when businessmen become optimistic once more.[38]

The tendency for businessmen to over-react is also the cause of the cycle in W. H. Beveridge's theory.[39] The economic system is itself to blame for this, because of its lack of perfection. Lack of knowledge, and the resulting uncertainty during prosperity, make businessmen misjudge the market. Each tries to obtain for himself as much of any increase in demand as he possibly can. The aggregation of this reaction brings over-production, falling prices and depression. Business pessimism grows and this exaggerates the contraction.

In response to this psychological theory, Robertson firmly upheld that both optimism and pessimism must be induced by specific occurrences.[40] It was in discovering what these occurrences were that the true sources of the cycle lay. Optimism and pessimism alone could not bring industrial fluctuation. The underlying causes of both the cycle, and the over- or under- reaction of businessmen, rested with the real forces already discussed. Increased crop volume and value is seen to breed an 'infectious spirit of confidence'.[41] The gestation period of investment disguises the amount of investment taking place, heightening the uncertainty of the business environment, and consequently the probability of errors of judgement by entrepreneurs.[42] At the heart of every error by businessmen there is an underlying *real* cause. In a world of imperfect knowledge, errors will occur and may exaggerate the economic instability present throughout the cycle. Robertson did not seek to deny this. Indeed he was critical of models of fluctuation which did not afford this psychological interference. Of Harrod's model he states: 'we are conducted through a severely rational and frictionless world in which nobody ever loses his head or makes mistakes or finds himself in a bottleneck'.[43] Although otherwise largely sympathetic to Harrod's real theory, Robertson is critical of its neglect of psychological factors. There is thus a kind of halfway house for psychological forces, not totally innocent of damaging steady progress, but certainly not the first offenders.[44] However, whereas the capitalist system of production renders the economic cycle a permanent and justifiable feature in the interests of long-run economic progress, additional fluctuation at the hands of psychological forces is not, according to Robertson, justifiable and should be eliminated through government economic policies.[45]

All business cycle theories express views on the operation of monetary factors during prosperity and depression. Output, employment and economic activity in general are facilitated by the monetary system. Investment requires finance, consumption requires money income, the value of production is measured in money terms, and the whole process of exchange is undertaken using money. Since the cycle is concerned with these economic variables, a neglect of the role of money is a sad omission from any theory. So far the theories outlined have accepted the role of money as being a passive factor in the cycle, not actively causing prosperity or depression, but merely allowing or aiding the cycle to occur. Monetary theories give a much stronger active role to money. Dominant amongst these theories is that of R. G. Hawtrey,[46] which first appeared in 1913 and had a significant early influence upon Robertson's work.[47]

Consumers' outlay, which in Hawtrey's analysis means expenditure on both consumer and capital goods, is determined by the quantity of money. As the quantity of money varies, or more specifically as expansions and contractions of bank credit take place, so consumers' outlay is affected and the cycle is generated.[48] The onset of prosperity is brought about by an expansion of bank credit and will persist as long as the expansion of credit continues.[49] A cycle in bank credit is a consequence of: 'an inherent tendency towards fluctuations in the banking institutions'[50] through: 'the too ready acceptance of reserve proportions as a guide to credit policy'.[51] The theory rests upon the sensitivity of merchants to changes in the rate of interest. Thus, when the banks find that they are able to extend bank credit, they lower the cost of borrowing, and this stimulates the merchants to utilise credit. Merchants use the credit to increase their demands upon producers (increased orders). Stocks are run down, and producers respond by increasing output to match demand, and to replenish stock levels. To do this involves increased utilisation of the credit facilities offered by the banks. A general rise in employment acts in promoting wage increases which, in turn, lead to increased consumers' outlay. Finally the banks feel they are no longer able to offer cheap money, the rate of interest rises and this chokes off the expansion.[52]

The discussion of saving, investment and the rate of interest in Part II will make a more detailed enquiry into the behaviour of monetary forces in Robertsonian theory. It has been stressed that one dominant objective of the *Study* was to pull back the monetary veil and to observe the real forces causing the cycle; later work, particularly *Banking*, was to fit monetary factors into the cycle, but money remained of secondary importance.[53] An expansion of credit could not on its own initiate the cycle, but it could, in going beyond the expansion needed to finance justifiable investment, lead the cycle to higher peaks, and to even worse depressions. The manner in which this aggravation of the cycle occurred was not dissimilar from arguments found within the monetary theories.[54] In the *Study*, for example, an expansion of credit, or an increase in the volume of money, will raise the general level of prices and encourage additional investment. This inducement may come about in several ways,[55] by raising the confidence of the business community, by lowering the real burden of the debt of the businessmen, and more specifically the real cost of the utilisation of bank credit, and by lowering the real costs of production.[56] An excessive expansion of credit may also keep the money rate of interest at a relatively low level in comparison with the rate of return offered on new investment opportunities;[57] equally a contraction of credit, and an increase in its cost, could not of its own bring the down-turn. It could, however, take it beyond that level dictated by real forces through a fall in prices and a diminution in profit margins and also through an increase in the money rate of interest rendering marginal investments unprofitable.[58] The cycle in credit therefore aided and abetted psychological forces; the excessive follies of businessmen in the upswing may be facilitated by a ready supply of bank loans at low cost; their undue pessimism in the downturn is encouraged by a lack of finance available to undertake further investments, and by immoderate rates of interest on new loans. The principal deficiency of monetary theories was in not appreciating that the true limitation upon expansion was not the restricted ability of the banking system to create credit, but the real stock of consumer goods which the economy could draw upon whilst the structure of production was biased towards capital goods.[59]

ROBERTSON AND THE MARSHALLIAN TRADITION: SOME PRELIMINARY OBSERVATIONS

Natura non facit saltum[60] had been the motto of Alfred Marshall, and indeed could equally have been that of Robertson. As Marshall sought to develop the early economics of D. Ricardo and J. Mill, so too did Robertson strive to present his theory as a continuation of Marshallian economics. Thus, one would not expect Robertsonian theory to be markedly different from that of Marshall; the differences in fact are mainly differences of emphasis rather than sharp contrasts; but these differences are concentrated in the theory of fluctuation and are less pronounced in relation to the important Marshallian micro-economic topics of supply and demand analysis and producer/consumer surplus.

Whereas Robertson devoted most of his research to studying industrial fluctuation and economic dynamics, Marshall had been preoccupied with comparative statics and with microeconomics in his earlier writings. The *Economics of Industry*[61] had offered two chapters on crises and depression, but it was not until his final work, *Money Credit and Commerce*,[62] that Marshall chose specifically to study industrial fluctuation. This makes the task of interpreting the Marshallian theory of fluctuation more difficult, since it has to be assembled from isolated references to the trade cycle.

This tendency to neglect the trade cycle, in contrast to Robertson, may in some ways reflect the classical disposition towards theories of fluctuation. Such theories grew out of an attack upon Say's Law[63] which argued that there was no possibility of over-production. The classical economists in general had sought to uphold Say's Law, but at the same time did acknowledge that maladjusted production could exist (where, for example, investment took place in unprofitable outlets). Marshallian economics was also to take this approach; Marshall declared that: 'though men have the power to purchase they may not choose to use it';[64] but this was not sufficient evidence against Say's Law to encourage Marshall to devote more of his energies to a study of industrial fluctuation.[65] Nevertheless Robertson felt that his own treatment of the law of markets grew out of a less than exaggerated respect for it from his teachers.[66] Clearly he was prepared to go further in his disrespect for Say's Law than Marshall. The over-investment theory was indicative of the belief that an economy can produce more of particular kinds of commodities than it desires; there can be over-production in relation to individual types of goods. More significantly Robertson agreed with Aftalion that over-investment can in turn bring about a general over-production.[67]

Strictly in accordance with the Marshallian tradition and contrary to Keynesian analysis, the Robertsonian causes of the cycle influence the levels of output and employment by changing prices and hence profit margins; in Keynesian economics prices remain stable at less than full employment; the movement from depression, through recovery to boom, is not characterised by increasing prices until unemployed resources have been fully utilised.[68] That price movements occur in response to the underlying causes of fluctuation is a fairly widespread feature of trade cycle theories in 1915 and did not belong exclusively to Cambridge economists. Robertson had read of the role of fluctuating prices and profit margins in the works of, not only Marshall, but also G. Hull and W. Mitchell[69] in preparing his *Study*. Hull in fact regards the variability in the price of construction goods as the cause of the cycle; when this price falls entrepreneurs are willing to undertake 'optional construction'[70] and this creates the upswing. Mitchell highlights the role of profits in the business cycle;[71] the economic system functions on the quest for profits. In a depression, factor costs, and the cost of bank credit, fall; profit margins therefore increase. This sets recovery in motion as businessmen react to the high profit margins by increasing production. A cumulative expansion occurs and prices rise. Businessmen anticipate even higher prices in the future, and economic activity accelerates.[72] The downturn comes when stresses occur in the prosperity phase.[73] At the peak of the cycle the rate of increase in costs exceeds the rate of increase in prices; bank credit becomes more expensive and less abundant; profit margins fall, and recession takes place. Although Robertson may therefore have inherited directly from Marshall the inclination to use prices as a vehicle for transmitting fluctuation to aggregate output and employment, he was certainly not distracted from this course by much of the alternative literature available to him in 1915.[74]

The main ingredients of Robertsonian theory are in fact the same as those found in Marshall's work, it is in the proportions in which they are mixed where the two differ considerably. Marshall too had recognised that fluctuation tended to be concentrated in the capital good industries,[75] and that fluctuations may be caused by: 'wars and rumours of wars, by good and bad harvest, and by the alternate opening out of promising new enterprises . . .';[76] these are the *real* causes found in Robertsonian theory. But more important than the real causes are the psychological forces operating in the cycle, and here we do witness a clear division between Robertson and Marshall. Here the Marshallian view follows very

closely that of John Stuart Mill and John Mills. The chief cause
of fluctuation is the cycle in business confidence. The downturn
is the result of a lack of confidence, and the revival occurs:
'through the gradual and often simultaneous growth of confidence
among the many various trades'.[77] This emphasis is not that
of Robertson in 1915, or even in later work, except that is until
Lectures, where his argument bears a high degree of similarity
with that of Marshall. Robertson writes: 'more often recovery
seems to start with a gradual regrowth of confidence among the
consumption trades, the construction trades coming along later'.[78]
He is so convinced by Marshall that he quotes, at length, passages
in the *Principles* relating to business confidence in the cycle.[79]
But this support for Marshall in this respect, it must be stressed,
is more of an *exception* than a general rule if one surveys the
totality of Robertsonian literature.

Finally, in this exercise of comparison, it is essential to realise
the contrasting role of credit expansion and contraction in the
respective theories. Robertson found himself critical of Marshall's
contention that credit expansion could stimulate investment.[80] Additional credit may be provided for the revival, but it is a different
matter getting businessmen to utilise that credit. Marshall implies
that the act of credit creation itself can manipulate business confidence, and boost investment. Credit creation can also provide
the fuel for revival by expanding in response to business confidence
during the upswing.[81] This latter proposition would not be denied
by Robertson in that he did acknowledge that monetary forces
could exaggerate the cycle, as previously discussed.

This is as far as we need progress in this part. The following
chapters will cast more light upon the degree to which Robertson
developed the Marshallian approach, and will explore the links
between Robertsonian theory and alternative explanations of the
cycle.

Part II
Saving and Investment in the Trade Cycle

1 Introduction

The discussion of the trade cycle, and the economic problems it created, entered a different phase during the interwar period. Economists began to examine fluctuation in terms of the relationship between saving and investment; this is perhaps best illustrated by the contents of Robertson's *Banking* and Keynes' *Treatise*.[1]

Much of the debate on the behaviour of saving and investment in the cycle took place between Robertson and Keynes. Thus it is important to gain a clear understanding of their working relationship in this period. This is the subject matter of Chapter 2.

We need to go back to the *Study* to discover the initial Robertsonian approach to saving in the cycle. In Chapter 3 the degree of sympathy which Robertson showed to the 'shortage of *real* saving' doctrine in 1915 is discussed in detail. In the 1920s more attention was paid, particularly by Robertson, Keynes and Hawtrey in the U.K., to the concept of saving. In Chapter 4 we examine the Robertsonian concepts of 'lacking'. This is essential, for the forced saving doctrine is at the centre of Robertson's thoughts on, not only the cycle, but also the behaviour of interest rates and the price level. The proceeding chapters (5, 6) dwell upon the influences on the working out of the Robertsonian concepts of lacking, on the question of the originality of 'automatic' and 'induced' lacking, and also compare the role of saving in Robertsonian theory with its role in the work of A. C. Pigou and F. von Hayek.

This is followed by an examination of the Robertsonian theory of interest (Chapter 7). The loanable funds theory seeks to establish the connection between saving, investment and the interest rate, and the interference to the determination of the interest rate brought about by changes in hoarding habits, and newly-created money. Again we will explore the origins of Robertsonian theory, in particular its similarities with the Marshallian theory of interest (Chapter 8). This leads into a discussion of the role of interest rates in either causing or allowing cyclical movements in output, employment and prices to take place (Chapter 9). Continental economists, notably K. Wicksell and F. von Hayek, considered industrial fluctuation in terms of the relationship between the 'natural' and the 'market' rate of interest. This was also an approach developed by Keynes in the *Treatise*. It is therefore important to determine Robertson's reaction to this aspect of trade cycle theory.

Keynes' *General Theory*[2] provided, for many economists, a revolution in economic thought. Again it was particularly concerned with the relation between saving and investment, and the influence of this relation upon the level of employment. In many ways it appeared to be contrary to much of what Robertson had to say before 1936. It was intended as an attack upon the 'forced saving' thesis, and upon the loanable funds theory of interest. The consumption function, relating consumption to income, gave rise to the multiplier process and replaced the strong link in classical economics between saving, consumption and the rate of interest. In Chapters 10, 11, 12 and 13 we will examine in detail Robertson's response to the *General Theory*. Chapter 10 explores the implications of the multiplier for forced saving; Chapter 11 examines the liquidity preference theory and begins to assess Robertson's views upon it; Chapter 12 considers the liquidity preference versus loanable funds debate which proceeded the *General Theory*; Chapter 13 assesses the revolutionary nature of the *General Theory* in relation to the contents of Robertsonian economics before 1936.

Chapter 14 concentrates upon Robertson's explanation of how the price level is determined, and gives some indication of the behaviour of prices over the trade cycle.

It has been necessary to omit a number of topics from this part of the book; in particular there is little detailed coverage of the debate concerning the definitions of saving and investment which followed Keynes' *Treatise*, neither is there a detailed discussion of the similarities between Robertson's loanable funds theory and that of the Swedish School. Interested readers will find these topics already adequately covered in Conard's *Theory of Interest*.[3]

2 Background to the Robertson-Keynes Debate

'In the early 1910s and again in the 1920s I *did* do a bit of scrambling towards the frontier (of economic thought), firmly roped to the man of genius who has perished there. Sometimes I venture to think, I was even a little bit in front of him; but in the end he went on beyond me, and it is my belief — an unpopular one, I know, but I cannot help it — that he got a bit off the track and set the flag in places where it is not destined to rest'.[1]

Much of what follows is not only a comment upon the work of Robertson, but an examination of the work of Keynes in the inter-war period, and the Keynesian Revolution which followed the *General Theory*; for this reason it is essential that, before embarking on these excursions, a general overview of the working relationship between Robertson and Keynes be presented, and an indication of the parallel development of their theories given.

Robertson turned to the economics tripos at Trinity College, Cambridge in 1910. Immediately he came into contact with Keynes, who, in the same year, had become Director of Studies for undergraduates reading economics at Trinity College. Keynes was Robertson's elder by seven years. He had graduated from Cambridge in 1905 with a first in mathematics, and, after spending two years in the Indian Office, gained, in 1908, a Lectureship in Economics at Cambridge University, and, in 1909, a Fellowship at Kings College, Cambridge. Both remained in Cambridge, Robertson as a Fellow of Trinity College from 1914 onwards, Keynes as a Fellow and Tutor in Economics, and from 1924 as the Bursar of Kings College, until 1939 when Robertson took the Chair in Banking at the London School of Economics. Keynes often combined his duties in Cambridge with work elsewhere, such that he remained in Cambridge for, at most, four days each week.[2] The only interruption to their close proximity in this period came during the first world war when Robertson served in the army and Keynes worked as a Civil Servant in the Treasury.[3]

In the early years Robertson undoubtedly still thought of himself as a student of Keynes. In 1920 he described Keynes as his master.[4] Later, although this great respect for Keynes remained, it is evident that Robertson became much closer to Keynes, regarding himself more as a colleague and friend. Not even the most forthright of students would dare to challenge his master's voice in the way Robertson did that of Keynes from 1928 onwards. Robertson and Keynes had similar views on a number of issues, not always connected with economics in this inter-war period. As an example one can cite their views on German reparations after the first world war. In a review of Keynes' *Economic Consequences of the Peace*[5] Robertson supports Keynes in a flattering manner and agrees with him that the financial burden put upon Germany was too excessive and that this excessiveness was caused partly by the other clauses of the Treaty; but he disagreed that these other clauses were unwise and suicidal.[6] Robertson and Keynes also felt similarly about the return to the Gold Standard in 1925.[7] Their political outlooks were also very compatible. Keynes took an active part in Liberal Party policy proposals in the 1920s and later;[8] Robertson, who had been president of the Liberal Society in Cambridge as an undergraduate, was less actively engaged, but did contribute to the Liberal Party Summer Schools[9] and to policy documents.[10] Keynes has been called an 'opportunist and an operator', who applied his theory when it aided a 'proposal that might win current political acceptance, and dropped along with the proposal when the immediate purpose had been served or had failed'.[11] Robertson could not be branded so, he was not the same political animal as Keynes.

THE EXCHANGE OF VIEWS ON ECONOMIC THEORY — EARLY AGREEMENT, LATER CONFLICT

How fruitful their collaboration and friendship became can now be satisfactorily judged by reading the correspondence between them contained in the *Collected Writings of John Maynard Keynes*.[12] The only major interruption in correspondence between 1913 and 1937 came during the first world war, and in the period of six years following it. The letters are on matters of substance, often extending to several thousands of words. Much of the debate between them in the period however did not take place on paper. Harrod remarks: 'They had many a long talk, chasing the truth'.[13] Unfortunately the spoken word is lost to us for ever. All that can be said is that the printed word, formidable as it is, is possibly only the tip of the iceberg of the interchange between them.

The earliest dialogue relates to Robertson's early draft of the *Study*. Keynes was extremely flattering about Robertson's work, despite having not been able to recommend it,[14] above all else, as evidence of Robertson's worthiness of a Trinity Fellowship in 1913.[15] In a paper,[16] which was stimulated by the reading of Robertson's thesis, Keynes was critical of over-investment theories of fluctuation of the Robertsonian type; he accused them of two incorrect arguments, that more capital can be invested than is physically available, and that investment will proceed beyond the point of profitability. Yet he proceeds to put forward his own over-investment theory, with much more emphasis upon banking operations and the creation of credit in yielding over-investment, and comes close to a theory of forced-saving,[17] which Robertson was later to elucidate in *Banking* under Keynes' influence.

The war interrupted any further development of ideas, and it was not until the 1920s that a renewal of the collaboration between them occurred. Throughout the 1920s they worked very closely together on the integration of interest rate and savings/investment analysis into trade cycle theory, although there was primary concern with one phase of the cycle; both were anxious to understand the causes of unemployment. In turn this led to an examination of the role of banking policy in regulating the cycle. The two worked very closely together on four books, *Tract on Monetary Reform*,[18] *Money*, *Banking*, and the *Treatise on Money*;[19] although none of the books were published under joint authorship. There was considerable, but not total, agreement between them in this period; Keynes' *Tract on Monetary Reform* was viewed by Robertson as placing too much weight on the ability of monetary policy to get rid of fluctuation.[20] Keynes upheld the Cambridge orthodoxy much more than Robertson was to do in the 1920s. Writing in 1948, Robertson admitted to having no great respect for Say's Law of Markets in his early writings.[21] However, led by Robertson in the 1920s, neither was to respect the traditional boundary between monetary theory, dealing with the demand for output as a whole, and price, or value theory.[22] There were differences of opinion over the drafts of *Banking* and especially over the *Treatise*.

Over *Banking* the differences between them were largely differences of emphasis and method, not of substance.[23] By 1926, the two had appeared to reach common ground at last.[24] Robertson was obliged to write: 'I have had so many discussions with Mr. J. M. Keynes on the subject-matter of chapters V and VI, and have re-written them so drastically at his suggestion, that I think neither of us now knows how much of the ideas therein contained is his and how much is mine'.[25] This agreement was crucial to the development of the theories of both Robertson and Keynes. These two chapters outlined the Robertsonian definitions of various types of saving, discussed the role of saving in the cycle, developed the theory of forced saving and laid down the guidelines for an effective banking policy to counteract the cycle.

That their agreement at this stage was almost total is supported by Keynes' declaration: 'I like this latest version, though God knows it is concise'.[26] And later: 'I think that your revised chapter V is splendid, — most new and important. I think it is substantially right and at last I have no material criticism. It is the kernel and real essence of the book'.[27] But he felt that very few economists would have the capacity to understand what Robertson was saying.

In the 1928 edition of *Money*, Robertson still saw fit to write: 'my debt to Mr. J. M. Keynes ... has reached a sum which is no longer capable of expression in words'.[28] He goes on to argue that much of it should not have been published without Keynes' name alongside his own taking a share of the credit,[29] particularly chapter VIII which related to banking policy in the cycle and which, in a simplified fashion, introduced the forced saving thesis of *Banking*. However, as we move through this period, their respective views on the behaviour of saving and investment in the cycle, and on banking operations, and their implications for economic policy, grew wider and wider apart, such that by the time the *Treatise* was published there were already signs of the irreparable breach which was finally to appear with the *General Theory* in 1936. Whilst Robertson was to remain faithful to the theory of forced saving developed in chapter V, Keynes was to depart from it very rapidly, and to be extremely critical of such a theory as it was to be found in Hayek's *Prices and Production*.[30] Forced saving was very roughly handled in the *General Theory*,[31] its demise in the eyes of Keynesians being brought about by the development of multiplier analysis after 1936.[32]

THE TREATISE ON MONEY

The gestation period of Keynes' *Treatise on Money* was to last for six years.[33] In September 1924 Keynes invited Robertson to discuss with him theories of the credit cycle which: 'go half-way to meet you'.[34] The debate which was to follow was detailed and complex. In the early drafts of Chapter 23, which later disappeared from the final version of the *Treatise*, Keynes followed the analysis of *Banking*[35] and maintained compatibility with the forced saving doctrine. This was in 1928. But by 1930, in 'the published work, forced saving played little part in Keynes' thesis. This change of mind by Keynes brought with it differences in the definitions of saving and investment, differences in their relationship through the cycle, and ultimately a divergence of views on the objectives and nature of banking policy in the cycle. Although, before publication, Robertson partially disguised his inability to accept the *Treatise*,[36] he could not resist writing: 'I am disappointed to find myself still full of resistances on certain parts, — not, I think on the main structure'. Even after its publication Robertson still offered it a certain amount of flattery, — describing it as: 'marvellously full of new meat ... I think the whole of Book VII, most of which is new to me, splendid',[37] but he did not go so far as to say that he agreed with its thesis.[38]

The substance of this disagreement will be seen in detail at various points throughout the following pages; it is sufficient at this stage to isolate the main areas of disagreement. These stem from the departures of the *Treatise* from the analysis of *Banking*. Clearly the key to the disagreement was to be found in Keynes' neglect of the forced saving doctrine which they had put forward together in 1926. This was felt deeply by Robertson; looking back in 1949 he remarked how disappointed he was that his own approach had never: 'got under his (Keynes) skin'.[39] He was perhaps thinking in particular of Keynes' failure to develop the period analysis of *Banking*. This led to differences of definition and terminology. Keynes' analysis used aggregate concepts of saving and investment, while Robertson preferred to divide saving into its voluntary and forced components, and investment into that relating to fixed capital and that relating to circulating or working capital.[40] Both argued that saving and investment need not be equal, but whilst at the time of writing *Banking* they agreed as to why such inequality might result, in the *Treatise* Keynes found new explanations for their divergence. Robertson saw Keynes' *Treatise* as being much nearer to the classical tradition. He objected to Keynes' contention that money receipts would always be spent.[41] Looking back on this period again in 1949, Robertson wrote that Keynes played down the: 'gravity of the objections which I thought I had discovered to the policy of monetary stabilisation'.[42] and defended the orthodox view calling for price stabilisation as an objective of monetary policy. This showed a fundamental conflict with *Banking*. Robertson argued there, and continued to argue, that it was the role of the banks to create credit to finance the working and fixed capital needed for *appropriate* fluctuations in output during the cycle. This credit creation might bring about instability in the price level.[43]

Even so, it would be justifiable to argue that Robertson and Keynes were closer together on theoretical and policy issues than either were to the classical tradition at this time. Saving and investment need not necessarily be equal. In fact Keynes went so far as to argue that disparity between saving and investment was the most important influence on fluctuations, claiming originality for this argument.[44] But the origin of the recognition that saving and investment need not be equal can be traced back to *Banking*, although Robertson never advocated that the excess of saving over investment was the cause of a trade depression. It was merely a symptom of a depression brought about by movements in the productivity of investment.[45]

The debate in the learned journals[46] which followed the *Treatise* proved an arduous task for even the participants to follow. To Robertson and Keynes was added a third major contributor, F. A. von Hayek, who reviewed the *Treatise* in 1931.[47] The complexities of the debate arose from differences concerning the definitions of saving and investment.[48] The debate had the outward appearance of a difference in terminology, but in fact it was much deeper than that.[49] Keynes clearly represented the issues in the following words: 'When you were writing your *Banking Policy and the Price Level* and we were discussing it, we both believed that inequalities between saving and investment — using those terms with the degree of vagueness with which we used them at that date — only arose as a result of what one might call an act of inflation or deflation on the part of the banking system. I worked on this basis for quite a time, but in the end I came to the conclusion that it would not do. As a result of getting what were, in my opinion more clear definitions of saving and investment, I found that the salient phenomena could come about without any overt act on the part of the banking system. My theory as I have ultimately expressed it is a result of this change of view, and I am sure that the differences between me and you are due to the fact that you in substance still hold the old view. But I only reached my new view as a result of an attempt to handle the old view with complete thoroughness'.[50] This had a considerable bearing on specific issues. Robertson's initial post-publication reaction was to view the crux of the dispute as being connected with the: '"price level of investment", the functioning of the rate of interest, and the synthesis of the new equations with those which bring in quantity and velocity'.[51]

The debate is encountered in several parts of the discussion which follows, in the examination of definitions of saving and investment (and their possible inequality), the behaviour of saving in the cycle, the crucial question of forced saving, and also the determination of the price level and banking policy.

TOWARDS THE GENERAL THEORY

Whilst the debate over the *Treatise* was still taking place in the learned journals, Keynes was already preparing his next and most important work — the *General Theory*.[52] Despite their inability to come to terms over the *Treatise*, Robertson and Keynes continued to work together. However, Keynes' main source of comment on the drafts of his new work, were not, as for his earlier works, to come from Robertson, but from the young generation of aspiring Cambridge economists, members of the so-called Cambridge 'circus'.[53] Robertson was the first person to see proofs of the

General Theory outside of the 'circus'. He provided copious, but unsympathetic, comment upon it in February 1935.[54] Keynes was anxious to avoid the terminological debate of the *Treatise*.[55] Before its publication Robertson found the *General Theory* difficult to comprehend,[56] and complained: 'a large part of your theoretical structure is still to me almost complete mumbo-jumbo!'[57] Not surprisingly Keynes was offended by this last remark,[58] and in March 1935, apart from minor correspondence, discussion between them ceased until after the *General Theory*.

One of the burdens which Robertson took upon himself in his critical comments on the *General Theory*, before and after its publication, was to act as defender of the Marshallian tradition against Keynes' criticisms. He himself had not fully accepted the neo-classical views in the 1920's, in fact one could go so far as to argue that he was perhaps its most consistent critic in that period. He did not accept the validity of Say's Law, he disputed the existence of any automatic mechanism generating full employment in advocating his over-investment theory of the cycle with its emphasis on real causes, and he disputed the existence of equality between saving and investment; but at the same time he never departed from a faith in the Cambridge equation, and the real cash balance approach, nor from the loanable funds theory of interest.[59] Nevertheless, he felt it his duty to support Cambridge orthodoxy against Keynes and the ensuing Keynesian Revolution. He regarded his own theoretical innovations as developments out of the Cambridge orthodoxy, and was anxious to convince Keynes that much of what was contained in the *General Theory* had its origins in Marshall's *Principles of Economics*[60] or in Pigou's *Industrial Fluctuations*.[61] His defence did not arise from any personal loyalty to Marshall and Pigou, he was much closer to Keynes than to either of them. Indeed, it was Robertson who had taught Keynes to stray from the neo-classical path in the 1920s, for Keynes described Robertson as his: 'parent in the path of errancy'.[62] Rather he believed Keynes to be mistaken on a purely intellectual level. For his contacts with Marshall and Pigou were not close.

Marshall had retired from the Chair in Cambridge in 1908, and had been succeeded by Pigou, before Robertson became a student of Economics. Therefore, he had not been taught by Marshall. He saw Marshall on one occasion only,[63] although Marshall remained in Cambridge until his death in 1924.[64] Although Robertson never corresponded with Marshall, Marshall did write to Robertson twice, to inform Robertson that he often used his *Study* in his preparation of *Money, Credit and Commerce*,[65] and to compliment Robertson on *Money*.[66] Robertson continued to be impressed throughout by Marshall's work above that of everyone else. It is indicative that for his lectures in Cambridge, from 1946 onwards, he recommended students to read Marshall's *Principles*, Pigou's *Economics of Welfare*,[67] as well as Keynes' *General Theory*. He remarked about the *Principles*: 'nobody has succeeded in replacing it'.[68] Robertson had more contact with Pigou; the influence of Pigou on Robertson's thesis has already been indicated,[69] and out of their work of the 1920s came very similar views on certain issues.[70] Even so, it is doubtful that Robertson was closer to Pigou than to Keynes, even in the post-*General Theory* period.[71]

His reaction to the *General Theory* was no more than a desire to see justice done, an attempt to make Keynes give credit where credit was due. He was always anxious to show to his readers the source of his arguments. In the original edition of his *Study* he failed to acknowledge a debt to an article written by Marcel Labordère.[72] He felt such self-reproach over this that in the 1948 reprint of his book he reproduced the complete article as an appendix, writing himself a brief biography of Labordère as an introduction to the article.[73] He thought that correctness in economics was often a question of degree, that all theories were to some extent true. Therefore it was wrong to completely condemn theories in the manner in which Keynes had condemned parts of the Cambridge theories in the *General Theory*. Robertson could never forgive what he saw as Keynes' disrespect to Marshall; for he, as much as Pigou, was a firm believer in the view that if one looks closely enough, 'it is all in Marshall'.

Robertson's pre-publication comment on Keynes' handling of the Cambridge orthodoxy were mild in comparison to what followed.[74] Keynes accused him of not sloughing his 'neo-classical skin' as his theory developed; Robertson retorted that Keynes had sloughed his 'neo-classical skin', but at the same time put on a pair of blinkers so that he was unable to take account of neo-classical doctrine in his *General Theory*.[75] Keynes believed that one of his intentions in writing the book had been to lay open the main differences of opinion between himself and his teachers and former pupils.

This form of attack upon the *General Theory* never mellowed. Shortly after publication Robertson claimed that the *General Theory* merely rearranged existing theory and did not put: 'some new piece on the board'.[76] It was criticised for exaggerating differences with existing orthodoxy, and for representing theory as a new addition to knowledge, not a development of what had gone before. Such an approach Robertson felt: 'doesn't breed a scientific spirit but the reverse — a blind scramble to acquire the new orthodoxes for fear of being out of fashion'.[77] This criticism had not diminished even in *Lectures* in the 1950s.[78]

Keynes accused Hayek of not giving him the 'measure of goodwill' that an author deserves from a reader in his reviews of the *Treatise*.[79] One cannot help but feel that Keynes was guilty, as far as Robertson was concerned, of the same offence. The Keynes of the *General Theory* chose to over-emphasise his departure from the doctrines of Marshall, Pigou and others and not to extend to them sufficient credit for the development of his thought. This was the offensive aspect of the *General Theory* to Robertson. The following passage admirably summarises how Robertson felt: 'You (Professor T. Wilson) say I have found it difficult to appreciate the revolution in thought *which followed* the publication of the G.T. ... No I haven't! I have disliked and mildly ridiculed the phrase "The Keynesian Revolution", because I think it suggests that the innovations in the G.T. *constituted* a bigger advance in thought on what had gone before than in fact they did. But that "in the end it was his rhetoric and his new mystique which carried the day" is indisputable! The truth is that they spread error as well as truth. In other words, not only did Keynes fail to acknowledge what had gone before, but many aspects of his work which had not gone before represented erroneous argument rather than the economic truth'.[80]

The defence of the Marshallian tradition can be seen primarily in his attack upon Keynes' liquidity preference theory of interest. Keynes' monetary theory of interest neglected the real forces acting upon the rate of interest, the neo-classical forces of productivity and thrift. Much of the post-*General Theory* debate was centred upon this particular issue. In addition Robertson sought to convince Keynes and others that Marshall and Pigou had been as much concerned with effective demand as Keynes had been in 1936, and that Marshall had recognised the multiplier process.

A PREVIEW OF CRITICAL COMMENT ON THE
GENERAL THEORY

Robertson has been accused by Hicks, amongst others, of examining
the *General Theory* like: 'a man examining a Seurat with a microscope, and denouncing the ugly shapes of the individual dots'.[81]
One of our objectives must be to determine how far this was
true. Were Robertson's criticisms fundamental? Should Keynes
have paid more attention to the individual dots rather than 'flinging
a pot of paint in the public's face' as Professor Wilson accused
him of doing?[82]

Moggridge[83] believes that the *General Theory* rests upon four
building blocks. The first is the consumption function, the second,
the multiplier, the third, the theory of investment and the fourth,
the liquidity preference theory of interest. Few economists would
dispute that these four blocks are the fundamental features of
the *General Theory*. For the moment at least it is convenient
to discuss Robertson's criticisms in relation to these building blocks.
It is upon these blocks that the strength of the *General Theory*
depends. If Robertson showed severe cracks in these, his criticisms
could be regarded as fundamental.

It is not surprising from the exchanges on theoretical matters
in the earlier inter-war period that a major part of this post-1936
controversy between Keynes and Robertson should be concerned
with the relation between saving and investment. Keynes attached
considerable importance in his *General Theory* to the consumption
function; from it was developed the multiplier, the proposition
that investment determines output and saving, and that the change
in output will be a multiple of the change in investment (that
multiple depending on the propensity to spend). This was regarded
by Keynes as an attack on the classical view that saving and
investment would be brought to equality via the rate of interest.
Keynes stood this theory on its head. Investment determines saving
not vice-versa, the connecting variable being real income and not
the rate of interest. Robertson had a number of criticisms relating
to this theoretical approach — each of which will be dealt with
in detail in due course. Suffice it now to say that these criticisms
related primarily to Keynes' definitions of saving and investment,
and to the influences upon spending and saving.

The interpreters of the *General Theory* derived two approaches
to saving/investment analysis. One is to be found in multiplier

analysis, where saving and investment are instantaneously equated (because of the use of comparative statics). The finance required for investment to take place is instantaneously provided by voluntary saving, so there is no need either for the banks to create credit to finance the investment or for forced saving to be imposed on the public. Indeed, in Keynes' thesis there is no such thing as forced saving. Even if credit is created by the banks, prices need not rise significantly so long as unemployed resources exist. In the forced saving doctrine prices rise even at less than full employment. Given the multiplier, and a static approach, the equality of saving and investment is guaranteed. Robertson did not dispute that consumption and saving were partly determined by real income, as well as by the rate of interest; this had been part of his own theory for at least ten years before the publication of the *General Theory*. But although he accepted this, in his own dynamic approach to the question, there was a one period lag in this relationship. Robertson's main criticism fell on the static nature of Keynes' analysis, *the instantaneous equality*, with its implication that positions of equilibria are more worthy of discussion than disequilibria, and on the fact that Keynes gave no role to the rate of interest in determining the equality of saving and investment. To Robertson the propensity to consume/save was not stable, it was influenced by changes in the rate of interest, and by banking policy and the creation of credit affecting the desire to hoard (changing 'K' in the Cambridge equation). The multiplier could not be regarded as being precise. To this one can add criticism of the third building block — the theory of investment. Keynes failed to allow the accelerator to work alongside his multiplier.[84]

The second approach to the saving/investment question is to be found in the 'ex-post' analysis of the *General Theory*. In this saving and investment are always equal by definition. This represents a total reversal of the argument of the *Treatise* that the inequality of saving and investment are responsible for industrial fluctuation. Again much of the controversy which surrounded the *General Theory* related to the definitions of saving and investment. Robertson believed that definitions which made them irredeemably equal: 'takes us all back to pre-Withers, pre-Wicksell days, and obscures instead of clarifying what happens when an act of investment takes place'.[85]

To Robertson therefore, the multiplier was no more than a

'potentially useful little brick',[86] not the cornerstone of some great monument. Keynes had used his savings/investment analysis as a substitute for the cash balance approaches of the classical and neo-classical economists.[87] One of the intentions of Robertson's work throughout his life had been to develop definitions of saving and investment, and their subsequent analysis, which were compatible with the 'money' and 'real' cash balance approaches.[88]

Having upheld a connection between saving and investment via the level of income, and not through the rate of interest, Keynes was forced into the position where he could not support the loanable funds theory of interest; that is, unless he advocated a theory where the rate of interest continually changed due to the influence of income changes upon the demand for, and supply of, loanable funds. This latter alternative would have only weakened his multiplier analysis by causing instability in the propensity to spend. His fourth building block therefore was his liquidity preference theory of interest. It was the purpose of Keynes' theory to deny that productivity and thrift had any major role in the determination of interest rates.[89] This was a central proposition in Marshallian theory, as it was in Robertson's own loanable funds theory of interest.[90] To Keynes the rate of interest was determined by the demand for, and supply of, money, by stocks rather than by flows. This was a purely monetary theory of interest. Robertson's loanable funds theory emphasised that the rate of interest was determined by flows of loanable funds; these flows were influenced by *real* as well as *monetary* factors. It was a *dynamic* not a *static* theory; the supply of, and demand for, loanable funds both change over time in accordance with changes in banking policy, in productivity (and hence income), and in thrift.[91] The controversy ranged over several issues, including, most importantly perhaps, the effects of changes in productivity, thrift, and the money supply on the rate of interest; but it also covered the relationship between short- and long- term rates of interest, the determinants of the demand for money, and the meaning of liquidity preference.

This section began with a quotation from Hicks, decrying Robertson's criticisms of the *General Theory*. Yet it is interesting to note that later on in that review he states: 'the effect on Mr. Kaldor's mind, as well as on my own, of the *General Theory* has been profound; but we have each of us been led, sometimes consciously, sometimes unconsciously, through Keynes to Robertson'.[92] One can take the view that some of the most important developments of the *General Theory* really take us back to the pre-*General Theory* writings of Robertson. The use of dynamic analysis can be seen in most of Robertson's earlier work; the reconciliation of the liquidity preference and loanable funds theories of Robertson and Keynes, take us back nearer to Robertson than at least the Keynes of the *General Theory* would have wished; the pitfalls of the multiplier were there to be seen in Robertson's work — in the influence of the accelerator, in the lagged relationship between consumption and income, and in the other influences upon saving and investment. On policy issues Robertson had been recommending public works programmes to cure depression as early as 1915, and stressing that depression resulted from a lack of effective demand.

The following pages will discuss in more detail the issues tentatively raised here. It may well be at the end that the conclusion reached is that of Robertson on the *General Theory* — that Keynes was: 'sharpening the wrong axes and running along the wrong streets';[93] that the correct and more worthwhile development of theory may have been along the Robertsonian path; the steps may have been more difficult to follow, (*Banking* was a less digestible book than the *General Theory*) but the path shorter. In so far as theory can be judged by its ability to fit the facts, and the success of the economic policies which it recommends, our conclusion on the latter must wait until the final pages.

That there was a lack of common ground between Robertson and Keynes over important parts of the total theory is beyond dispute; but it would be wrong to leave this discussion with this conclusion alone. If one takes an overall picture of the *General Theory* it is not so dissimilar from Robertson's theoretical and policy beliefs as the literature would lead us to suppose, particularly on the question of effective demand and fiscal policy. This view has also been taken by such eminent economists as T. Wilson and A. Hansen.[94] Robertson had always maintained, and continued to maintain, that effective demand was the main determinant of the level of employment. He warned Pigou in 1945 that the implication of his latest book[95] was that it was in favour of attacking unemployment by manipulating wages: 'rather than manipulating demand',[96] a proposal with which he disagreed. This emphasis on aggregate demand was also the most important message of the *General Theory*.

The correspondence also reflects this agreement on a general policy and theoretical level. On 13th December 1936 Keynes wrote: 'after reading your two American papers, I do feel that there is not a great deal that is fundamental which divides us — even less perhaps than you think. For I agree with a greater proportion of what you say than you give me credit for. As regards your Harvard paper and practical applications, you will find that two articles which I am writing for the *Times* early next year go a considerable way along this same route'.[97] Robertson replied in a like manner. On liquidity preference, Keynes acknowledged the debt he owed to Robertson in the development of his ideas in the inter-war period, but at the same time doubted the debt he owed to Marshall and Pigou.[98]

Nevertheless Robertson was not prepared to stay in Cambridge in the heat of the Keynesian Revolution. In 1939 he left to take the Chair in Banking at the London School of Economics. This must have been a wrench for him for he loved Cambridge dearly; it is perhaps indicative of the strength of the animosity he felt for some of the leading members of the Keynesian Revolution. E. A. G. Robinson has recently reflected on Robertson's departure from Cambridge: 'Dennis, an immaculate scholar, had been for years in a sense the keeper of his (Keynes) conscience. If he could convince Dennis, he felt that he was right. I find it harder to look at this through Dennis Robertson's eyes. In retrospect I think Robertson felt more acutely than any of us imagined at the time the constant strain of being used as Keynes' conscience. Inevitably Keynes was arguing vigorously in defence of his ideas. And Robertson, was curiously diffident for one of his great ability, was unsure whether he was yielding to good argument or to pressure of friendship, and unsure whether Keynes' attempt to restate really met the legitimate points that he made. One recalls what he had written to Keynes ten years earlier, when they were both arguing about *Banking*: "I am afraid of being swayed into publishing by the desire to avoid disappointment and loss: but I am also afraid of being swayed against publishing by my tendency to believe you are always right! Sometimes when I have stood out against this weakness I have been justified! ... I am so unconfident that I should always like to put at the top of everything that I write nobody must believe a word of what follows. Is that a hopeless frame of mind?" I believe, that is to say, that when Robertson decided to take a chair in London in 1939 he was anxious to be released from the still continuing responsibilities of being the keeper of the conscience, the touchstone'.[99] One cannot doubt the truth of this, but one may suspect that the last straw for Robertson in making his decision to depart was the bitter conflict he had with some of the Keynesians, not Keynes himself.[100]

AFTER THE GENERAL THEORY

Robertson remained in the Chair in Banking at the London School of Economics for only one year before he departed for wartime duty. Hence the War brought the debate over the *General Theory* between Keynes and Robertson to an end, at least for the time being.

Robertson became a civil servant in the Treasury, whilst Keynes was appointed advisor to the Chancellor of the Exchequer; the two therefore came into contact within the Treasury. Robertson acted as economic advisor to Sir Frederick Phillips who was the Third Secretary in the Treasury, responsible for the Balance of Payments. This task included the management of the country's gold and foreign currency reserves. The American Alliance and Lend–Lease brought Robertson into contact with the Americans. In 1943 he went to Washington to discuss Lend–Lease arrangements, and later on he was to work on the preparations for the Bretton Woods negotiations. When this Conference began he found himself a member of the British delegation.

It was at the Bretton Woods Conference that Robertson was again to work with Keynes. There followed a reconciliation between the two, but not over matters relating to the *General Theory*. The Conference was to establish a new international monetary system, and the International Monetary Fund to aid its operation. Keynes and Robertson had never been at loggerheads over matters of this kind; Keynes was to write to his mother: 'Dennis Robertson is perhaps the most useful of all — absolutely first class brains do help!' Others also regarded Robertson's contribution as important: thus according to Sir Richard Hopkins: 'if anyone is picked out, I think it would have to be Dennis, whose help has been absolutely indispensible'.[101] Indeed Robertson and his American counterpart, Bernstein, had been responsible for drafting an agreeable text from the multitude of decisions which had descended from the committee meetings.

But there was not sufficient time available to Keynes and Robertson to allow them to discuss the *General Theory*, and time in future was to prove short. Robertson, after the war, found himself back in Cambridge, in Pigou's chair. He was back in the heat of the Keynesian Revolution, but in a Cambridge without Keynes. Keynes died on April, 21st, 1946. Robertson introduced his lecture to Cambridge undergraduates on the 25th April, 1946 in the following words: 'I am thankful that it was my privilege in the last years of the war to work under him (Keynes), in London and Washington and at Bretton Woods, in the old relation of admiring, though not uncritical discipleship, in furtherance of purposes which we both had much at heart. I had hoped that in quieter years ahead we might slip back into leisurely discussion of those matters of theory and of pedagogies over which we had failed to see eye to eye and which there has been no time to reopen in these crowded years'.[102] Nevertheless Robertson continued to be critical of the *General Theory*, as he promised in his early Cambridge lectures; he was: 'Scattering sparks of fire' against a theory which: 'quickly showed signs of crystalising into an orthodoxy no less rigid than that against which it was, or conceived itself to be a revolt'.[103]

CONCLUSION

It is against this background that the remainder of Part II must be read. This chapter has highlighted the strong personal and working relationship between Robertson and Keynes, the early close development of their respective views on saving and investment, and the trade cycle; this was followed by increasing academic disagreement from the *Treatise* onwards; there was never a total reconciliation of the disagreement relating to the *General Theory*, although their personal relationship always remained close. They both had a great respect for each other. Despite their academic disagreements, it is doubtful that their theories would have reached the sophistication that they did reach without the penetrating advice given by each other.

3 Saving in the Cycle: The Robertsonian Approach in the 'Study'

After our discussion of the relationship between Keynes and Robertson, we now turn to a detailed analysis of Robertson's work on saving and investment, and their role in the trade cycle. This will eventually lead to an elucidation of the differences and similarities between the two men; the content of this and the next seven chapters however will not allow us to lose sight of the major objective of this book — to present a thorough examination of the theory of industrial fluctuation. We begin in this chapter with a discussion of the Robertsonian analysis of saving in 1915.

The *Study* paid less attention to the behaviour of saving in the cycle than Robertson's work was to do from 1920 onwards. Nevertheless one can gain a clear interpretation of the movement of saving through crisis and depression; the message one gets differs substantially from the standpoint adopted by Robertson in the 1920s, particularly in *Money* and *Banking*.[1]

THE REAL SAVING THEORY

In the period 1912–15 Robertson was anxious to get behind the monetary exterior to the real forces operating, and causing, industrial fluctuation.[2] Although the *Study* was not concerned with presenting a thorough elaboration of the definition of saving, as later work was to, it is evident that Robertson equated the amount of saving available for investment with the *accumulated stocks* of consumer goods.[3] Savings are not to be found in the amount of loanable funds available, but in the *real* stock of goods available to support the community whilst a greater proportion of resources are diverted to the production of capital goods.

The inspiration for this view on saving at this time undoubtedly came from three sources, from an article written by a French 'eccentric', Marcel Labordère, which had sought to determine the cause of the American crisis in 1907,[4] an outline of the work of Spiethoff in Mitchell's *Business Cycles*,[5] and the paper delivered by Keynes on the theory of fluctuation in 1913.[6] This 'real saving' theory was to be developed later by Cassel and by Spiethoff amongst others,[7] and was to be commented on again by Robertson in 1926.[8]

The theory can best be illustrated by assuming a Robinson Crusoe island, the major implications of which are an absence of money, with both total production and consumption being undertaken by Crusoe.[9] Crusoe has a limited amount of time, he has to decide on how to divide this time between taking leisure, producing consumer goods and producing capital goods. If he devotes all his time to the manufacture of a fishing rod without first building up a store of consumer goods on which to live, he will starve. Therefore, before investment can be undertaken, a stock of consumer goods needs to be accumulated. This stock has to be sufficient to support subsistence through the gestation period of investment, and is hence the *real capital* needed to finance the investment. Even in a monetary economy, without this stock no amount of paper money could finance investment and at the same time allow the community, big or small, to survive. The store of food which Crusoe needs to enable him to devote the winter months to making his fishing rod is *real* saving. In 1915 Robertson applied this thesis straightway to a monetary economy without discussing the influence of banking policy on saving. He did not enquire as to the ability of the banks to *force* people to refrain from current consumption and in so doing to divert resources into capital good industries. This latter inquiry first appeared in *Money* in 1922.[10]

THE ORIGINS OF THE REAL SAVING DOCTRINE

Robertson could not claim any originality for the real saving doctrine. Labordère and Spiethoff had argued likewise before the

Study appeared, and indeed took the doctrine a good deal further by suggesting that the shortage of real saving was the cause of the crisis. Both defined over-investment in relation to the available supply of *real* saving, not as a deficiency in the demand for capital goods relative to their supply as in the Robertsonian theory of crisis.[11]

Spiethoff[12] argued that the over-production of machines and also durable consumer goods in the crisis was the result of an inability of prospective purchasers to raise sufficient capital to buy them at a profitable price. The lack of capital in the money markets disguised the real difficulty. There was a deficiency of labour and consumer goods needed to utilise the resources, materials and equipment, earmarked for the production of more capital equipment and durable consumer goods. Therefore, a shortage of capital is not a deficiency of monetary funds, but a symptom of an imbalance in the production of capital and consumer goods; capital and durable consumer goods (e.g. dwellings) are over-produced; consumer goods are under-produced. The solution to this shortage of capital is not to print more money, that is unless it can be transformed into the goods required to utilise the over-production.[13]

Labordère held similar views to those of Spiethoff, but being a non-professional economist, and not having read widely on the subject of fluctuation,[14] it is doubtful that he was influenced at all by Spiethoff. Undoubtedly, Labordère's article had much more impact on Robertson than any other at this time, as the original works of Spiethoff were not available to him. Robertson was particularly impressed by Labordère's description of a one-man crisis, which developed the Robinson Crusoe argument above.[15] In the following passage, drawn from the English translation,[16] the thesis is lucidly laid out; 'Towards the end of summer, he noticed that his supplies, his reserves of corn, wine and all the products, the abundance of which were his pride and joy, or in other words that his spare capital in kind, was running out. What was he to do? Should he stop the construction of a dam, half completed and risk the spring floods destroying work that, too weak yet by itself, would not fail to give way under the strain? With the winter snow what would become of the houses without roofs intended for the new inhabitants of his lands? A thing half finished dies and carries away with it all traces of the human labour that it represents'.[17] Crusoe has over-invested, he has put too much of a strain on the stocks of consumer goods that exist to finance the investment; the result must be a collapse, a crisis. Investment projects have to be abandoned never to be completed (the resources put into such projects being totally wasted). This is clearly the emphasis upon real saving which Robertson proposed in the *Study*.

The third source of inspiration of Robertson's view of saving in the cycle came from Keynes; but Keynes' thesis did not have the same clarity as that of Labordère, and, more importantly, it did not appear until after the early drafts of the *Study* had been written.[18] Nevertheless, Robertson acknowledged an obligation to Keynes for the provision of an insight into the possibility that crises may be caused by a too rapid utilisation of the existing stock of consumer goods in the investment process; but Robertson criticised Keynes for the over-certainty of this thesis. Robertson did not believe that the collapse of investment was always caused by the inability of the stock of consumer goods to maintain it at its current level; this was the implication of Keynes' thesis.[19]

REACTION TO THE 'MONEY' SAVING THESIS

These were the *positive* sources of influence upon Robertsonian theory; but theories are made, in addition, from negative reactions to the theories of others. The shortage of real saving thesis came from a desire to isolate the real causes of the cycle, and to counter what Robertson believed to be the over-emphasis upon the monetary forces acting upon fluctuation present in the work of Tugan-Baranowski,[20] and more so in the work[21] of R. G. Hawtrey.[22]

Hawtrey's theory is criticised in Part I:7, hence attention can be focused here on the theory of Tugan-Baranowski. He believed that there was a natural tendency in capitalist economies to accumulate savings[23] even during depression. This accumulation does not automatically lead to an equal accumulation of capital goods;[24] that is saving does not automatically flow into investment. This accumulation of saving takes place in the banks, and results, during a depression, in a lowering of the market rate of interest. As more and more savings are accumulated through the depression, so the greater becomes the pressure to find investment opportunities for them. Eventually this pressure reaches such a level that industries can no longer refrain from employing the available funds. There is a burst of expenditure on capital goods leading to prosperity. Prosperity continues through the expansion of investment which uses up more and more of the 'money' saving; over-investment occurs as the rate of increase in investment outstrips the rate of accumulation of saving. The rate of interest rises, a financial crisis ensues, investment falls, and recession occurs.

The fundamental criticism by Robertson of this thesis was that it placed too much emphasis on money savings, and made no reference to the real nature of the limit to investment, — the *real* consumer goods required to finance investment whilst it is taking place. There is thus a *significant* difference between 'shortage of capital' theories which concentrate upon fluctuation in money savings, and those which recognise saving in the form of stocks of real consumer goods.

The latter was the Robertsonian approach to the problem of financing investment in 1915; he did not remain faithful to this view of saving and was later critical of the way in which he had confused saving with the *stock* of consumer goods.[25] From 1920 onwards he was much more concerned with the ability of the commercial banks to extract saving from the public by increasing the creation of credit, hence raising the price level, and *forcing* the public to refrain from consumption, in turn diverting resources into the capital good industries. Saving could be manufactured through banking policy and was not entirely to be found in the existing accumulation of consumer goods. Attention is now focused on this in the following chapter.

4 Robertson on Saving (1918-1940)

INTRODUCTION

The development of trade cycle theory in terms of an examination of the relationship between saving and investment had proceeded in the 19th century without precision being given to the definition of these terms. As a result differences in theory often arose from different implicit meanings of saving and investment. The assumption that the theory could take for granted the definitions of saving and investment was challenged in the 1920s. In Britain it was Robertson who was responsible more than anyone else for this challenge.

In this chapter the Robertsonian approach to saving in the writings of the inter-war period is outlined and commented upon. This enables an examination of the role of saving in the cycle to be undertaken. The result of a redefinition of terms provides Robertson with a significantly different view of the behaviour of money in the cycle to that found in the *Study* — but not significantly different to the point where *monetary* forces win over *real* forces in determining cyclical fluctuations.

THE DISTINCTION BETWEEN VOLUNTARY SAVING AND GROSS LACKING

Crucial to an understanding of Robertsonian analysis is the clarification of the possible divergence of what most textbooks now refer to as 'Keynesian' saving, and what Robertson calls 'lacking'.[1] The two may be identical, but if money flows are changing, and consequently prices are variable, they will be unequal. It is also important to realise at the outset that this possible inequality is determined largely by the dynamic nature of Robertsonian analysis compared with the static analysis of Keynesian economics. The time lags in the adjustment of output to monetary expenditure flows, and the lag of some money incomes behind price changes, are responsible for saving being not only spontaneous and voluntary, but also forced.

Spontaneous saving or lacking is no more than simply the money saving out of income received which is voluntary and not *imposed* upon the public by banking operations. It is determined entirely by the level of income received and the desire to save, which is itself determined principally by the rate of interest. This type of saving therefore is identical to the conventional meaning of saving. But total saving may not be entirely comprised of spontaneous saving or lacking. The difference may be attributed to forced saving, or what Robertson calls in *Banking* 'automatic lacking', and to 'induced lacking'.[2] The elementary approach to spontaneous lacking was first developed by Robertson in *Money*. The analysis of *Banking* and later[3] became much more sophisticated as a result of the introduction of period analysis. The relation between income and spontaneous saving is based upon periods of a 'day', which is defined as a period when the income received on that 'day' cannot be spent on that 'day'.[4] Thus the amount of lacking on 'day' 2 is determined by the amount of disposable income received on 'day' 1 in relation to consumption on 'day' 2: more specifically:

$$S_t = Y_{t-1} - C_t[5]$$

Hence from this we gain a clearer definition of what constitutes lacking. Robertson writes: 'a man is said to lack, or to do lacking, if his consumption on any day falls short of the value, at the time of its receipt, of the income which he has at his disposal on that day'.[6] If a man has £X of disposable income and he spends £Y then he is lacking to the extent of £(X − Y). The major difference between this view of lacking, and that contained in the spontaneous saving of *Money* is that lacking on any 'day' is defined according to the individual's level of *disposable* income

on that 'day', which is the income *received* on the *previous* 'day'.
What is more important is the fact that spontaneous saving
and *total* saving or lacking need *NOT* be equal. The difference
is attributable to the existence of *automatic* lacking or dislacking.[7]
Voluntary saving can occur without automatic lacking; automatic
lacking can occur without voluntary saving.[8] If our individual
receives £X and spends £Y, then, *ceteris paribus*, voluntary saving
and total lacking are both equal to £(X − Y). However, if other
individuals expand their consumption, and this results in higher
prices, our individual can get less consumer goods for his £Y
of expenditure than previously; in this case he is saving £(X − Y),
but in addition he is *forced* to save, to the extent of the consumer
goods he loses through the rise in the price level. This is lacking
beyond that which is voluntary. Hence total lacking is in excess
of voluntary saving. If he increases his spending to £X, then
clearly he is not saving in the conventional sense; but lacking
may be imposed upon him if other individuals are increasing
their expenditure and are forcing up the price level, since then
he can buy less consumer goods than previously with £X. The
short fall in consumer goods represents the extent of automatic
lacking. Gross lacking is positive whilst voluntary saving is zero.
Alternatively, if other individuals reduce the flow of money they
are putting on to the market, prices will fall and our individual
can buy more goods for £Y than he could previously; here voluntary
saving will now exceed gross lacking. Dislacking is in fact taking
place.

There will be a need to delve more deeply into the distinctions
touched upon here, in particular to enquire as to the meaning
of automatic lacking which complicates the Robertsonian concep-
tions of saving or lacking. Before we do this, however, an essential
prerequisite is to discuss the meaning of capital in Robertsonian
literature.

THE MEANING OF CAPITAL AND ITS DETERMINATION

In *Banking* Robertson made a sharp distinction between the decision
to save and the decision to invest. The two acts were not synonymous. This represented a marked difference from the early classical
approach, but it varied little from the continental approach with
which D. H. Robertson was familiar at that time. Nevertheless,
it was something of a breakthrough in economic analysis in this

country, and was later to be developed not only by Robertson but also principally by Keynes in the *Treatise* and the *General Theory*.

Three types of capital are distinguished in *Banking* — fixed, circulating and imaginary capital. The function of lacking is to provide this capital. The fixed capital possessed by society is its stock of 'man-made material wealth',[9] which can be used to produce goods and services in the future. This includes: '*instruments* of all kinds, including buildings, and improvements to land such as drainage works or harbours'.[10] The lacking which is used up in the provision of such fixed capital is termed '*long* lacking'.[11]

The meaning of circulating (or working) capital[12] is not so straight forward. Robertson was influenced by Henderson[13] who had rebelled against the orthodox view of circulating capital; this held that circulating capital is to be found in the stock of consumer goods which the entrepreneurs and their employees have to consume whilst undertaking production.[14] The longer is the average period of production the greater will be the required stock of consumer goods. Alternatively, the greater is the stock of consumer goods the longer can be the production period and/or the volume of production. This is not inconsistent with Robertson's view in 1915. In the classical economic system this 'real capital' doctrine yields the equality of saving and investment; saving, the stock of consumer goods, determines the volume of investment possible, not vice versa.[15] It is by utilising the unspent income of one period, represented by the stock of consumer goods accumulated, that the output of the next period is generated. Henderson did not see the necessity for such a stock of consumer goods; it was sufficient that the community had the power to produce the required consumer goods as the need arose.

Robertson adopted a middle course. He believed that circulating capital did consist of a stock of consumer goods, but that this stock need only be a small proportion of the total circulating capital. In the Robertsonian definition it included also what statisticians might today call 'work in progress', and the raw materials used up in the production process.[16] For a Robinson Crusoe Island, circulating capital is shown almost totally in the stock of consumer goods available to finance the production process, but for a complex capitalist economy the major portion of such capital exists in the unfinished produce in whatever stage of production.

How much circulating capital is necessary for production to take place depends firstly upon whether the level of production represents a growth, contraction or stability of output compared with the previous level of production. Assuming a stable level of output it would depend upon the average production period and the character of the production period.[17] The production period of a commodity is the time lag between the commencement of manufacture and the final arrival of the commodity in the hands of the consumer. Given that the value added at each stage of production is evenly distributed over the production period, the amount of circulating capital required will be equal to one half of the value of production for each production period:[18]

$$W = \tfrac{1}{2}D \cdot R$$

Robertson chooses throughout his writings to maintain this distinction between fixed and circulating capital; thus one has a disaggregation of investment rather than an economic analysis based upon a concept of gross investment.[19] The justification for this distinction is to be found in the Robertsonian theory of banking policy.[20] Commercial banks in the earlier part of this century provided advances for the finance of circulating capital only; very little was given to finance expenditure on capital equipment, which was usually financed out of past profits, or by share issue. In exploring the repercussions of bank credit creation, Robertson felt it essential to separate the two forms of capital, since fixed capital played little part in the process. Each type of capital may thus react differently to changes in, for example, the rate of interest. Lacking which is converted by the commercial banks into circulating capital is termed 'short lacking'. But why is short lacking necessary? Simply, it is necessary because production cannot be *instantaneously* expanded. If there is a desire to expand output, entrepreneurs need first to enlarge their requirements of circulating capital; the provision of additional circulating capital can only be accomplished by the utilisation of existing resources, in particular by employing labour. The labour so employed has to be paid a wage, and so has purchasing power; but because of the *time lag* in the extension of production as a result of the increased *desire* for production there has not, as yet, been an expansion in the output of consumer goods. Remember that this addition to the employment of labour produces only more circulating capital

NOT more consumer goods. Hence we have a situation in which more employment creates, in the period needed for consumer good output to respond, greater competition for the existing volume of consumer good production. With a given volume of consumer goods this *must* involve some consumers doing without goods, or at least making do with less than they consumed previously before this increased competition for goods. It cannot be stressed too strongly that this lacking is generated because of the inability of production levels to respond immediately to changing circumstances; *the average period of production is greater than zero.* As most industries have unequal values of circulating capital at different times, this gives rise to variability in short lacking requirements throughout the trade cycle and is at the heart of the Robertsonian decision concerning the appropriate use of banking policy in the cycle. The differing nature of capital, as well as the differing means of financing the purchases of the two forms of capital, led Robertson to take a critical view of Keynes' general treatment of investment in the *Treatise* and also in the *General Theory*; Keynes in this respect did fling a pot of paint rather than sketch the intricate details of the provision of capital.

The third type of capital, and the least important in terms of its role in Robertsonian theory, is imaginary capital; this is represented by the stock of paper securities which are not backed by physical assets. These are largely in the form of transfers of spending power from the public to the government. Lacking which goes into this channel is termed 'unproductive' as distinct from the 'productive lacking' associated with fixed and circulating capital.[21]

In what follows the Robertsonian concepts of capital must be borne in mind. Capital is *not* to be used interchangably with loanable or investible funds; this latter definition of capital was employed by, amongst others, Tugan-Baranowski.[22] Likewise the Robertsonian concept of 'capital' is not that which most individuals conceive as capital, that is their stock of assets of all kinds.[23]

THE FORCED SAVING DOCTRINE — AUTOMATIC LACKING AND INDUCED LACKING

Much of what Robertson has to say during and after the inter-war period on the question of economic policy and the control of industrial fluctuation, and on the theoretical controversies of the period, is derived from one central, and extremely important, theory. This is the 'forced saving' theory. An understanding of this therefore is an essential prerequisite to a clear interpretation of what follows. The remainder of this chapter will concentrate upon an explanation of this aspect of Robertson's work, but the full importance of this forced saving thesis will not be appreciated by the reader until the final chapter has been read.

Forced saving is the link between the Robertsonian theory of prices and the theory of interest. If banks create credit, prices in general rise and at the same time the supply of loanable funds is increased, keeping down the market rate of interest. Should the productivity of investment increase, creating an increase in demand for loanable funds, the advent of forced saving in the wake of more credit creation will prevent the market rate of interest moving towards the natural rate of interest. Forced saving can be blamed for the divergence between the two rates of interest. Forced saving is doubly important because it represents an original and substantial contribution to the debate on saving and investment in the 1920s; Robertson was the first British economist to thoroughly develop the concept of forced saving although he was quickly followed by Pigou.[24] Later the doctrine was rediscovered in early classical writings although, even so, the Robertsonian concept of induced lacking represented a substantial refinement of this doctrine.[25] Interest is also stimulated in this topic by the fact that the working out of the theory was undertaken with the invaluable assistance of J. M. Keynes. Remember that Keynes had put his stamp of approval on the forced saving doctrine in 1926 and had been responsible for the introduction of induced lacking into *Banking*.[26] However, it was Keynes who later became its keenest critic.

THE FORCED SAVING THESIS IN MONEY (1922)

The forced saving thesis was introduced in the first edition of *Money*,[27] it was not part of the *Study*. The contribution of loanable funds to support capital, working and fixed, was not to be found entirely in the difference between current disposable income and current spending, nor in the accumulated stock of consumer goods at the beginning of the period in question, as Robertson had argued in 1915; loanable funds for investment were available in addition through the forced saving provided by banking operations. Given excess liquidity, commercial banks will make net additions to loans as a result of continuous pressure on them to do so from optimistic businessmen: this increase in loans may be several times as large as the original expansion in deposits. Additional loans will create an increase in the flow of money onto the goods market in competition with the flow of money already coming from the public. This increase in demand will force up prices, and the general public will be 'forced' to share the available real output of consumer goods with those financing expenditure via the commercial banks. The general public are forced to abstain from consumption they would otherwise have undertaken had prices remained static.

The validity of this forced saving process partially depends upon the acceptance of Robertsonian *period analysis*. The time lags present in the process are essential if forced saving is to occur. Firstly, the increase in bank loans will initially raise prices; only after a lag will the level of output be affected.[28] Secondly, as a result of the increase in prices brought about by the additional bank loans, the real income of some households will decline; that is, for a proportion of the population, there is a lag of money income changes behind the increase in the price level. It is this section of the community which provides the forced saving for investment.[29] Forced saving therefore is not to be found in a stock of loanable funds held by the individual which can be used for future consumption, as with *spontaneous* saving. Real resources have been transferred from one group of individuals to another. One may view this as a shift of resources from creditors to debtors, since those borrowing from the banks have net gains in terms of the real resources which they consume. Alternatively, it may be viewed as a shift of resources away from fixed income groups to entrepreneurs.[30] Robertson saw the process as being very precise in *Money*; an X per cent rise in the volume of bank loans would yield an X per cent increase in the general price level; that is the real value of money would decline by X per cent.[31] The accompanying diagram summarises the forced saving thesis expressed here, and highlights the step by step approach, the period analysis more thoroughly developed in *Banking* and beyond.

The Forced Saving Process

STEP 1 | Increase in the demand for loanable funds (e.g. as a result of an increase in the marginal productivity of capital)

STEP 2 | Demand for loanable funds exceeds supply

STEP 3 | Inadequate VOLUNTARY saving to support desired investment at existing rate of interest

STEP 4 | BANKS respond to provide finance for the additional investment

STEP 5 | LOANS are utilised to finance the production of CAPITAL goods — not consumer goods. The volume of consumer good production is FIXED at this stage

STEP 6 | The WAGEBILL in the CAPITAL GOOD INDUSTRIES will increase

STEP 7 | There is increased COMPETITION for the available output of consumer goods

STEP 8 | The PRICE LEVEL will rise

STEP 9 | SOME INDIVIDUALS are FORCED to save i.e. to consume less than they would have done before prices rose (= the AUTOMATIC LACKING of BPPL)

THE RECOGNITION OF INDUCED LACKING — AND THE
DEVELOPMENT OF THE CONCEPT OF AUTOMATIC
LACKING — '*BANKING*' (1926)

The forced saving doctrine put forward in 1926 by Robertson
is much more refined. It is found in the Robertsonian concepts of
automatic and induced lacking.[32]

Automatic lacking is difficult to define although it represents
no more than a refinement of the previous forced saving process.
It requires an understanding of what Robertson meant by 'automatic
stinting'. This arises where individuals are prevented from consuming
goods as a result of an increase in the aggregate stream of money
onto the consumer good market. Again its existence depends upon
the time lags operative in the consumer good market. Prices respond
to an expansion of bank loans, output follows after a lag. The
increase in the stream of money is caused by either net dishoarding,
where some individuals are spending more than the value of their
current output on consumer goods, using past hoards to finance
their expenditure, or by an increase in the money supply via
the commercial banks. Automatic lacking occurs if this automatic
stinting reduces the consumption of some individuals below their
intended level of consumption and below the value of their current
output.[33] It is the equivalent of the forced saving introduced
in *Money*, except insofar as Robertson made explicit the view
that a change in hoarding habits could generate forced saving
as well as the creation of credit.

Induced lacking represents an innovation in Robertsonian theory.
As a result of an increase in the flow of money onto the goods
market, prices will rise and forced saving will occur; but additional
saving may be *induced* through the rise in prices. The real value
of the individual's money stock declines as prices rise and as
a consequence individuals may refrain from consuming to the
full value of their current output in order to restore this real
value. Alternatively, the individual may be encouraged for several
reasons to achieve a new real value for his money stock.[34] The
lacking which results has been induced by the change in prices;
it is voluntary and designed unlike automatic lacking, but it is
the result of a change in the money stream as is automatic lacking.
The general public therefore supply the lacking required to finance
capital, not the owners of the deposit in the banks, from whence
the additional loans are created.[35]

There are two further, and extremely important, characteristics of this process of forced saving. Firstly, it involves a change in the structure of production with resources being diverted from consumer good industries to capital good industries. The expansion in bank loans provides entrepreneurs with the funds to buy capital goods and labour. There will be an increase in the demand for capital goods relative to the demand for consumer goods and hence the price of capital goods will rise at a faster rate than that of consumer goods. Resources will be encouraged to move from consumer into capital good industries.[36] This has a repercussion on the nature of the cycle.[37]

Secondly, Robertson *is not assuming that full employment exists* in the economy and that output cannot be expanded. What he proposes is that, utilising period analysis, the expansion of output can only follow a rise in the price level, not precede it. The argument runs as follows. If output is to be expanded then this can only come about through an increase in the availability of circulating capital. Circulating capital cannot be made available unless the activity of lacking is similarly increased. Spontaneous saving or lacking may not be sufficient to meet the demand for circulating capital, hence it is left to the banks to increase the amount of credit creation; but an increase in the amount of credit will enlarge the flow of money competing for the existing available output which cannot change in the current time period, bringing an increase in the general price level, but particularly in the price of capital goods. This imposes lacking on the public, through the change in prices. The extended volume of lacking must always *preceed* an expansion of output. This could be viewed as a sustained rise in the price level, since an increase in prices will necessitate an increase in the value of circulating capital required to finance an expansion of output. This, in turn, will call for a further expansion of bank credit and a further rise in the price level. The problem which then arises is that of controlling the rise in the price level.[38]

Three questions are worthy of being answered. The first is to enquire as to the originality of Robertson's forced saving thesis, and the influences upon it. The second is somewhat of a digression at this point, but it becomes extremely relevant in later discussion. What role did Keynes play in the development of Robertson's views on forced saving? The third question asked in the next chapter is: How valid is the forced saving thesis? These will be taken in order.

THE ORIGINALITY OF THE ROBERTSONIAN FORCED SAVING THESIS AND THE INFLUENCES UPON IT

Although there is no evidence to suggest that Robertson was aware of the fact during the preparation of either *Money* or *Banking*, the forced saving doctrine had already seen the light of the day in the work of numerous writers.[39]

It is now generally accepted[40] that the forced saving doctrine had its origin in the work of the pre-classical writers Potter and Law, and possibly also in the work of one of the physiocrats, St. Peravy.[41] By the early 19th century it was clearly expounded in the work of Bentham and Thornton. Bentham introduced the concept of 'forced frugality' which went some way towards Robertson's automatic lacking.[42] Similarly Thornton recognised that an increase in the money supply, by raising prices, may force labour to reduce its consumption.[43] This doctrine was developed in the first half of the 19th century in the classical literature alongside Say's Law, even though it was inconsistent with it. (It was inconsistent in the sense that saving and investment, as a consequence of forced saving, need not be brought into equality by movements in the rate of interest. Hence supply may not create its own demand). It was a much less mechanistic explanation of the link between changes in the money supply and prices than the Quantity Theory and the Cambridge Equation which was to be developed later in the work of Marshall, Wicksell and Pigou amongst others;[44] the simple versions of these approaches argued that a change in the money supply would bring an equi-proportionate change in prices. The forced saving doctrine argued that the change in prices which transpired would depend upon whose holdings of money the change in money supply affected. This is most explicit in the work of Thornton and Mill.[45] An exhaustive coverage of the treatment of forced saving in classical literature would be too time-consuming and would be subject to the law of diminishing returns in relation to its relevance to the development of Robertsonian thought, particularly as it has been surveyed in other literature. The point has been adequately made that automatic lacking had been recognised by classical writers in the period 1800–1850, by Malthus, Ricardo, Dugdale Stewart, Torrens and Lauderdale, in addition to those already cited.[46]

However, the work of T. Joplin in the 1820s and later merits a special mention because of its relevance, not only to the pre-Robertsonian expression of forced saving, but for its attempt to relate forced saving to the theory of interest which was also a feature of Robertson's work.[47] Joplin distinguished between the natural rate and the market rate of interest, attributing the cause of any difference between them to forced saving. The consequence of this would be an inequality of saving and investment and a fluctuation in prices not interest rates.[48] Joplin proved to be a voice in the wilderness; the doctrine of forced saving and its association with the difference between natural and market rates of interest was not a feature of classical and neo-classical literature until the advent of Robertsonian theory in the 1920s.

This period of inactivity in the development of the forced saving doctrine however, did not stretch to the continental economists. Leon Walras developed a theory of forced saving in 1879 and this in turn was to stimulate Knut Wicksell[49] to extend the analysis along the line of enquiry introduced by Joplin; but there is nothing to indicate that Wicksell was familiar with Joplin's work. The significant feature of Wicksellian work was that it not only propounded a forced saving doctrine, and made forced saving responsible for the divergence between natural and market rates of interest, but it went on to state that the divergence of natural and market rates of interest was responsible for the credit cycle. If the imposition of forced saving meant that the market rate of interest was less than the natural rate, then monetary demand for factors of production would increase. The ensuing competition for labour would increase wage rates, consumer demand would increase, as would the demand for credit coming from producers, and a cumulative expansion would result.[50] This was the inspiration for later work by Von Mises, Schumpeter and Hayek.[51] Forced saving, therefore, played a much more important role in Wicksellian and indeed in Hayekian theory as the cause of the cycle than it did in Robertson's theory of fluctuation.[52] It represented an attack on the classical literature from which the forced saving doctrine had matured; the classical literature had failed to recognise that the forced saving thesis was not in harmony with the classical theory of interest.

In conclusion therefore, what is missing from the pre-Robertsonian treatment of forced saving is the concept of induced lacking, the additional saving which may result from the rise in prices because of a change in hoarding habits ('K' in the Cambridge Equation). This was in fact the main point made by Robertson in his comments upon Hayek's article on the development of the forced saving doctrine.[53] Robertson did not have access to that continental litera-ture which recognised forced saving and its influence upon the cycle until the 1920s; but the classical writings were available to him. However it is not surprising that he failed to find the origins of automatic lacking in this literature; forced saving was not a central thesis of classical economics; it was buried in footnotes and very infrequent page references in the major classical writings. It was not a topic covered in its own right, but an occurrence occasionally referred to in the discussion of current economic pro-blems.

The inspiration for the forced saving doctrine in Robertsonian theory is not entirely evident. This is a rare occasion on which it can be said that this aspect of Robertson's work was not to be found 'in Marshall'.[54] There is no evidence of any recognition by Marshall of forced saving in any of his publications, but one would suspect that his analysis of the effects of changing prices on income distribution had some influence upon Robertson.[55] Schumpeter had employed the forced saving doctrine in 1911 but this work was not available to Robertson in English until 1934.[56] H. Henderson had introduced a concept of involuntary saving which went some way towards the forced saving doctrine, and Robertson was familiar with this when writing *Money*.[57] The exam-ple given by Henderson was of a municipality, embarking on an investment project, which borrows from its public — they are compulsorily forced to save as a result of higher rates charged; but this specific case does not involve credit creation, nor a general rise in the price level of consumer goods; both of which are features of the Robertsonian forced saving doctrine. The work of Aftalion, reviewed by Robertson in 1914 had suggested a quasi-forced saving process.[58] Aftalion had argued that the entrepreneur was able to *impose* saving by keeping stocks of consumer goods off the market, forcing up the price level and' hence reducing the real income of the consumers. This, in turn, led to a transference of purchasing power from consumer to producer and to a diminution in consumption; but again this argument omitted the credit creation process and a general movement in the prices of consumer goods.

One is left wondering whether or not it was Keynes who aided Robertson in the working out of the role of forced saving. No correspondence remains between them over the drafts of *Money*, although the debt which Robertson owed to Keynes has already been indicated.[59] The clue lies in Keynes' paper on fluctuation in 1913,[60] which Robertson had used in the preparation of his *Study*. In this Keynes distinguished between deliberate and undeliberate saving. Investment can be financed from either source. Deliberate saving is the amount set aside by individuals for the purpose of investment; that portion of their resources which is put aside by individuals, into commercial bank deposits, is undeliberate saving. There is no intention on the part of the individual for it to be used for investment. If this is fed by the banks into investment projects via bank advances the amount of saving used for investment might exceed the amount deliberately saved for this purpose. This is as far as the Keynes' thesis goes; however, the next logical question is to ask what effect bank advances might have upon prices, and the division of resources between capital and consumer goods industries. We have already seen how Robertson took this step.

THE KEYNES/ROBERTSON DEBATE ON FORCED SAVING

Keynes, in the *General Theory*, took a very critical view of the forced saving doctrine. He regarded what he called the neo-classical attempt to link saving with investment through the forced saving doctrine as one of: 'the worst muddles of all' within the theory of interest.[61] He could see no clear meaning of the concept of forced saving unless it was measured against a specified rate of saving. This might be the rate of saving consistent with full employment; the forced saving would be measured by the excess of actual saving over that consistent with full employment (in the long run). Although this definition was consistent with that of Bentham's forced frugality,[62] it was inconsistent with Robertson's view that forced saving could arise at less than full employment. Keynes' definition would yield a forced short-fall in actual saving not a positive contribution to total lacking at less than full employment. He saw little possibility of successfully applying a forced saving doctrine in conditions of less than full employment and did not believe that contemporary economists had actually attempted to apply the forced saving thesis assuming conditions of less than full employment. Clearly Keynes memory was short; this was precisely what Robertson had been trying to do in *Banking*, with Keynes' assistance.[63]

The real Keynesian attack on forced saving came with the development of multiplier analysis.[64] The fundamental problem which the forced saving doctrine attempts to solve is to explain how funds are provided to meet the demands for fixed and working capital during the boom. The simple answer given by the multiplier process is that additional savings are *automatically* yielded by the initial change in investment; the change in investment instantaneously (in static analysis) yields an equal increase in saving which is voluntary, and is generated by the increase in income/output and employment created by the addition to investment. Prices need not rise to finance investment, additional bank credit need not materialise.[65] There is no need for forced saving. This was Keynes' ultimate standpoint on forced saving, but it disguises an earlier flirtation he had during the 1920s with Robertson's similar concept of lacking. This we will now consider.

Mention has already been made of Keynes' paper on industrial fluctuation in 1913 in which he distinguished between deliberate, or what might be more conventionally called voluntary saving, and undeliberate saving. It would be incorrect to suggest that this undeliberate saving matched the later concept of automatic lacking, but there are a number of similarities. Keynes believed at this time that saving and investment need not be equal; during a boom investment would exceed voluntary saving, during a depression investment would fall short of such saving. The discrepancy between the two was made possible by banking operations. It is within the scope of the banks to transmit the 'community's reserve of free resources' towards those responsible for capital expenditure. In other words the banks could put funds deposited with themselves to productive use. Clearly this is a long way from a forced saving thesis; there is no necessity for prices to rise to impose saving on the public via credit creation; but Keynes had accepted that saving and investment need not be equal and this was a step forward from orthodox thinking in 1913; he had recognised that banks could play a role in supplying the funds needed to finance the expenditure.

The forced saving doctrine was not supported in any of Keynes' publications in the years that were to follow, but there is considerable evidence in Keynes' correspondence to uphold the view that the Robertsonian approach to saving was acceptable to Keynes right up to the publication of the *Treatise on Money*. Robertson gave Keynes a major acknowledgement for help received in the preparation of *Money*, but no correspondence survives to determine whether or not Keynes agreed with the section within its pages on the imposition of forced saving. The most illuminating correspondence however is to be found in relation to Keynes' comments on the drafts of *Banking*. In the earliest surviving chapter draft of the *Treatise* Keynes had already moved nearer to the forced saving thesis by accepting that banks may create additional money in excess of the purchasing power entrusted to them and as a consequence prices would rise in the boom. The reverse would hold true of the depression, but he did not relate this to its effects on saving.[66] This preceeded Keynes' comments on the drafts of *Banking*.[67] Not only did Keynes accept the Robertsonian view of lacking in the cycle, but he was responsible for introducing induced lacking into Robertson's thesis and partly responsible for working out the implications of hoarding and automatic lacking.

In the early drafts of *Banking* Robertson had tried to make a distinction between the act of hoarding and what he called 'forced effective short lacking'. A change in hoarding arose where an individual altered his stock of money holdings. An increase in hoarding was a source of additional saving which could be transmitted to investment through the banks. Robertson initially believed that forced short lacking would not involve a change in the stock of money held by individuals, hence it could be distinguished from the lacking available through a change in hoards. Keynes convinced him otherwise.[68] Without admitting to this increased hoarding brought about by an expansion of bank loans, Keynes could not accept that resources would be released from the consumer good industries to capital good industries, since without it there would be no diminution of aggregate spending power as inflation proceeded. Robertson was to accept this,[69] but he maintained the distinction between the types of hoarding which were undertaken. In general a change in hoarding is voluntary; that which arises from an expansion of currency is not voluntary, but imposed on the public; it is instantaneous and inevitable.

KEYNES AND INDUCED LACKING

More important than this was Keynes' contribution of induced lacking, which is the most significant difference between Robertsonian theory and that of others advocating a forced saving doctrine.

Robertson had begun by assuming that 'K', the proportion of the individual's holdings of money to his level of real income, would remain constant over time. Keynes felt that this assumption led Robertson to neglect an important source of additional saving which was reflected in changes in 'K'. As a by-product of automatic lacking, there would be a certain amount of induced lacking. The increased flow of money, and increased prices characteristic of the process of automatic lacking, might induce some individuals to alter 'K'; that is to increase or decrease their real hoardings; this in turn might divert more or less funds to investment. Robertson would not initially relax his assumption, believing that even if he did allow 'K' to vary, it would only strengthen his argument;[70] later he was convinced by Keynes.[71]

Keynes gave three reasons why new hoardings would take place as prices rise:[72]

  i) The real value of bank deposits may fall below the minimum required by depositors and therefore they may desire to restore this real value rather than maintain their consumption levels.
 ii) Inflation may bring a redistribution of income in favour of individuals whose propensity to hoard is greater.
iii) If inflation is accompanied by a higher bank rate, this may provide additional incentive to hoard by raising the reward for abstinence.

However, working against these forces, Keynes recognised that inflation may breed expectations of higher prices. This would accelerate spending and reduce the incentive to hoard and also lead to the impoverishment of certain sectors of the public causing a fall in their capacity to hoard.

Undoubtedly this exhaustive list of the effects of inflation on hoarding was more than sufficient to persuade Robertson that 'K' might change. In fact Robertson goes so far as to employ the redistributive, the real balance, and the expectations arguments in the final version of *Banking*.[73] The implication of induced lacking is that the naive version of forced saving found in *Money* required amending: no longer is it possible to argue that an X per cent rise in the money supply will bring a similar change in the price level. As prices rise so hoarding habits may change producing a change in 'K'. An increase in 'K' would dampen down the change in the price level, a reduction in 'K' would accelerate inflation.[74] The debt Robertson owed to Keynes therefore was very substantial.[75]

Keynes was not overpowered by his discovery of induced lacking, remaining doubtful as to the degree of its importance.[76] By the time *Banking* was ready for publication (1926) Robertson and Keynes were in total agreement on the forced saving doctrine.[77] After *Banking* Keynes was to lose faith in the forced saving doctrine, and in particular with the recommendations derived from it for the appropriate use of banking policy during boom and depression.[78] Robertson had concluded that in order to finance justifiable investment during the boom forced as well as voluntary saving would be required. This could only come about if prices were allowed to rise (as banks expanded loans to meet the increased demand for circulating capital). Keynes, in the *Treatise*, believed that the 'orthodox' objective of price stability should *not* be sacrificed entirely in the interest of the demand for circulating capital during the boom.

Although the final draft of the *Treatise* omitted any comprehensive discussion of the forced saving doctrine, it is evident that as late as August 1929 Keynes was contemplating including a chapter which displayed support for it.[79] During the boom the banks would be called upon to finance an increased demand for working capital. Unless voluntary saving was forthcoming the expansion of bank credit would result in a rise in prices.[80] Keynes listed five possible solutions which could be employed to bring equality of saving and investment. If voluntary saving could not be adjusted to meet the demand for investment, if resources could not be gathered from abroad, if investment could not be manipulated or saving and investment brought into equilibrium, then the only remaining solution was for the banks to bring about a 'forced transfer of purchasing power'. In outlining the solution Keynes follows the Robertsonian path completely. Automatic lacking is explained, as well as induced lacking.[81]

The real break with the forced saving doctrine was to come in the debate following the publication of the *Treatise*; it is most visible in Keynes' attack[82] upon Hayek's *Prices and Production*,[83] in which Hayek had put forward a similar theory of forced saving to that found in *Banking*.

What has been gained from this discussion? Two conclusions stand out. Keynes supported Robertson's forced saving thesis right up to the publication of the *Treatise* in 1931 and indeed was responsible for a good deal of its sophistication in *Banking* compared with its statement in *Money*. In particular one can credit Keynes with the working out of the concept of induced lacking and its implications for price movements in the cycle and appropriate banking policy. Secondly, the hostility which Keynes later directed to the doctrine was really an attack upon *his own previously held views* in the mid, and late, 1920s and not simply an assault on the views of Robertson, Pigou and Hayek amongst others.

5 Critical Comment on the Forced Saving Thesis

It is not the objective of this chapter to question whether or not a government should allow a period of forced saving to develop. This question has been more than adequately discussed elsewhere.[1] Here we are primarily concerned with the validity of the thesis itself. Can forced saving actually arise in a period of expansion?

The various criticisms of the thesis are directed at the different stages of the process. One ancient criticism which has been adequately covered in the literature[2] is to question the means by which bank loans are created. Do new deposits create loans or vice-versa? Robertson, in 1926, was arguing against Taussig's proposition: 'So far as deposits are created by the banks ... money means are created, and the command of capital is supplied, without cost or sacrifice on the part of any saver'.[3] If one accepts that new deposits create loans how do these deposits arise? The assumption which Robertson had to make was that they emanated from government policy, from, for example, the buying of securities from the public. It is the attack upon the second link in the chain of reasoning which is perhaps more substantial, the link between an expansion of bank loans and the rise in prices generated.

There are three major criticisms of this link, two are related and might be described as Keynesian in nature, though one at least was recognised long before the Keynesian period in the work of the early classical writers. The non-Keynesian attack is best illustrated in the work of R. G. Hawtrey.[4] This was directed at Hayek's version of forced saving, which was almost identical to that of Robertson with the exception that induced lacking was not introduced into his analysis.[5] Hawtrey disputed the existence of forced saving. If businessmen increase their borrowing from banks then they will purchase additional resources *before* the rise in price takes place. The additional demand created will not automatically result in a rise in the price level and the imposition of forced saving. This additional demand will fall upon the *stocks* of consumer goods which have been accumulated out of past saving (prices remain constant even though the money supply may be expanding). Even if loans are spent on new production, the income so created may be spent on goods which can be drawn from existing stocks of consumer goods.[6] If stocks are depleted far enough prices will ultimately rise; but Hawtrey argues that it is impossible to link the losses which occur in some sections of the public with the loans given to businessmen for the purchase of additional resources and what is called forced saving. Stock levels are replenished as prices rise, but this is carried out by utilising excess profits created by such price rises (from voluntary not forced saving).[7]

Robertson had taken account of the availability of stocks in his original formulation of forced saving.[8] In many ways he agreed with this latter Hawtrey criticism, but he did not believe that it invalidated his argument. Increased demand may initially reduce stocks rather than raise prices, but eventually prices would need to rise to ration out goods between competing demands. If prices rise, forced saving must come about: some individuals would suffer a decline in real income and have lacking imposed upon them through the price rise. Insofar as Hawtrey admits that excess profits through higher prices are at the expense of consumers[9] he has a weak case against the forced saving doctrine.

The second, and what has the appearance of a Keynesian criticism, is to question whether prices will rise as additional credit is created in the presence of unused resources. Thus it is found in the modern day exposition of demand pull inflation. Prices will only rise where a position of full employment has been reached and not before.[10] Robertson made no reference to the state of employment in *Money* but there is an implicit assumption in *Banking*, and in later work, that unemployed resources could exist where forced saving was taking place; that is, prices could and would rise at less than full employment. Forced saving would take place in the movement from depression to boom, where some resources are assumed to be idle.

The answer to this criticism is to be found in the sequence of events in the Robertsonian theory. A rise in prices must *precede* a rise in employment. If businessmen wish to expand output and to increase employment, this can only come about by utilising more working and circulating capital, which is required in the production process. Voluntary saving is insufficient to finance this increased demand for circulating capital and therefore businessmen have to borrow from the banks. Loans are expanded and this swells the flow of money competing for the *existing* level of output. There has *not* yet been a change in output, because circulating capital is needed to bring this about. (Again the time lags are all important). If the flow of money increases, prices must rise. Output will only expand after a time lag, in response to this movement in prices. Keynes, in the debate surrounding the *General Theory*, was to argue that the supply of output would be *elastic* at less than full employment, and therefore the prices of consumer goods would not rise as demand and output rose in both the capital and consumer good industries. The forced saving thesis rested upon the belief that the supply of consumer goods is less than perfectly elastic, and that price rises are inevitable with an increase in demand.[11]

The final major criticism came directly from the *General Theory* and the so-called revolution which followed it. A thorough discussion of this will follow a later outline of Robertson's views on the multiplier process.[12] Keynes' neglect of forced saving was justified by his use of static analysis. If businessmen sought to increase expenditure on capital goods (of whatever kind), the extra saving required to finance this increment in investment will be brought about by that investment itself. As Joan Robinson was to argue, more clearly than Keynes,[13] extra investment will instantaneously create an equivalent amount of additional saving through its effect on the level of income. If the real world was static Robertson would not dispute this; but, as Robertson had maintained throughout his writings, there are time lags to be taken into account in the real world. Such time lags severely limit the validity of the Keynesian attack. It takes time for the additional saving to be generated to finance the increment of investment; the question remains: how is investment financed in the meantime? This is a question to be answered after a later discussion of the multiplier.[14] One would suspect that Keynesians rest too easy in their beds in accepting the multiplier and dismissing the forced saving doctrine, but let the suspicions remain for a few pages more.

Further questioning of the validity of forced saving arose from the work of Professor Strigl.[15] He disputed that a transfer of purchasing power would yield an increase in the production of capital goods. The fall in consumption of those whose real income is reduced by inflation would be offset by the increase in consumption of those whose real income is improved, leaving no additional resources for capital formation. The Robertsonian answer to this would be that forced saving will bring a transfer of purchasing power, but it will be a transfer to those in the community who are seeking to undertake relatively more expenditure on capital goods, not upon consumer goods. Resources will be diverted from consumer to capital good industries.

Theoretically there still is support for a forced saving doctrine, in that the various criticisms outlined above can be countered by a detailed examination of the Robertsonian process of forced saving. The argument against Robertson's theory, if there is one, is surely to be sought not in the above criticisms, but in the view that output cannot expand without an initial increase in the provision of circulating capital. This is the proposition which leads Robertson to believe that price changes, and forced saving, must precede variability in output and employment.

6 Saving in the Cycle

Robertson continued to defend his belief in the forced saving doctrine throughout the Keynesian Revolution and into his Cambridge Lectures in the late 1940s and 1950s. In *Lectures* he dropped the terminology of lacking and reverted to the Marshallian term 'waiting' but still employed the argument of imposed lacking.[1] It is now possible therefore to visualise the Robertsonian approach to saving in the cycle which he held from the time of *Banking* (i.e. 1926) onwards. It will be instructive, in addition, to compare his approach with that of Pigou and Hayek; these were the two eminent Robertsonian contemporaries, pre-*General Theory* writers, who utilised the forced saving doctrine in their theories of fluctuation.[2] Again it cannot be emphasised too greatly that Robertson always examined saving in a dynamic setting as part of cycle theory and this goes some way towards explaining why he was later critical of Keynes' attempt to 'deal with the savings–investment complex in terms of a theory of static and stable equilibrium'.[3]

In *Banking* Robertson conceded that some, but not all, crises were caused by a shortage of saving even in the presence of the forced saving mechanism. Thus he was partially able to agree with the conclusion of both Cassel and Spiethoff who wrote that crises were caused by the over-production of capital equipment in relation to the volume of savings.[4]

To Robertson it was not the deficiency of the accumulated stock of consumer goods which caused the crisis, an argument he had recognised but not accepted in 1915, nor a deficiency in loanable funds available for investment; it was a deficiency in the provision of lacking needed to finance circulating and fixed capital.[5] Such a deficiency he believed was responsible for the crisis of 1919–20 and perhaps this is why he accorded it some importance in 1926 compared with his dismissal of the theory in 1915;[6] but even so, in *Banking* he remained faithful to the causes of fluctuation suggested in the *Study*.[7]

If one examines his later work on fluctuation, particularly his comments upon the Austrian School,[8] he again emphasises the theory contained in the *Study* and omits the concession that a deficiency of capital *may* be responsible for crises. Crises are caused by over-investment, by a decline in the desire to purchase the flow of capital goods coming on to the market. This will arise no matter what level of activity of lacking is forthcoming. The enquiries which Robertson failed to follow through in *Banking* were firstly to ask what forces were responsible for the initial increase in demand for circulating and fixed capital at the end of depression, (which set off the process of forced saving) and secondly, what forces were responsible for the downturn in demand for circulating and fixed capital. Such enquiries would have led him straight back to the *Study*, to the forces of agricultural change and invention working on the investment decision, and to the causes of over-investment; but one must remember that *Banking* was not intended as a comprehensive study of the cycle, but as an examination of the monetary forces operating in the cycle; it specifically intended to investigate the justifiable behaviour of banks and the appropriate movements of the price level through the cycle. That Robertson remained faithful to his view of the cause of the crisis in the *Study* comes out most forcibly in his review of Ropke's *Crises and Cycles* in 1936.[9] In this he argues that even if spontaneous saving were provided in sufficient quantity to support investment: 'over-investment would be over-investment none the less'.[10] An expansion of credit and additional forced saving would merely postpone an inevitable downturn.

In examining the dynamic behaviour of saving over the cycle, as Robertson expressed it in 1926, it is essential to recognise the time lags present in the relationship between variables which give the process its dynamism. The differences in the time lags acknowledged in competing theories are often the major expression of differences between theories;[11] the main concern here is with the behaviour of forced and spontaneous saving over the cycle.

Beginning in depression, the first time lag is to be found in the response of output to an increase in the demand for circulating capital. This increased demand will be reflected in an increase in the price of the goods which constitute circulating capital and will be a signal to producers to extend production. Neither the spontaneous saving available, nor the degree of dishoarding in the economy, may be sufficient to cope with the demand for finance; businessmen must therefore turn to the banks for assistance, and the consequent expansion of credit will bring the forced saving required. Automatic lacking arises because circulating capital requires labour to be employed in its production. This labour is paid a wage, but it is not producing consumer goods. However, because it has the purchasing power to buy consumer goods, it will compete for the available consumer goods with that labour which is actively engaged in producing consumer goods. At this stage consumer good output has *NOT* expanded, the prices of consumer goods must rise; but Robertson implicitly assumes that the rate of increase in consumer good prices is not as high as that of capital good prices. The newly created credit falls into the hands of entrepreneurs who are seeking to expand their circulating capital. Thus there is an increase in the demand for capital bringing an increase in the price of capital goods; but to gain more circulating capital involves employing more labour, this swells the wage bill and in turn leads to an expansion in the demand for consumer goods. Prices of both capital and consumer goods will rise in a forced saving process, but the former will outstrip the latter. This early phase of the recovery process is summarised in the diagram on p. 124.

Forced saving will take place as some will have to forego consumption they would previously have undertaken before the change in the price level. It is here where the most crucial time lag is found in the Robertsonian process. Forced saving can only arise insofar as the real income of some individuals in the economy declines, that is the change in their money income lags behind the rise in the price level.[12] The classical writers had regarded wage earners as the class of income receivers whose income adjusted to prices only after a lag. Robertson believed the classes of income receivers who had lacking imposed upon them were the rentier class, and the salaried part of the labour force.[13] It may not be the wage earner who suffers in the Robertsonian forced saving process. Part of the expansion of credit would be used to employ

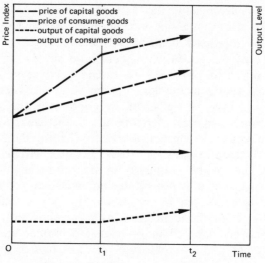

FIG. Initial phase of recovery

more labour with the result that the total consumer demand may not decline as previous writers had suggested; a greater proportion of consumption may in fact find its way to the wage earning sector of the economy.

The amount of forced saving required is enlarged by several factors. As prices rise, those entrepreneurs, who were not initially seeking a rise in their real circulating capital, will need to increase their money expenditures on capital in order to maintain that capital at its existing level. Again there may be a call upon the banks to finance this, creating further increases in the price level and forced saving. As loans are repaid to the banks new loans will be made, but there is no guarantee that the former is equated with the latter. The process of expansion of output will bring with it a lengthening in the production process for two reasons; firstly, if prices are expected to go on rising, merchants will hold stocks for longer periods; secondly, as output rises, so 'physical obstacles and delay'[14] will occur in the production process. In addition, as prices rise, so dishoarding can be expected to take place. Price rises breed expectations of further rises and expenditure will accelerate thus reducing the available savings. Those fixed income groups that suffer from imposed lacking may try to adjust their real hoarding in the face of price rises in order to maintain consumption; this again brings a fall in saving; but more important than this is the behaviour of entrepreneurs. If they anticipate that prices will continue to rise they will be encouraged to dishoard by keeping stocks of goods rather than cash balances. This again stems the flow of forced saving in the expansion and necessitates, alongside the other arguments expressed here, the imposition of further forced saving and further price rises if the expansion is to continue.

How is expansion brought to an end? An expansion of this kind, involving an initial increase in the demand for circulating capital and hence increased demand for short lacking, will reach a crisis when the supply of short lacking, forced and spontaneous, fails to meet the demand for it. Thus this is a 'shortage of saving' theory of fluctuation.

Robertson did not wholeheartedly back this theory in 1926. Most cycles were to be explained by an examination of variations in the demand for, and supply of, long lacking, that is in the saving which goes towards the financing of fixed capital as opposed to circulating capital. This did not involve the process of forced saving initially since long lacking was provided, not by the banks (to any degree), but by *voluntary* decisions on the part of individuals and corporations. Most periods of expansion are preceded by an expansion in the demand for long lacking. This may, for example, come about through invention which raises the productivity of investment. Past profits earned by entrepreneurs, private or public companies, and the purchase of new securities by individuals, are the main sources of this supply of lacking. This supply is voluntary, but as the expansion develops it may be insufficient to match the demand for long lacking. At this stage the banks may be called on to bridge the gap between demand and supply, exhorting lacking from the public by an expansion of credit which raises prices; again this leads to automatic lacking as with the provision of short lacking.

In putting forward the view that voluntary saving might not be sufficiently forthcoming in the boom, Robertson was influenced by the reasoning of Cassel.[15] Following Cassel, Robertson believed that expansion brought with it rising input costs which diminished profit margins and the available lacking from this source. In addition the voluntary supply of lacking may be curtailed by the substitution of hoarding for the productive use of profits in financing investment as entrepreneurs recognise that bad times are to follow, and that a pool of funds must be accumulated to pay future dividends.[16]

If the banks fail to respond to the demand for long lacking a premature downturn of the cycle may occur. Thus Robertson suggests a 'deficiency of capital' theory of the crisis in the same mould as that of Spiethoff and Cassel.[17] But such a crisis is the exception rather than the rule in Robertsonian theory. Some crises may be caused by a shortage of capital, but this merely disguises an inevitable downturn which would have occurred later irrespective of the state of the supply of long lacking. Eventually during the boom the point would be reached where the: 'revaluation of the advantage of acquiring instruments would in any case have soon arrived'.[18] At this stage the marginal utility of acquiring capital goods declines, and the *demand* for lacking diminishes. This is the true cause of the crisis in Robertsonian theory. The correct banking policy may be one of restricting the demand for lacking rather than procuring the funds needed to match demand.[19] The cause of the downturn therefore is to be found on the demand side for long lacking, not on the supply side: having led his readers someway along the path of the Spiethoff and Cassel theory of crisis, Robertson ends by performing a somersault which leaves his theory facing in the opposite direction. A somersault, however, which was to be expected if the consistency with the *Study* was to be upheld regarding the causes of crises.

A COMPARISON OF VIEWS ON FORCED SAVING — ROBERTSON, PIGOU AND HAYEK

Two other notable economists were to use the forced saving doctrine in their theses on the causes of industrial fluctuation; these were A. C. Pigou and F. A. von Hayek.[20] Their work on forced saving came after that of Robertson, and both were apparently aware of, and influenced by, Robertson's work on forced saving, Pigou more so than Hayek.

A. C. PIGOU ON FORCED SAVING

The major work of Pigou on industrial fluctuation was published in 1927.[21] His discussion of forced saving was very close to that of Robertson and indeed was partly represented as a comment upon *Banking*.[22] Pigou had been convinced by the forced saving argument in *Banking*; but he was not seeking to answer the same question as Robertson, or Hayek for that matter, as to the impact of a shortage of saving on the boom.[23] His main concern was to provide a correct *measure* of the amount of forced saving, or real levies, over the cycle.[24] He did however, frame his view of appropriate banking policy in the cycle in the light of forced saving; his conclusions and proposals on banking policy again were greatly influenced by Robertsonian argument.[25] But he did not admit to the possibility that *some* crises may be attributed to a shortage of saving, forced or otherwise, as Robertson had done.

To Pigou industrial fluctuation was mainly the result of non-monetary causes.[26] Banking operations might interfere so as to extend the amplitude of the cycle.[27] Forced saving was associated with rising prices; which in turn exaggerated the cycle by, amongst other things, affecting businessmen's expectations. This created optimism or pessimism and brought unjustified investment decisions. This led Pigou to conclude that monetary disturbances of this kind could be eliminated if forced saving was prevented. This elimination could be achieved by keeping the price level stable.[28]

The Pigovian view of forced saving in the cycle was therefore not so divorced from that of Robertson. Pigou had accepted Robertson's process of forced saving, but he had not accepted that some cycles might be caused by a shortage of saving; however this had been the exception in Robertson's theory rather than the general rule. The downturn would follow inevitably even with a glut of saving. His own work had led him to the Robertsonian conclusion that monetary forces could only exaggerate the cycle not cause it. Hayek's theory of fluctuation was in marked contrast to this Robertsonian approach, forced saving was recognised, and it was given prime importance in Hayek's explanation of the causes of industrial fluctuation.

HAYEK ON FORCED SAVING

Hayek was the person chiefly responsible for bringing the earlier work on forced saving to the attention of contemporary economists.[29] Despite his obvious thorough grounding in the historical development of the doctrine, he was unable to mould this into a clear statement of what he meant by forced saving.

There are several inconsistencies in his references to forced saving. He appears to have a totally different concept to that employed by Robertson and Pigou at one stage where he proposes that forced saving will occur whenever the *volume* of money is increased, and this does not necessarily involve a decrease in the *value* of money.[30] Robertson believed that a decrease in the value of money was responsible for forced saving. This Hayekian approach was to imply that saving would be forced whenever additional credits, the only discernable characteristic of the process, were offered by commercial banks — irrespective of the effect on prices. There was no indication that any one would suffer from declining real income and declining consumption.

This contrasts with a second statement of his theory in *Prices and Production*.[31] Here he shows a more traditional approach to forced saving, identical with the automatic lacking of *Banking* in that prices are seen to rise as credit creation expands, some incomes lag behind prices, and hence some individuals have to go without consumption. This interpretation of the Hayekian theory[32] is visible in the work of Hawtrey and Haberler, but is one upon which Hicks has more recently failed to cast his eye.[33] Hicks' survey of the Hayekian theory is indeed very interesting in that it attempts to highlight Hayek's failure to provide a time lag which would yield a dynamic process. Most of Hayek's work is consistent with Hicks' interpretation that Hayek had in mind a lag of consumption behind wage rises, rather than a lag of wages behind prices.[34] *Prices and Production* is the exception to this.

The possible lag of consumption behind wage rises is a lag which is evident also in Robertson's theory and one which now bears Robertson's name in most modern macroeconomic textbooks; but it was not a lag which had any great role to play in the dynamic process associated with forced saving in *Banking*. This lag in Hayekian theory brought about the relative movement in prices between consumer and capital goods which stimulated the changing structure of production found in the theory of fluctuation; if consumption demand lags behind wages, consumer good prices will not rise to the same extent as capital good prices during the early stages of the expansion; thus resources will be diverted to capital good industries.

Therefore, it is impossible to come to any firm conclusion on a comparison of the two theories of forced saving — those of

Hayek and Robertson, because of the ambiguities in the writings of the former. One interpretation would suggest that they are identical, the other would leave them very different. Both interpretations must be borne in mind in what follows.

FORCED SAVING AND INDUSTRIAL FLUCTUATION

The second line of inquiry which is of interest at this point is to compare the role of forced saving in generating fluctuations in the theories of both Robertson and Hayek.[35] Later it will be shown that Hayek's theory is best explained in terms of the divergence between the natural and market rates of interest,[36] but here the position has not yet been reached where it is opportune to undertake this explanation.

Haberler classifies the Hayekian approach as a monetary over-investment theory of the cycle.[37] This is indeed a classification which Hayek would favour,[38] but the purist might not readily agree with this. The expansion comes when there is an increase in the provision of credit by commercial banks.[39] Now what is the cause of the expansion — the provision of additional credit (and the subsequent forced saving) or the factors creating the increased demand for credit in the first place? Hayek would conclude the former, Robertson would argue it is the latter. The fundamental difference between them is that Hayek believed that it is not the *initial* disturbance which is important in the explanation of the cycle but the way in which the economic system reacts to this disturbance; it is upon this that his theory must be classified. Robertson saw the cause of the cycle as the cause of the initial instability in the economic system. One finds in the Hayekian theory a list of causes of the increased demand for credit not dissimilar from that which Robertson had put forward in his *Study*.[40] However, Robertson held that such causes were the real causes of the cycle; crises would occur whatever happened in the monetary system; monetary forces could only exaggerate the amplitude of the cycle. Hayek believed that a crisis would not follow an expansion brought about by real forces unless additional credit came from the banks during the upturn (causing *excessive* investment activity). The determining cause of the cycle can be found in the elasticity of the volume of credit which causes a divergence between natural and market rates of interest. Forced saving is to blame for crises.[41] Therefore, much more importance is attached to forced saving as the villain of the piece in this theory compared with that of Robertson.

It is possible to detect a substantial change in the Hayekian thesis over the years. In particular, his work published in a 1939[42] shows marked contrasts with his earlier work on forced saving. In this he took two steps towards the Robertsonian theory. Firstly, he dropped the assumption of full employment which he had used in his two earlier books on fluctuation; this was an assumption which Robertson had never made. Secondly, and perhaps more fundamentally, he argued that the downturn in the cycle came, not from a shortage of forced saving and a subsequent increase in the rate of investment, but from a fall in the inducement to invest. This fall in inducement was not the result of a rise in the rate of interest, nor of an increase in factor prices, but came about because of a rise in the rate of return in consumer good industries relative to capital good industries. In other words, as in Robertsonian theory, it represented a revision of the marginal utility of acquiring capital goods by entrepreneurs.

However, this is where the similarity ends between the respective theories. Hayek, in his 1939 explanation of the cycle, was to utilise the 'Ricardo effect'[43] whereby a rise in real wages leads to a substitution of machinery for labour (and vice versa). Towards the end of the boom consumer good prices rise, real wages fall and labour is substituted for capital. Consumer good industries become more profitable relative to capital good industries. The economy moves to less capitalistic methods of production. The cause of the downturn therefore is the fall in *demand* for forced saving not the failure of supply to match demand — exactly Robertson's argument; but Robertson did not employ the 'Ricardo effect' in his explanation.

Whatever differences there might have been over the causes of fluctuation, Robertson and Hayek both had similar views on the nature of the cycle. Hayek saw the cycle as a continuing process of change in the structure of production and as a shortening and lengthening of the period of production. A depression has the main characteristic of a shrinkage in the structure of production, a movement away from capital good to consumer good production and a shortening of the production period. An expansion has the opposite characteristic.

This is more clearly spelt out in Hayek's writings than in those of Robertson. Changes in the structure are the consequences of changes in the relative prices of capital and consumer goods. During expansion, capital good prices rise relative to those of consumer goods. At the end of prosperity, consumer good prices rise relative to those of capital goods. Resources move to reflect this change. In *Prices and Production* Hayek tried to show that forced saving lengthened the productive process by creating an increase in investment; the structure of production changed in favour of capital goods. Robertson would have attributed this change in structure to the non-monetary factors increasing the marginal utility of acquiring capital goods. This lengthening of the production process could not last if the money supply failed to continue increasing. The failure to continue to provide forced saving shortened the production period. It is this latter argument which Hayek replaced in 1939 by the 'Ricardo effect'. During the expansion, investment rises, but the money spent on investment brings with it an increase in consumers' incomes; consequently the demand for consumer goods increases. Prices of consumer goods will rise, real wages will fall and it becomes relatively more profitable for entrepreneurs to divert resources to consumer good industries.[44]

In this chapter the importance of the forced saving process in the Robertsonian theory of fluctuation has been established. Forced saving is the *means* of financing the burst of investment during recovery, not the cause of the upturn itself. But Robertson did concede that a shortage of saving may, on occasion, bring the downturn in *advance* of an inevitable downturn which would result from a devaluation of the marginal utility of acquiring capital goods. We have also seen the high degree of similarity between the theories of Robertson and Hayek on the role of forced saving in the cycle. Now we must turn to the theory of interest.

7 The Robertsonian Theory of Interest

INTRODUCTION

The logical extension of the analysis of the preceding section is to explore the relationship which exists in Robertsonian theory between saving and investment. In this one encounters the theory of the rate of interest since the Robertsonian approach argues that changes in saving act upon investment via the rate of interest. First thoughts on this subject might lead one to believe that interest theory is straightforward — there seems little controversial in the proposition that savings will act on investment through changes in the rate of interest; but the 1930s saw the elevation of interest theory to a position of extreme importance in the theoretical debates surrounding especially Keynes' *Treatise* and the *General Theory* and the work of the Austrian and Swedish schools on industrial fluctuation.[1]

In the pre-1930 period Robertson had given little importance to the rate of interest, except insofar as his work on saving and hoarding was relevant to its determination. Indeed there is no formal statement of his theory of interest in any of his books until the publication of *Lectures*. The first task of this section therefore is to clarify the Robertsonian theory of interest. Most of his writings in the 1930s, and later for that matter, were comments upon the role and determination of interest rates in competing theories, rather than clear statements of his own views; but from this it is possible to assemble what is known as the loanable funds theory of interest — this is associated perhaps more with Robertson than with any other economist, principally because of Robertson's staunch defence of this theory against the Keynesian Revolution.[2]

It cannot be overstressed that in his work on interest rates Robertson was attempting to develop a theory which was consistent with his theory of money. It was an attempt to *integrate* the theories of interest and money. Later, the proposition that changes in the money supply will cause a change in the general price level will be explored in detail.[3] In the theory of interest a change in the money supply, or a change in the propensity to hoard, will be shown to have repercussions on the rate of interest through their effects on the supply of loanable funds. Robertson was at pains to uphold the compatibility of these effects by explaining the consistency of the changes in the rate of interest and the price level that would result.

The debate in the 1930s surrounding the theory of interest was detailed and complex. In what follows the more important aspects of the debate are selected for discussion. Having examined the Robertsonian theory of interest, and hinted at its resemblance or otherwise to Marshallian theory, it is compared with contemporary theories. The major concern is with industrial fluctuation and for this reason attention is particularly paid to the explanation of the cycle in terms of a divergence between natural and market rates of interest, (characteristic of the Austrian school of thought in the earlier part of this century), and Robertson's comments upon it. Post-Keynesian criticisms of the loanable funds theory have often been developed on the assumption that it is a *static* theory, yielding an equilibrium rate of interest. This is not true of Robertsonian theory. To Robertson the loanable funds theory was a dynamic theory, with the schedules of supply and demand for loanable funds continually changing such that equilibrium was never attainable.

A further extremely important question worthy of discussion is that of the possible inequality of saving and investment and the implications of this for cyclical fluctuations. This ultimately brings us to a consideration of the *General Theory* and to the Robertsonian criticism of the multiplier and the liquidity preference theory of interest; each of which were major assaults on the validity of the loanable funds theory of interest.

As in relation to most other subjects, the Robertsonian theory

of interest is entirely consistent throughout his publications; the
chapters on interest in his *Lectures* have a content compatible
with perhaps his earliest, and most illuminating, article on the
rate of interest in 1934.[4] His views on interest were not to be
changed by the *General Theory* or by the Keynesian attack on
his theory. He remained unconvinced by the liquidity preference
theory, and indeed was responsible for a good deal of the pressure
which led Keynesians to rethink the theory and to support the
reconciliation of loanable funds and liquidity preference theories in
the form of the Hicks-Hansen, IS-LM curves. It will be argued later
that this reconciliation led Keynes' theory back towards the neo-classical theory of interest — nearer to it than the Keynes of the
General Theory would have intended. That Robertson was prepared
and determined to uphold the loanable funds theory in the face
of the sharp Keynesian criticism shows the strength of his conviction
to it. This is not to argue that Robertson did not develop his
theory over the years; he was convinced by certain innovations
in interest rate theory; and this was particularly so in relation
to the work of A. Lerner on the demand side of the money
markets.[5] But he continued to regard his theory as being in line
with accepted economic doctrines before 1936 and as a branch
of the general theory of pricing.

THE MEANING OF INTEREST

The first problem encountered in a survey of interest theory is
in establishing a definition of the rate of interest. This is problemati-
cal for a number of reasons. In reality there exists a wide range
of interest rates not a single rate. There is a short-term and
long-term money market where the short-term rate tends to be
less stable than the long-term. There is a market for gilt-edged
securities and one for non gilt-edged securities. Some money markets
are more competitive than others. Theory has to proceed by assuming that there is a single representative rate. The justification for
this is partially based upon the empirical fact that the variety
of interest rates which do exist tend to move in the same direction
as each other, even though they may not be identical. One particular
controversy in which Robertson became involved was in the determination of the relationship between short-term and long-term

interest rates; does the long rate determine the short rate or vice versa?[6] Of great relevance to the theory of industrial fluctuation is the distinction which some economists have attempted to make between a natural and a market rate of interest, and the relationship between the two.[7]

Therefore, to argue that Robertson believed the rate of interest to be the price of loanable funds, and like other prices to be determined by supply and demand is somewhat of an oversimplification of Robertson's thesis; but Robertson did state this on several occasions. In 1931 he wrote that the rate of interest is the: 'market price of the hire of something which Marshall called "free or floating capital" ... and which recent writers seemed to have settled down into calling "loanable" or investible funds'.[8] In *Lectures* he was similarly disposed to argue: 'it is the price of the use of investible funds, arrived at in the market, like other prices as the result of the interaction of schedules of demand and supply'.[9] However, the actual market rate of interest need not necessarily coincide with the natural rate of interest. The two will coincide if the demand for, and the supply of, loanable funds are equated; although even so, this would be a very unstable position, both rates quickly changing. Robertson was keen to point out that banking operations could bring an inequality of natural and market rates of interest (e.g. through the forced saving process).[10]

Of necessity we must determine the meaning of the natural as opposed to the market rate of interest; it will be necessary to explore the Robertsonian belief that this natural rate itself is not a stable rate of interest, but is continually moving; finally it will be essential to explore the relationship between natural and market rates of interest; does the market rate have a tendency to move towards the natural rate or vice versa in the long run? These complexities arise because Robertson believed that his theory of interest was a dynamic theory and that the rate of interest would be continually changing; as a consequence he needed to examine the reasons for the continual movements in the supply of, and demand for, loanable funds which would be taking place. The loanable funds theory is *not* a static theory yielding an equilibrium rate of interest. It will be necessary to treat it as such in the survey of Robertsonian theory which follows in order to isolate the sources of supply and demand for loanable funds; that is, one must make an assumption of *ceteris paribus* which Robertson was loathe to make.

Finally it must be stressed that the loanable funds theory examines the flow of loanable funds. Robertson is seeking to establish the sources of the supply of, and demand for, loanable funds in a defined time period, and the factors determining their magnitude; he is not concerned with a stock of loanable funds existing at some point in time. This stock approach was the form in which Keynes developed his theory of interest in the *General Theory*.

THE SUPPLY OF AND DEMAND FOR LOANABLE FUNDS

The Robertsonian theory of interest emphasises the role of both monetary and non-monetary factors in the determination of the rate of interest. In this way it can be distinguished from the real theory of interest found in the work of, for example, Boehm-Bawerk[11] and from the monetary theory of interest found in Keynes' *General Theory*.[12] The monetary factors dominate in the determination of the supply of loanable funds. The real factors, in particular the forces of invention and agricultural change, act principally upon the demand side by changing the marginal productivity of capital and in turn changing the demand for loanable funds. Together demand and supply, hence monetary and non-monetary factors, act upon the rate of interest.

THE SUPPLY SIDE

Although Robertson did not specifically refer to the term loanable funds in the first edition of *Money*, his discussion of the operation of the banks and saving habits leads one to believe that the supply of loanable funds came from three sources, from voluntary saving by individuals or companies, from net dishoarding on the part of the public and from newly created money by the commercial banks (thus giving rise to forced saving). Exactly the same proposition is contained in several of the ensuing publications,[13] and finds its final expression in *Lectures*.[14] However, in later writings, beginning in 1938, Robertson also stressed a fourth source of supply, what he called 'disentanglings'. He defined these as savings which had been undertaken in the past which were currently being disembodied from fixed capital or from working capital, and were being freed for further use on the money markets.

DISPOSABLE INCOME AND THE SUPPLY OF LOANABLE FUNDS

The amount of voluntary saving forthcoming will not be entirely determined by the reward for saving, that is by the rate of interest offered. In 1926 Robertson put forward the view that the individual undertakes voluntary saving when he does not spend all of the income received in the preceding period on consumer goods in the current period. Thus it is determined in part by the individual's previous level of received income; this gives a lagged relationship between saving and income (Robertsonian lag).[15] The amount of voluntary saving depends upon the: 'margin of income over necessary, or at all events customary expenditure'.[16] Similarly the amount saved by business enterprises is dependent upon the amount of gross profits less the necessary payments in the form of dividends. Such saving may be directly invested back in the business without being offered on the money market; hence part of the saving is directly offset by the demand for loanable funds, although it is possible that some businesses will offer their savings to the money market, at least temporarily. Hence for each rate of interest the amount of voluntary saving forthcoming will vary according to the aggregate level of disposable income in the economy in that time period.

If a constant level of aggregate disposable income is assumed, not all of the difference between this level of disposable income and current expenditure will manifest itself in the flow of loanable funds on to the money market. Some individuals or businesses may prefer to keep part of their saving in the form of hoards; they may express a preference for liquidity, keeping part of their money income by them rather than offering it to the money market. The aggregate supply of loanable funds will therefore be affected by the desire to hoard and by changes in the factors influencing this desire. New hoarding will diminish the flow of loanable funds onto the market. This may be counteracted by dishoarding where saving undertaken in previous periods is released from hoards onto the money market.[17] The total supply of loanable funds is, as a result, not only dependent upon the income level of the preceding period but also upon income levels of all preceding periods. However, one would suspect that the further one moves from the current period the less that level of income will have an influence upon current amounts of hoards available for dishoarding. There was a continual debate in the inter-war period on the concept of hoarding between Robertson and Keynes and others. This need not occupy our attention now, but it will be necessary to return to it later when discussing the loanable funds versus liquidity preference controversy.[18]

Excluding the rate of interest and income, four further influences on the supply of loanable funds were recognised by Robertson in *Lectures*. Firstly, saving will depend upon the opportunities that are available for the use of saving. Such uses can vary in the amount of safety, or alternatively the degree of risk, attached to them, and in their liquidity.[19] The availability of only high risk, low liquidity, assets in exchange for loanable funds would be a disincentive to supply these funds to the market. Secondly, the nature of the expected future needs of the individual, and his dependents, will determine the extent to which he is prepared to utilise current disposable income for consumption. Most individuals recognise a need to save — this need takes many forms — the need to provide for the upkeep of one's family, if not increase the standard of living in the household, the need to provide for the time when current earning power has diminished and the need to be in a financial position where one is able to meet unforeseen expenditure on illness, or other misfortunes. Related to this is the variability in the capacity of individuals to undertake their assessment of future needs; these would stem from differences in the degree of certainty relating to future events, and presumably, different educational backgrounds. Finally Robertson isolates a number of psychological factors influencing the saving decision; these are equivalent to the psychological factors propounded by Keynes in 1936.[20] It is important to emphasise that these four factors were introduced by Robertson in his post-*General Theory* publications and did not form part of his earlier published work on the theory of interest.

THE ELASTICITY OF THE SUPPLY OF LOANABLE FUNDS

Robertson followed in the classical and neo-classical tradition by concentrating much of his discussion of interest rates on the question of the elasticity of the supply of loanable funds to changes in the rate of interest. His earlier work on this lacked the usual Robertsonian thoroughness. In 1931[21] he was led to question the law of supply whereby a rise in the rate of interest, by increasing the reward for saving, will encourage a greater supply of loanable funds. This was the justification for the conventional classical argument for a direct relationship between the volume of loanable funds supplied to the market and the rate of interest. Robertson questioned this direct relationship by introducing an argument employed by Marshall[22] and Cassel[23] before him. Some individuals have an inelastic demand for income; thus if the rate of interest rises they will save less since less saving will now guarantee them the same given future income. Individuals are regarded as having a *fixed saving objective*. If the rate of interest falls more saving will take place. Marshall had regarded this argument as unimportant and as such it did not interfere with the direct relationship between interest rates and saving; Cassel had not been so convinced.[24] Robertson failed to reach a firm conclusion on the importance of this particular argument. The direct relationship was maintained in Robertsonian theory by an unconvincing argument; by the argument that higher rates of interest will: '. . . swell the source in which a large part of the saving that is done in fact originates — namely, large incomes derived from investments. Very rich people will find it hard to think of anything to do with an increase in income except save it'.[25] There is implied a relation between the level of interest rate and the distribution of income in the economy. Robertson is clearly not assuming *ceteris paribus*. Higher rates give more income to the top income groups who can do little else but save this income. Robertson himself was later unconvinced by this argument for it disappears from his subsequent writings on interest. He continues to employ a direct relationship between the supply of loanable funds and interest rates, but later is more willing to accept the classical reasoning as to why it should be a direct relation.[26]

Again Robertson's most sophisticated discussion of this relationship is to be found in his *Lectures*.[27] In this he traces the development of the loanable funds theory and comments upon the refinements introduced into it. It is therefore possible to gain some impression of his later views on contemporary loanable funds theories.[28] On the issue of the sensitivity of saving to changes in the rate of interest, Robertson accepts the neo-classical approach. The individual is regarded as seeking an equilibrium where he equates the marginal utility of spending a unit of money on consumption with the marginal utility he would gain by saving that unit of money.[29] The relation between saving and the rate of interest can be seen as a problem of assessing these respective marginal utilities. The solution will be reflected in the amount of interest which can be accumulated by saving a unit of money rather than spending it, counteracted by the individual's rate of time discount.

In neo-classical literature this has been treated partly as a problem of growth theory; Robertson commended the Ramsey model where the theory of saving was used to explain growth within the economy.[30] In the context of the supply of loanable funds forthcoming in a given period, the conclusion reached by Robertson was that if 'R', the rate of interest, exceeded 'P', the rate of time discount, then saving would be positive; if 'P' exceeded 'R' then saving would be negative. Thus if the rate of interest increases, given that the rate of time discount is constant, the supply of loanable funds will increase. An inverse relationship would only materialise in the case of the 'sargant man',[31] which is the exception rather than the general rule. If future income is expected to decline by a constant proportion 'G' per time period, saving will be positive even if 'P' is greater than 'R', since the individual may be encouraged to save to meet future needs in the advent of declining income. Mathematically Robertson argued that if:

$$G > \frac{A}{1-A} \cdot P \,.$$

where 'A' is the elasticity of his desire for consumption, the supply curve for the individual becomes backward sloping. However, the aggregate supply of loanable funds bears the classical inverse relationship with the rate of interest in Robertsonian theory.

HOARDING AND THE RATE OF INTEREST

So far the discussion has proceeded in terms of the relationship between saving and the rate of interest. The second source of loanable funds, dishoarding, and the negative source, hoarding will also depend upon the rate of interest. A rise in the rate of interest increases the marginal disutility of hoarding and encourages positive saving; a fall acts in the reverse direction. Robertson's early pronouncement on this relationship shows the danger involved in talking in terms of a single rate of interest. It is important in *Banking*, for example, to distinguish between the rate of interest offered on deposits in commercial banks, and the rate of interest available in the money markets, (e.g. the bond rate). In Robertsonian theory, increased hoarding can take the form of increases in the current account deposits at commercial banks; thus, if the bank raises its deposit rate, this: 'diminishes the temptation to Dishoard',[32] and reduces the supply of loanable funds. Quite the contrary conclusion to that above results if no distinction is drawn between types of interest rates. If the interest rate in the money markets is raised relative to that in commercial banks, dishoarding will take place. Therefore the behaviour of hoarding depends upon which interest rates are being moved and what relationship these movements have to each other.

Keynes introduced the concept of liquidity preference in his *General Theory* to replace the kind of approach to hoarding characterised by Robertson's work. There was considerable disagreement over the similarity of the two concepts.[33] Robertson did regard the liquidity preference approach as being superior in one respect; this was in relation to the attention it focused on the psychological factors influencing the various demands for money. Robertson had never developed fully the causes of changes in hoarding in the manner which Keynes had done in his examination of the speculative and precautionary demands for money.

Previous analysis makes further discussion of the forces acting upon hoarding unnecessary; induced lacking, an element of the Robertsonian forced saving doctrine, is represented by changes in hoards, and this has been shown to be influenced by price expectations and actual price movements in Robertsonian theory.[34]

NET ADDITIONS TO THE SUPPLY OF MONEY

Last, but by no means least, additional money created by the commercial banks, perhaps on the basis of conscious government policy directed via the Bank of England, is a source of loanable funds. In many ways this is probably the most important element with regard to later discussion. As such it is the only source of supply of loanable funds which can be regarded as being independent of a conscious decision to save on the part of individuals.

For this reason it is not subject to the range of influences upon it which arise in relation to voluntary saving and which have dominated this discussion. As a source of supply it has an elevated position in Robertsonian theory for a number of reasons; it gives rise to forced saving, generated by price changes, and it yields the possibility of an inequality between the actual market rate of interest and the natural rate; alternatively it prevents the equality of voluntary saving with the amount of investment taking place.

To summarise, the Robertsonian supply of loanable funds takes three forms: firstly, the voluntary saving on the part of individuals and companies within the economy, determined largely by the level of disposable income available to be saved, and the market rate of interest, secondly, the amount of net hoarding taking place, determined by the range of factors influencing also voluntary saving, and finally, the net addition to the money supply created by the commercial banking system.

THE DEMAND SIDE

Although the supply of loanable funds was discussed thoroughly in the early Robertsonian writings, the demand side was not explored in any detail until after 1936 in the debate surrounding the interest rate controversy.[35] However, it is clear that in 1931 Robertson regarded the demand for loanable funds as coming from businessmen who wished to undertake investment, and as such was dependent upon the profitability of the possible investment opportunities. This demand, as with the supply of loanable funds, is regarded as a flow of funds between two points in time and not as a stock at any given point in time. The behaviour of demand would depend upon the behaviour of the marginal productivity of the industrial uses to which the funds could be put. Robertson felt that this marginal productivity would decline as investment rose: hence the demand for loanable funds for industrial uses would be inversely related to the rate of interest; that is, to be encouraged to demand more loanable funds, in the face of a declining marginal productivity in the uses to which these funds can be put, businessmen must be enticed by lower rates of interest. Although this argument remained central to Robertson's later writings on interest theory, the treatment of the demand for loanable funds became appreciably more sophisticated over the years.[36] Robertson never claimed any originality for his treatment of the demand for loanable funds; indeed his later statements followed closely the work of Ramsey and later that of Lerner,[37] whom he regarded as 'distinguished scavengers' tidying up the classical approach to the demand for loanable funds.[38]

The argument that all loanable funds need not necessarily flow into the financing of investment appears for the first time in Robertsonian theory in 1938.[39] Robertson distinguishes between four potential uses in which funds may be employed. In addition to expenditure on fixed and working capital, they may be spent on the maintenance or replacement of capital goods, they may be put into store, or they may be utilised by the consumer to finance expenditure in excess of current income.[40] Despite this fourfold classification Robertson continued to regard the first use as the most significant in the determination of the behaviour of the demand for loanable funds, and this dominates his discussion of this topic.[41]

Following the early work of Lerner on the demand side, Robertson recognised two curves of marginal productivity which had previously been used by economists in seeking to explain the level of interest rates.[42] The first, the marginal productivity of capital, is less important than the second, that which Robertson prefers to call the marginal productivity of investible funds (which Lerner refers to as the marginal efficiency of investment). Indeed there is a good deal of confusion as to what the marginal productivity of capital means. The more logical interpretation is that of Robertson, derived from the early work of Lerner. Here it is regarded as a stock concept showing: 'For each hypothetical size of stock of machines, what would be the rate of return ... which would be incurred on the replacements which would be needed to keep the stock of machines constant at just that size'.[43] This approach is converted into a numerical example in *Lectures*, yielding a curve showing the marginal productivity of stocks of fixed capital at different sizes.[44] In later work[45] Lerner chose to interpret the marginal productivity of capital as showing the rate of change of income with respect to capital.

Although Robertson did not discard the marginal productivity of capital in his *Lectures* and maintained its original meaning, he clearly saw it as being of relatively minimal importance in the determination of interest. The second concept, the marginal productivity of investible funds, which Robertson saw as equivalent to Keynes' marginal efficiency of capital, is that which yields the sensitivity of the demand for loanable funds to the rate of interest. The investment decision is made in any time period by taking into account the current necessary expenditure on investment and the rate of return on that investment. The marginal productivity of investible funds curve shows for any period the behaviour of the net rate of return derived from employing investible funds in expenditure on capital goods. What relationship then will the demand for loanable funds have with the rate of interest? Robertson believed that the net rate of return from employing investible funds would decline as more funds were employed, since the greater the rate of output of capital goods, the greater would be the cost of producing one more unit of capital.[46] This was exactly the reason given by Keynes for the negative slope of the marginal efficiency of capital curve. However, in addition, Keynes argued that the investment process uses up the most profitable outlets first of all and leaves the less profitable investment opportunities for later utilisation. Robertson believed that this decline in the profitability of investment, as the stock of capital increased, would be reflected in a declining marginal productivity of capital and would bring a shift in the marginal productivity of investible funds curve, and hence in the demand for loanable funds over time. Indeed, with a given state of technology and level of population, there would be a tendency for the marginal productivity of investible funds to decline over time, hence the demand for loanable funds curve would shift in each successive time period nearer and nearer to the origin.[47]

It is impossible to come to any firm conclusion as to which is the correct approach. If the marginal productivity of capital can be regarded as being fairly constant over the range of investment opportunities which are available in the time period assumed by the loanable funds theory, then Robertson's approach is acceptable. If it varies with each extra unit of investment undertaken, or is expected to vary by businessmen who may have a regard for the future as well as the present capital stock, then the Keynes' approach has validity. Because of this difference, Robertson was incorrect in arguing that the marginal productivity of investible funds and the marginal efficiency of capital were identical concepts.

Despite these minor technical differences between Keynesian analysis and his own, Robertson was able to endorse the earlier views on the inverse relation between the demand for loanable funds and the rate of interest.[48] But did Robertson really intend to move towards the Keynesian stagnation thesis by arguing that the marginal productivity of investible funds would continually decline over time? Surely not, for there are in Robertsonian theory several forces in operation which have a tendency to displace the demand for loanable funds curve to the right rather than to the left, bringing higher levels of investment; these forces can be viewed as acting upon the average period of production in the economy. The greater is this average period of production, the greater is the amount of working and fixed capital needed in the production process; consequently the greater will be the demand for loanable funds. In *Lectures* there is an emphasis upon the impact of population changes and invention and research upon the demand for loanable funds.[49] If the population is expanding then capital must be widened, as the demand for consumer and capital goods increases alongside the population change. Similarly if invention and research is taking place which reduces production costs or introduces new products, then capital deepening will occur.[50] This is not to say that invention and research need always lead to an increase in the demand for loanable funds. Some developments may lead to less capital-intensive processes being introduced; however it would be true to argue that this has not been the more common development. What is fundamental with respect to the rate of interest is that the demand for loanable funds emanating from invention and research is responsive to changes in the rate of interest.[51]

DEMAND AND SUPPLY WORKING TOGETHER

It would be an unforgivable sin in the eyes of Robertson to take the curves showing the demand for, and supply of, loanable funds and depict them in a static unchanging manner on a diagram. Nevertheless this sin is openly committed with the plea that it will aid in the clarification of Robertson's theory of interest. The analysis proceeds with the warning that Robertson preferred not to use the simplifying assumption of *ceteris paribus*; for Robertson, the rate of interest would never reach an equilibrium level but would be continually changing throughout the course of the cycle, as a symptom, and not a cause, of the cycle. This would be the result of unending shifts in the demand and supply schedules over time; in other words, the Robertsonian theory of interest is a *dynamic* and not a *static* theory.

This approach is represented in the diagram below:

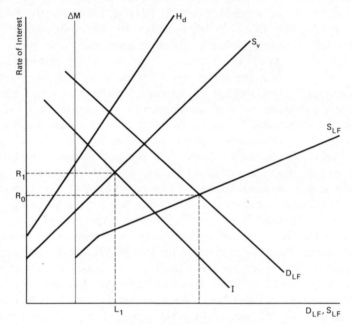

FIG.   Interest-rate determination

The supply of loanable funds comprises:

$$S_{LF} = H_d + S_v + \Delta M.$$

Where H_d represents net dishoarding,[52] ΔM is the new creation of money by the commercial banks,[53] S_v is the extent of voluntary saving out of current disposable income.

It is convenient to divide the demand for loanable funds into two components — that part going towards the financing of invest-ment projects (I) and that to be otherwise utilised (J) hence:

$$D_{LF} = I + J.$$

Given the assumption of *ceteris paribus* the demand for, and supply of, loanable funds are equated where:

$$H_d + S_v + \Delta M = I + J.$$

From this it can be seen that, even if Robertson had argued that supply and demand could be equated and equilibrium achieved, — which he steadfastly refused to argue — saving and investment need not be identical in the medium-term unless by some coincidence:

$$H_d + \Delta M = J.$$

This would be a coincidence in that there is no argument in Robertsonian literature which supports this equality. This would only be the case in the diagram if S_v and I intersect at a rate of interest R_0 and not R_1. Movements in the rate of interest will not necessarily act so as to equate saving and investment, such that investment always fills the gap left between income and consumption by the desire to save.

One final point should be made while the luxury of static analysis is afforded. Robertson was disposed to accept that there may be a minimum below which the rate of interest will not fall. The supply of loanable funds may be zero at a positive rate of interest.[54] Thus he shared the proposition put forward by Keynes in the form of the liquidity trap region. But this was not of Keynes' inspiration, but an acceptance of arguments put forward by Cassel which Robertson had first acknowledged in 1929.[55] At some low rate of interest Robertson believed that saving became zero because the desire to reach a fixed saving objective is quashed by the minimal reward of saving. It takes twice as long to gain a fixed saving target if the rate of interest is 1 per cent than if it is 2 per cent. In other words one needs to save twice as much at 1 per cent to reach the saving objective in the same time; as a consequence such low rates of interest act as a disincentive to save, and saving objectives are abandoned. If this leads to zero saving at a positive low rate of interest as Robertson suggests, then clearly he regards the achievement of a saving objective as the key motive for saving. This is an important argument for it demonstrates the pre-*General Theory* Robertsonian belief in the possible existence of a *minimum* rate of interest. Keynes was *NOT* the first economist therefore to recognise a level below which the rate of interest would not sink.[56]

8 Origins of the Robertsonian Approach to the Theory of Interest

It is particularly in relation to the theory of interest that one can productively investigate the claim that 'it's all in Marshall'. Two distinct areas of inquiry can be laid open. Firstly, one must explore the extent of Robertson's knowledge and understanding of the Marshallian theory of interest, and secondly it is important to compare the two theories. There is an element of truth in Keynes' assertion that Marshall did not provide any consecutive discussion of the rate of interest in any of his published writings.[1] But this does not mean that it is impossible to gain some insight into his theory of interest, although the task is made much more difficult, and the insight fringed with a certain amount of confusion and interpretive licence![2]

Robertson invariably quoted Marshall on the meaning of the rate of interest, agreeing that it was the market price for the use of what Marshall called 'free or floating' capital, or what Robertson preferred to call loanable or investible funds.[3] The strict Marshallian definition of the rate of interest was taken by Robertson to be: 'the payment which anyone received in return for a loan'.[4] This definition of interest was one of two definitions of the rate of interest used by Robertson, corresponding to the market rate of interest.[5] But Robertson did not fully understand Marshall's meaning of interest. This was because he failed to recognise that Marshall meant by the expression 'free capital', not the supply of, and demand for, loanable funds, but *real* capital or resources not yet employed in any particular use and therefore available to businessmen for investment.[6] There were therefore two rates of interest in Marshallian theory: a real rate of interest determined by the demand for, and supply of, free capital or real resources and a market rate of interest determined by the demand for, and supply of, floating capital or loanable funds. Robertson recognised only the latter in Marshallian theory.

Had Robertson not misinterpreted Marshall in this manner he would undoubtedly have been in even more agreement with Marshall, for Robertson was also to put forward the proposition that there were two rates of interest: the market rate of interest and also a quasi-natural rate of interest which corresponded closely to Marshall's real rate of interest. This latter rate was principally influenced by the demand for capital goods, which in turn depended upon the productivity of investment.[7]

Despite this failure to come to grips with Marshall's real rate of interest, Robertson did not neglect the role of the productivity of investment in Marshallian theory. This would act not only upon the real rate of interest, through the demand for real capital, but also upon the market rate of interest through the demand for loanable funds. He was in fact keen to emphasise, in his post-*General Theory* defence of classical theory, the role and importance of real factors in interest rate determination (including the productivity of investment). Marshall believed that the real and market rates of interest need not be identical through time, the real rate being the dominant rate pulling the market rate towards it. This is exactly the relationship which Robertson saw between his own quasi-natural and market rates of interest.[8] However, Marshall argued that their equality represented an equilibrium position, Robertson believed that the coincidence of his two rates of interest would not be a stable position.

That confusion did arise in Robertson's interpretation of Marshall's theory is understandable for, as Eshag has pointed out,[9] Marshall often implicitly assumed that the real and market rates were equal, and proceeded to use real capital and loanable funds interchangably in his explanation of interest rate determination.

There is some reason to believe that in his treatment of loanable funds Marshall was referring to the flow of funds within a time period and not to the demand for, and supply of, the existing stock of floating capital.[10] Robertson himself was critical that Marshall wrongly placed flow and stock concepts side by side in his discussion of interest rate determination, talking at times of a flow of saving, and at other times of a stock of past savings.[11]

Of the forces acting upon saving on the supply side, Robertson followed the Marshallian path particularly on the influence of interest rates.[12] But on the question of the sensitivity of saving to changes in the rate of interest this was not treated with the same importance in Marshallian theory as it was by Robertson. The influence of income on saving, which Robertson strongly denied was a Keynesian discovery, again was to be found in Marshall's work.[13] What Robertson failed to appreciate was that Marshall was not concerned with the influence of short-run changes in income upon saving, but with long-term secular changes in income.[14] But the influence of changes in hoarding habits, and net additions to the money supply (and the resultant forced saving), on the supply of loanable funds is not to be found in Marshall; although the latter, unknown to Robertson at the time, was to be found in the writings of the earlier classical economists.

In relation to the demand for loanable funds, Robertson's approach again reflected what he saw as a development, or refinement, of the Marshallian position. He accused Marshall of imprecision, of generally arguing that only net investment is important in determining the demand for loanable funds, but at other times including the use of finance for replacement investment purposes within demand.[15] This inconsistency in turn led Marshall into confusion between stocks and flows.[16] Marshall saw the demand for loanable funds increasing as the rate of interest declined within the individual firm because of the diminishing marginal productivity of capital; at the aggregate level demand was determined by the 'profitableness of business'. This might have been more precisely defined as 'anticipated profitability', since Marshall was anxious to emphasise the impact of businessmen's expectations on the demand for loanable funds. He argued that the rate of interest would be high if: 'as a result of expectations, whether well-founded or not, the general prosperity is likely to be high ... the rate of interest often rises rather high under the influence of hope, in an ascending phase of industrial and commercial activity and prosperity.'[17] Robertson also was to refer to the movement of the rate of interest brought about by hope or by fear,[18] but he paid much less attention to the influence of expectations on demand than did Marshall (or Keynes for that matter in his discussion of the marginal efficiency of capital). As to the influence of the marginal productivity of capital on the demand for loanable funds, Robertson was to minimise its importance in later writings, concentrating instead upon what he called the marginal productivity of investible funds.

Therefore, in many ways the Robertsonian theory of interest represented no more than a logical development of Robertson's interpretation of Marshallian theory, an interpretation which was not strictly correct on all counts. But this was clearly the most important source of influence on his theory at least in his earlier writings. In this way Robertson merely extended the classical tradition as Marshall had done before him. Robertson's most significant contribution to interest theory was to be found in the examination of the impact of hoarding and new money on the rate of interest, enlarging upon Marshall's treatment of hoards in his discussion of the demand for money. But, as Robertson pointed out in 1937,[19] he was not alone in including monetary as well as non-monetary factors in the theory of interest rate determination; the classical theory of interest could not be adequately represented by Fisher's loanable funds theory which excluded the monetary influences upon supply, as Keynes had argued in the *General Theory*.[20] All those economists who had developed a forced saving doctrine were to some degree or other emphasising the effects of banking operations and credit creation upon the market rate of interest.

To Robertson the loanable funds theory of interest was a 'common sense account of events', a theory which was an attempt to give precision to the views of neo-classical writers — in particular the work of Lavington and Hawtrey on capital and credit, as well as the general writings on capital and credit in 'a thousand newspaper articles'.[21]

9 Natural and Market Rates of Interest and the Trade Cycle

As has been hinted at on several occasions, an increasing number of economists from the early part of the 20th century onwards attempted to explain cyclical fluctuations in terms of a divergence between the natural and the market rate of interest. This stimulated Robertson to devote an article to an examination of this explanation of the cycle in 1934.[1] This chapter begins with a brief historical picture of the distinction that has been made between natural and market rates of interest, it then explores the use made of this distinction by the Swedish and Austrian schools in explaining the cycle, and ends with Robertson's own views on the natural rate of interest and its role in the cycle.

THE CLASSICAL ECONOMISTS AND THE NATURAL RATE OF INTEREST

The idea of a natural rate of interest is to be found in early classical writings. Although not explicitly stated, the classical definition of a natural rate of interest would be that rate which in the long-run yields the equality of voluntary saving and investment;[2] this equality would result in an equilibrium level of income.

In the long-run the quantity of money cannot influence the rate of interest. Adam Smith wrote that an increase in the quantity of money would increase prices but because it did not affect the rate of profit it could not affect the rate of interest.[3] Similarly John Stuart Mill was disposed to write that the most common error of the businessman was to suppose that changes in the quantity of money brought with it changes in interest.[4] In general most classical writers felt that in the short-run the market rate of interest could be influenced by monetary forces.[5] Those economists who recognised the forced saving doctrine also generally accepted that in the short-run there could be a difference between the natural and market rates of interest, brought about by banking operations; although, as Ricardo argued, whatever the volume of loans by the banks, it: 'would not permanently alter the market rate of interest'.[6] The regulation of the rate of interest was not to be imposed by variations in the rate of lending by the banks, but was determined by the rate of profit to be made by employing capital. It is the natural rate of interest which is commonly held as the dominant rate, pulling the market rate of interest towards it. The market rate of interest may be under the influence of monetary forces in the short-run. Marget refers to the sophisticated understanding of economists from Thornton to Marshall of the way in which changes in the quantity of money affect prices through the rate of interest; but most felt that the rate of interest could not be held for very long by monetary policy at any rate other than the natural rate.[7]

Patinkin has interpreted the classical and neo-classical economists in a different fashion. He suggests that because of the forced saving doctrine, they were quite prepared to accept the permanent influence of monetary changes on the rate of interest.[8] This may be true of the neo-classical economists, as the Robertsonian approach will show, but it is not typically true of the classical economist. The work of T. Joplin is a good example of this. He clearly saw that forced saving would interfere with the equality of saving and investment. If changes in productivity or thrift occurred, shifting the saving and investment schedules, the natural rate of interest would change. But if the market or actual rate of interest is prevented from moving by changes in credit creation, Joplin believed that the likely consequence would be fluctuations in economic activity not in the rate of interest.[9] Saving could be cancelled or manufactured by the banks, and consequently the actual rate may be above or below the natural rate.

NATURAL AND MARKET RATES OF INTEREST — WICKSELL, HAYEK AND KEYNES

Robertson was not familiar with the classical discussion of natural and market rates of interest when he first turned his attention to this in 1934. His work then was simply a comment upon the writings of three economists in particular — Wicksell, Keynes and Hayek.

Wicksell was inspired by the work of Thornton, Malthus, Ricardo and Joplin. His own theory was developed fully within the Swedish school, in the writings of Ohlin, Lindahl, Myrdal and B. Hansen; it also influenced the Austrian school approach to trade cycle theory, particularly the work of Hayek. The innovation in Wicksellian theory was the application of interest theory to the cumulative processes of expansion and contraction. Wicksell described fluctuations in terms of the divergence between the natural (or normal) rate and the market (or money) rate of interest; any divergence would show itself in fluctuations *in prices, not in output and employment*; but he did not suggest that this divergence was a cause of price fluctuations. Indeed he was at pains to point out that *real* causes were responsible for the price cycle, not the divergence of natural and market rates.[10]

Wicksell defined the natural rate as that: 'at which the demand for loan capital and the supply of savings exactly agree'.[11] This would correspond to the definition already assumed above. However, at various times it is also referred to as that rate which corresponds approximately to the expected yield on the newly created capital, as the rate at which commodity prices are stable, or as that rate which would exist if real capital were loaned 'in natura'.[12] Each of these definitions are consistent with one another, except insofar as the first alternative fails to take into account the supply of savings acting on the natural rate and therefore neglects the effect of thrift, but not productivity, upon the rate; the final alternative creates problems by assuming a barter economy. Hence the natural rate is the normal rate, the rate to which the market rate will move, the divergence between the two being caused by banking policy. If the market rate is less than the natural rate then *prices* will rise under the influence of a low desire to save as a consequence of a low reward for saving. This leads to a growth in consumer demand. The divergence between the two rates brings with it increased expectations of profit, which bring a greater demand for factors of production; higher factor incomes will result if full employment already exists (as Wicksell assumed) and there will be further increases in consumer demand. These reasons are additional to the fact that the demand for loanable funds needs to be partly financed via forced saving, which itself is inflationary. Clearly in Wicksellian theory it is the *price* level which fluctuates not the level of output and employment.

Tooke, in particular, had been critical of theories which had not matched the empirical observation that rising prices in a period of expansion are associated with rising interest rates.[13] The Wicksellian approach was to avoid this criticism by arguing that it was the natural rate of interest which tended to change frequently, whilst the market rate remained sluggish in response to changes in the natural rate. Hence an expansionary situation would be characterised by an increasing natural rate of interest with the market rate gradually following behind it. Rising prices and rising interest rates were compatible in this theory. The boot was not on the other foot, it was not the natural rate which remained unchanged over time and the market rate which danced around it. The message was there for all to see, it was only where market and natural rates of interest coincided that money had a completely neutral relationship with the price of goods and services; any divergence between the two would bring price movements. It was a message with which Robertson took issue. He was to argue forcibly[14] that the rate of interest which keeps the price level constant is not necessarily the natural rate of Wicksellian theory, the rate at which the supply of saving and the demand for capital are equated.[15]

The development of this Wicksellian approach leads once more to that now familiar economist — F. von Hayek. The divergence between natural and market rates of interest was lucidly linked by Hayek to the variability in forced saving and taken to be the cause of cyclical fluctuation.[16] Hayek's 'additional credit theory' placed the cause of the divergence between the natural and market rates upon newly created money. This, in the face of the increased, anticipated profit from investment in an expansion, and the subsequent increased demand for loan capital, increases the supply of loan capital with little or no increase in the market rate of interest. Investment therefore surpasses the amount of voluntary saving taking place and a cumulative expansion results. Initially the increased investment changes the relative prices of capital and consumer goods in favour of the former; the structure of production consequently changes in favour of capital goods. In the latter stages of expansion factor incomes rise, bringing a rise in the demand for consumer goods; this may lead to increased withdrawals from bank accounts driving up the market rate of interest and leaving some investment projects already begun unprofitable. This will bring a turnabout in the structure of production; relative prices now move in favour of consumer good industries and against expansion in capital good production.

Wicksell had assumed full employment in his model; Hayek was to do the same in his earlier writings. Later he dropped this assumption[17] and examined the Wicksellian cumulative process in terms of the fluctuations in output and employment that it might generate over the cycle. The conclusion he reached was in contrast to that of Wicksell. A stable price level will not provide a total disappearance of cyclical fluctuations.[18] This could only occur if bank deposits could be kept stable, but such a policy was not justifiable in Hayek's thesis. Stability would be at the expense of economic progress; innovation would be hindered and the psychological forces working for progress would disappear. If economic progress was to be encouraged, banks could not remain inactive and credit must be used to supplement voluntary saving.[19] Wicksell had given priority to maintaining a stable economy, Hayek had seen the need for economic progress. Different objectives required different banking policies.[20]

Amongst the British economists, it was Keynes who sought to develop the Wicksellian process in the *Treatise* published in 1930.[21] This had the same objective as *Banking*. It was a discourse on the causes of industrial fluctuation, with the aim of establishing the conditions necessary for monetary equilibrium in the economy; Robertson had similarly, in *Banking*, sought to plot the justifiable course of banking policy over the cycle. The *Treatise* saw the cycle as arising from fluctuations in the rate of investment relative to the rate of saving, that is in the inequality of saving and investment.[22] As such this was a descendent of the over-investment theories of Robertson and others; in fact Keynes went so far as to agree with the role of innovation in the cycle put forward by Schumpeter. As with Wicksell's cumulative process, investment increases when the natural rate of interest exceeds the market rate and vice-versa; the divergence between the two rates is responsible for price movements. If saving and investment could be continually equated by maintaining the equality of market and natural rates of interest, prices need never move. Entrepreneurs would neither be encouraged nor discouraged to expand or contract their scale of operation. The *Treatise* was no more therefore than an attempt to spell out the appropriate banking policy which could maintain this monetary equilibrium. Wicksell had chosen not to give his cumulative process mathematical precision. It was Keynes who sought to introduce this mathematical precision by manipulating his 'fundamental equations' to yield an explanation as to why differences between natural and market rates would bring the inequality of saving and investment, and subsequent price movements.

Keynes' final conclusion was that prices would fluctuate around a value $E \div 0$, this fluctuation depending upon the volume of Q (equals $I - S$), which in turn is dependent upon the divergence between natural and market rates (where $E =$ Income paid out; $O =$ Output; $Q =$ Windfall profits; $I =$ Investment; $S =$ Saving).[23] It would appear that there is little dissimilarity of view between Wicksell and the Keynes of the *Treatise*, other than in the degree of mathematical rigour attached to the analysis. However, this is not the case. It is apparent that Keynes was thinking in terms of a short-run equilibrium in the *Treatise*. One must remember that the *Treatise* contained static analysis, no time lag was introduced; the discussion as such was no different from the *General Theory* which was to follow, even though it purported to relate to fluctuation. The most serious criticism of it was perhaps its attempt to gain conclusions concerning dynamic phenomenon from static equations. In contrast, Wicksell was attempting to explain the possibility of some long-term equilibrium in the economy. Both failed to take account of the state of unemployment in their analysis, equilibrium was defined exclusively in terms of price stability irrespective of the level of employment; hence price stability would materialise if saving and investment were identical, whether employment was low or high.

Hicks has interpreted the *Treatise* differently. He suggests that, although Wicksell would not support the possible existence of an equilibrium at less than full employment if prices and wages are perfectly flexible (as they would be in the long-run), Keynes would accept that short-run equilibrium could exist at less than full employment.[24] In other words the scale of operation of entrepreneurs defined in the equilibrium of the *Treatise* need not necessarily be that consistent with full employment. This may be so, but it is not explicitly stated in the *Treatise*.

NATURAL AND MARKET RATES OF INTEREST —
THE ROBERTSONIAN VIEW

This is the background against which Robertson was to put forward his own interpretation of the relation between natural and market rates of interest.[25] The major problem, and one which was not satisfactorily resolved by Robertson, was to define the natural rate of interest.

The Wicksellian approach had been to define equilibrium and then to argue that the natural rate was the rate of interest which would maintain this equilibrium. The difficulty for Robertson was to accept a meaningful definition of equilibrium. His own approach to the study of fluctuation led him to adopt dynamic and not static analysis. It was illogical to assume that equilibrium could be defined as a situation where prices were stable and full employment existed. Economies were not stable but were continually progressing under the capitalist system of production. Economic progress takes place with the symptom of cyclical fluctuation. Robertson believed that the natural rate of interest should reflect this fact, and therefore he could not accept Wicksell's definition of the natural rate.

There is, as Professor Davidson has argued,[26] not one but two natural rates of interest; one keeps the average price level stable and the other brings the equality of the demand for, and supply of, savings. Full employment and price stability may not be possible within a single definition of equilibrium.

Robertson gave his equilibrium three characteristics; wages and profits are at a 'normal level', but he failed to indicate what was meant by normal; secondly, capital will be growing and consequently equilibrium is not of a static nature; thirdly, because cyclical fluctuation is taking place, full employment will not be a feature of equilibrium; unemployment will be at the *average* level it attains over a full cycle. These characteristics are in marked contrast to the meaning of equilibrium in earlier Wicksellian theories. Here price stability is not the chief feature; indeed it is more probable that falling prices may be occurring at equilibrium. Equally the money supply may not be constant, but will, with an increasing population, be increasing at equilibrium; in other words, money may not be neutral where the natural and market rates of interest coincide. The natural rate of interest is the rate which will maintain this dynamic equilibrium — an equilibrium which has different qualities at different times. Robertson had in mind, not the short-run equilibrium of the *Treatise*, nor Wicksell's long-run equilibrium, but a middle period analysis suitable to the study of fluctuation and consistent with his earlier introduction of period analysis in *Banking*. There is no such animal as a static natural rate of interest towards which the market rate will be drawn. The natural rate of the Robertsonian thesis is a moving equilibrium rate never attainable as there are always *endogenous forces operating to alter it*.

Robertson was to emphasise that equilibrium and the natural rate had been studied from the viewpoint that equilibrium existed; analysis then proceeded by examining how this equilibrium could be maintained. A more realistic, and worthwhile, approach was to assume initially a position of disequilibrium and to seek an answer as to how the economy may be restored to equilibrium.[27] Keynes was to state in the *General Theory*: 'there is . . . a *different* natural rate of interest for each hypothetical level of employment'.[28] This was the very message which Robertson was trying to get across two years earlier, inspired by the drafts of the *General Theory*.[29]

The natural rate, was clearly, as for Wicksell, the dominant rate, the one about which the market rate would fluctuate. Similarly Robertson was disposed, as Wicksell had done before him, to argue that the natural rate was not an immobile rate of interest, but one which would be chiefly affected by fluctuations in the marginal productivity of using investible funds (through, for example, innovation and discovery and changes in thrift affecting the supply side).[30] The Blondinians[31] had chosen to highlight the monetary forces which created a divergence of natural and market rates and had argued in varying degrees as to the powerfulness of monetary policy in maintaining equilibrium.[32] According to Robertson, what the *General Theory* was to do later to this debate, other than to play upon the inter-dependence of investment and saving through the level of income, was simply to introduce the possible impact of liquidity preference upon the market rate; a force which the Blondinians failed to fully examine, but one which Robertson had accounted for, in his discussion of changes in hoarding habits on the rate of interest.[33]

This is not where the story ends. Robertson was anxious to comment fully upon the Wicksellian approach. He could only do this by utilising a diagrammatic scheme which would take him partway back to static analysis.

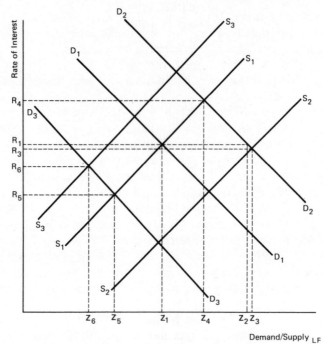

FIG. Industrial fluctuation and the natural rate of interest

It will be worthwhile to follow the argument of the article written by Robertson in 1934 very closely because it brings together his views on a number of topics discussed so far. These are:

i) the role of forced saving in the trade cycle,
ii) the importance of the divergence between natural and market rates of interest on the course of the cycle,
iii) the role of investment in the cycle and of the forces of invention and discovery in influencing investment,
iv) the validity of the 'shortage of saving' version of the over-investment theory of the cycle.

It represents a survey of the Robertsonian position up to the publication of Keynes' *General Theory* in 1936, a position which remains substantially intact in the post-1936 era.[34] In addition it throws some light on how the theory of interest is integrated with price theory in Robertsonian literature through the forced saving doctrine.

Let us assume that in the diagram above S_1 shows, for a given time period, the amount of voluntary saving forthcoming at each rate of interest, and D_1 the amount of investment during the time period corresponding to different levels to the rate of interest (reflecting a declining marginal productivity of investment). Excluding principally any net hoarding which might take place, and the possibility of any newly created money coming from the banks, the rate of interest equating S_1 and D_1 is representative of the classical natural rate in a static economy. Robertson would maintain that R_1 would not be a stable natural rate of interest, neither would there be any automatic tendency to return to that rate once a disturbance of the system has arisen.

THE UPSWING OF THE CYCLE

Robertson's dynamic interpretation can be imposed upon this analysis by assuming, for example, that an increase in the marginal productivity of utilising saving occurs.[35] As a consequence the demand curve will be displaced to the right (D_2). The impact of this upon the relationship between natural and market rates of interest will depend upon the reaction of the clearing banks to the increased demand for loans. It would appear that the natural rate of interest has risen to (R_4). If the banks keep the market rate of interest at R_1, they will need to create additional money to finance the increased demand for loans for investment purposes ($Z_2 - Z_1$). It will be difficult for the banks to sustain this rate of interest; indeed the newly created money will set in motion forces which will act upon both the market, and what appears to be, the natural rate of interest. These forces result from imposed lacking generated by newly created money. From our earlier discussion[36] it was seen that money incomes will rise alongside the money supply, prices will rise, and income will be redistributed in favour of entrepreneurs. If it is assumed that the entrepreneurial class have a higher propensity to save than the salaried class,[37] this redistribution will lead to a shift in the saving curve to the right (S_2).[38] The natural rate of interest now appears to be R_3. Robertson concluded that there would be a natural tendency for the market rate of interest to move to this rate (R_3). A number of important conclusions arise from this Robertsonian analysis.

i) saving and investment schedules are not stable, and therefore the classical natural rate of interest will not be stable.

ii) the banks can interfere to create a divergence of market and natural rates of interest,

iii) this interference (through changes in the amount of newly created credit) will have some influence upon the classical natural rate of interest. This influence manifests itself through the forced saving process. In 1934 Robertson chose to emphasise the redistribution effects of income upon induced lacking. Earlier, in *Banking*, several reasons for induced lacking were recognised. These would tend to shift the supply curve. What is most significant is that this analysis distinguishes Robertson's work from that of the early classical writers who saw only a short run influence of monetary changes upon the rate of interest. In the long run they believed the rate to be invariant to changes in the money supply,[39]

iv) the natural rate of interest, unstable though it may be, will pull the market rate towards it.

THE DOWNTURN OF THE CYCLE

But R_3 is only, what Robertson calls, a quasi-natural rate of interest. It is not a stable equilibrium because there are two forces operating within the system causing it to change. It is to these forces we look for an explanation of the downturn of the cycle. The first, and less important, force (in Robertson's opinion — although emphasised by the Austrian school of economists) is the eventual tendency during the boom for wages to catch up with prices and for profit levels to fall. The redistribution effect of newly created money is reversed and the supply curve will shift to the left (S_1). The natural rate will rise relative to the market rate, the demand for loanable funds for investment purposes will fall $(Z_3 - Z_4)$, and the recession will occur. The Austrian economists[40] blamed the rise in the rate of interest, the divergence between natural and market rates that occurred during the boom, for the downturn. It could be interpreted as a 'shortage of saving' theory of crises, admittedly more sophisticated in argument than that of Spiethoff and Labordère,[41] but having the feature of an inadequacy of funds to sustain investment at the boom. In classifying this theory of crisis however Robertson prefers to go further back in the causal chain. The cause of the crisis is not the shortage of saving, or even the increase in the natural rate of interest, but the source of the original change in thrift. In his 1934 article this was the redistributive effect of differential movements in wages and prices; but equally he might have emphasised any of the possible causes of a change in lacking expressed in *Banking*.

However much more fundamental to Robertson as the cause of the crisis is the saturation of the economy with capital goods which will arise in the vast majority of boom periods. This is brought about by the forces discussed in Part I, principally by the gestation period of investment, and by the indivisibility and longevity of investment. On rare occasions this saturation may be absent from the boom if a shortage of saving has occurred first. But invariably, according to Robertson, saturation appears first and represents the *only* cause of the crisis. On other occasions it works alongside the first cause, but invariably dominates it. Even where saturation does not arise, Robertson argues that it would have eventually arisen had not the first cause been present. It will result in a decline in the marginal productivity of investment, bringing a shift in the demand curve to the left (D_3). The quasi-natural rate of interest falls to R_5, with a substantial falling off in the demand for loanable funds ($Z_3 - Z_5$) and, in turn, investment. But there is also a secondary effect. Not only will income and output contract, but income will be redistributed from entrepreneurs to wage earners. Again this may lead to a leftward shift in the supply curve raising the quasi-natural rate (R_6) and dampening investment even further.

Robertson was anxious to stress that the two causes of crisis were not incompatible;[42] they could operate side by side; but the second cause was of significantly more importance than the first as an explanation of most crises.[43] In most crises it was not the high rate of interest which was the cause of the downturn in investment, but the saturation of the economy with capital goods which brought a situation where, relative to the boom, very little investment would take place whatever the rate of interest might be.[44]

What conclusions can be added to those above? Although Robertson is the first to admit to the oversimplified nature of the above analysis,[45] it does demonstrate a number of Robertsonian beliefs:

i) not only is the natural rate not stable over the cycle, and hence termed the quasi-natural rate by Robertson, not only does the natural rate dominate and pull the market rate towards it, but it is also never a rate at which prices are stable — nor is it a rate at which full employment is attained. A quasi-natural rate exists in both boom and slump. There exists a tendency to move towards it, but no sooner is this tendency followed then the quasi-natural rate is itself displaced. We have a moving equilibrium situation which is never reached because of the time lags inherent in the system,

ii) the cycle is not to be explained by monetary forces — by, for example, a divergence between natural and market rates of interest. Such a divergence is merely a *symptom* of the cycle not a cause of it. The real cause is to be found, in terms of interest rate theory, in the forces which cause the supply and demand curves to shift — the real forces recognised in Part I in the over-investment theory of the cycle,

iii) the disequilibrium situation, and the processes involved in moving from one disequilibrium to the next, whether or not the economy is moving nearer to ultimate equilibrium, is more worthy of discussion than a simple comparison of static equilibrium; that is, there is a reluctance to develop a static approach,

iv) the forces of productivity and thrift should be emphasised as acting in the long run upon the level of activity; in the short-run monetary factors (via the clearing banks), would interfere with the level of economic activity and with the movement in the rate of interest, but the underlying forces of productivity and thrift are dominant.

v) there is no automatic tendency over time for voluntary saving to be equated with investment through movements in the rate of interest. This was a conclusion strongly disputed by Keynes in the *General Theory* who believed that saving and investment must be equated but through variations in the level of income, not via the rate of interest as in classical theory. This equality was at the centre of Keynes' dispute with the loanable funds theory, and stemmed from his recognition of multiplier analysis. This failure to propose that saving and investment would be equated by interest rate movements is one of the major distinctions between Robertsonian economics and the economics associated in modern macro-economic textbooks with the classical straw-man.[46]

10 Saving, Investment and the Multiplier (1936 and after)

The next major step in the saving-investment debate came in 1936 with the publication of Keynes' *General Theory*. This section begins by surveying the relationship between saving and investment found in this great work; from this one can then appreciate why the forced saving and multiplier theories were incompatible; but which had greater validity? Robertson was not convinced by Keynes and Keynesian argument. The main objective of this chapter therefore is to examine why Robertson remained unpersuaded by multiplier analysis and why he remained faithful to the forced saving thesis.

THE EQUALITY OF SAVING AND INVESTMENT IN 'THE GENERAL THEORY'

Keynes did not accept the Robertsonian proposition that saving and investment need not be equal. This proposition was central to the forced saving thesis and, in turn, to Robertson's loanable funds theory. The inequality of saving and investment was practically guaranteed by the interference of changes in the money supply and hoarding habits upon the supply of, and demand for, loanable funds. If they were equal it was purely coincidental. The *General Theory* offered its interpreters two explanations of why saving and investment should be equal — either they were equal by definition or were equated via the multiplier process. Thus Keynes was at odds with Robertsonian theory, and, in this respect, with his own *Treatise* in which the inequality of saving and investment gave rise to cumulative movements in the economy.

The two explanations of saving/investment equality in the *General Theory* arose from Keynes' failure to distinguish between ex-ante and ex-post concepts, between actual saving and attempted saving. The first tells us that saving and investment are identical by definition.[1] Actual saving must always be equal to actual investment. This is a truism, an identity. Robertson saw that nothing was to be gained by maintaining such an identity for it told nothing of the causal sequence between saving and investment.[2] If the equality of saving and investment always existed by definition — the result of how the terms were defined — then there was nothing to be learnt of how independent human responses on the part of consumers and businessmen might bring about the equality in reality. This criticism was also to be voiced by Ohlin,[3] and by Lutz[4] who argued that such a definitional approach not only was impotent in relation to causal analysis, but that it led to a neglect of the role of credit and hoarding in the financing of investment. This latter point was made by Robertson in his comment upon Keynes' multiplier analysis.

But Keynes avoided this Robertsonian criticism in his second approach to equality.[5] In this he attempts to show how saving and investment are equal via the multiplier process.[6] An increment in investment generates an equal increment in saving. Additional investment creates additional income, part of which will be spent, part saved; this spending will create further income, part of which again will be spent, the rest saved; so the process will continue. The additional income created by the original increment in investment will depend upon the size of the propensity to spend. The greater is the propensity to spend, the greater is the value of the multiplier and the greater is the total change in income brought about. Contrast this with the classical relation between saving and investment, where saving influenced investment through the rate of interest, and where no reference was made to the influence of income changes.

A simple numerical example demonstrates the multiplier and also helps clarify some of the later Robertsonian criticisms. Although such a numerical example was not part of Keynes' *General Theory*, it does lucidate the main conclusions reached by Keynes; but at the same time it leaves the multiplier open to a dynamic interpretation. This was not part of Keynes' thesis.

The Operation of the Multiplier

Round	ΔI £m	ΔY £m	ΔC £m	ΔS £m
1	100	100	$\frac{1}{2}(100)$	$\frac{1}{2}(100)$
2		$\frac{1}{2}(100)$	$(\frac{1}{2})^2(100)$	$(\frac{1}{2})^2(100)$
3		$(\frac{1}{2})^2(100)$	$(\frac{1}{2})^3(100)$	$(\frac{1}{2})^3(100)$
4		$(\frac{1}{2})^3(100)$	$(\frac{1}{2})^4(100)$	$(\frac{1}{2})^4(100)$
5		$(\frac{1}{2})^4(100)$	$(\frac{1}{2})^5(100)$	$(\frac{1}{2})^5(100)$
6		$(\frac{1}{2})^5(100)$	$(\frac{1}{2})^6(100)$	$(\frac{1}{2})^6(100)$
n		$(\frac{1}{2})^{n-1}(100)$	$(\frac{1}{2})^n(100)$	$(\frac{1}{2})^n(100)$
TOTAL	100	200	100	100

In this table the initial change, and only change, in investment is £100m; the marginal propensity to consume is .5 and consequently the marginal propensity to save is equal to .5 (assuming a simple economy). A higher marginal propensity to consume of, for example, .75, would yield additional income of £400m. The multiplier in which case would be 4 not 2;[7] but the extra saving generated, whatever the marginal propensity to consume might be, would always equal £100m; that is, starting from a position where saving and investment are equal, the change in investment will always create an equivalent increase in saving ($\Delta I = \Delta S$). A stable level of income can only exist where saving and investment are equal; if the two are not equal then income must still be changing — the multiplier process will still be in operation. What was crucial about Keynes' treatment of the multiplier was his insistence upon static analysis, the neglect of lags within the multiplier process between additional spending and the creation of income, and between receiving income and spending it. He was concerned entirely with a comparison of static equilibria, without analysing how the economy moved from one equilibrium to the next.[8] It was this neglect which shouldered much of Robertson's criticism. It has already been concluded in the last chapter that the equality of saving and investment in this manner did not signify stability of output or employment in Robertson's thesis.

It is important to dwell upon Keynes' multiplier theory, for it is the base from which Keynesian policy recommendations follow. The cure for unemployment is increased spending; the amount of additional spending required depends upon the value of the multiplier, which in turn depends upon the propensity to consume. A stable marginal propensity to consume yields a stable multiplier value. Instability in the propensity to spend damages the usefulness of the multiplier as a policy guide since any change in autonomous expenditure as a result of government intervention may not have the desired effect on total demand if such instability persists.

THE MULTIPLIER AND THE FORCED SAVING DOCTRINE

Robertson's reaction to the multiplier can be anticipated if we consider the implications that it has for the validity of the forced saving doctrine. The forced saving process results from the impact of an increase in the desire to buy capital goods upon the level of prices. This increase in demand for capital goods brings forth an additional demand for bank loans. If additional credit is created, competition results for the available output of goods and services, prices rise and some individuals in the economy are forced to save; that is they are forced to lack, to consume less than they would otherwise have done in the absence of the additional credit created. Prices rise even though the economy may be at less than full employment. The finance for additional investment is to be found, not in additional credit created by the banks, but in the forced saving which additional credit creation has brought about, and the induced changes in hoards resulting from price changes.

In Keynes' analysis, at less than full employment, the multiplier process provides the additional saving required to finance the increment in investment without a change in the general price level, and without the need for additional bank credit creation. The act of investment automatically, instantaneously in Keynes' analysis, provides the funds to enable the investment to be undertaken.[9] Forced saving is not required — voluntary saving responds with just sufficient funds to match the investment. Output responds and not prices. The multiplier amounts to a complete condemnation of the forced saving doctrine which, as we have seen, is central to Robertson's conception of macroeconomic theory — the role of the banks, the operation of the cycle, the movement of prices and so on. Furthermore, it gives the conclusion that a stable economy can exist if saving and investment are equal, stability conditions which are alien to Robertsonian theory.

The conflict between the multiplier process and the forced saving thesis comes out most clearly in correspondence between Keynes and W. Beveridge.[10] Here the conflict is seen in terms of the repercussions of a change in investment upon the demand for, and supply of, consumer goods. Keynes argues that the act of investment will not raise the price level at less than full employment because the supply of consumer goods is *elastic*. The Robertsonian forced saving thesis recognises that the supply of consumer goods is less than perfectly elastic such that the additional demand created by employing more labour in capital good industries cannot be met by additional supply at the *existing* price level. If the supply of consumer goods fails to respond instantaneously, and in a like manner, to changes in demand, prices must change and forced saving must ensue — at *less than full employment*.

In later correspondence Keynes concedes that his theory depends upon the supply of consumer goods being elastic. If it is not then a large part of his theory is invalidated,[11] and the case against forced saving is less certain. Keynes admits that if he were to rewrite the *General Theory* he would need to re-define full employment as that point where the supply of output becomes inelastic.[12] To Robertson this would be an admission that full employment can be achieved with any amount of the labour force unemployed.[13] This is clearly an untenable position and a major limitation to the usefulness of much of the *General Theory*.

ROBERTSON'S REACTION TO MULTIPLIER ANALYSIS

Robertson reacted to Keynes' multiplier analysis in three ways. He began by disputing the originality of the multiplier as it appeared in the *General Theory*. Secondly, he attacked the static nature of Keynes' argument, providing his own dynamic interpretation and consequently remoulding the implications of the dynamic multiplier for the forced saving thesis. Thirdly, he disputed the stability of the propensity to spend and consequently the usefulness of multiplier analysis.

1. THE ORIGINS OF MULTIPLIER ANALYSIS

Our earlier preview of Robertson's criticisms of the *General Theory* indicated that Robertson felt Keynes claimed too much originality for his work. The components of the *General Theory* were not new, but simply rearrangements of existing theory, rearrangements which distorted and exaggerated the 'fruitful body of doctrines'[14] inherited by economists in the 1930s. The least convincing argument in this respect in Robertson's armoury was his assertion that the multiplier had been seen before in Marshall's work, and also in the work of J. Lescure. However, Robertson's statement of the so-called 'theory of repercussions' associated with Lescure indicates that it is an acceleration, not a multiplier, theory in that it relates to the impact of a change in consumer demand upon the level of investment. No one would now dispute that Keynes' multiplier analysis, developed from an article by R. Kahn,[15] had appeared before in the work of Johannsen and Wulff.[16] Indeed the idea that investment stimulates consumption is regarded by Haberler as being almost as old as business cycle theory.[17]

But was the multiplier recognisable in Marshallian economics? The answer depends upon what constitutes the multiplier process. Keynes believed that in increment of investment had a multiplied effect upon income and that the multiplier was determined by a stable propensity to spend. As a consequence there existed a precise relation between increments of investment and increments of income, output and employment. This was certainly not to be seen in Marshall's work. The multiplier is much more than a proposition that various trades are interdependent. If it were not then we need look no further than Marshall's *Principles* for its discovery. Marshall here states that one effect of the cycle was: 'the effect of growing unemployment in one trade reducing sales in another so causing unemployment',[18] and that when: 'there is but little occupation in any trades which make fixed capital. Those whose skill and capital is specialised in these trades are earning little, and therefore buying little of the produce of other trades'.[19] Clearly this is one step towards a multiplier theory, but the ultimately important features of Keynes' analysis were its precision, its consequences for the financing of investment, and its implications for economic policy. Marshall's treatment is no more than a general statement on the interdependence of trades which is common to many pre-Keynesian writers. What cannot be disputed is that Marshall saw a relation between consumption and income. But the propensity to spend out of income would not be stable since saving, and hence consumption, would depend upon the rate of interest.[20] As for the consumption-income relation, Robertson himself proposed a lagged consumption function in *Banking*.[21]

Even if we acknowledge that Marshall's theory relating to the interdependence of trades is equivalent to the multiplier process, there cannot be any doubt that Keynes gave multiplier analysis much more emphasis and overwhelming importance than Marshall gave to the quasi-multiplier in his view of the operation of the economic system.

2. A DYNAMIC INTERPRETATION OF THE MULTIPLIER

The theoretical argument against the multiplier, *vis a vis* the forced saving thesis, was lost so long as static analysis was maintained in Keynes' framework. If saving could adjust instantaneously to changes in investment via income and output changes, the multiplier would provide the finance for investment; there would be no need for prices to rise and no need for forced saving to take place; but the realistic interpretation of Keynes' multiplier analysis was not, according to Robertson, of a static kind.[22]

A failure by the multiplier to generate, through income changes, additional instantaneous voluntary saving, led Robertson straight back to the forced saving doctrine; finance had to come from somewhere. If voluntary savings were not available, savings had to be exhorted from the public through banking policy and price changes. Although Keynes regarded his attack on the forced saving doctrine through multiplier analysis as decisive in the *General Theory*, there is still a suspicion remaining that Keynes' saw the limitations of his static multiplier and that he himself hinted at a forced saving doctrine.[23]

The popularisers of Keynes' *General Theory* chose to interpret the multiplier in a dynamic manner. The notable example of this is to be found in the work of Mrs. Joan Robinson.[24] In this the rounds of the multiplier are clearly seen and the infinite series of income adjustments recognised, with each successive change in income becoming progressively smaller (the rate of progression depends upon the value of the marginal propensity to consume).

Clearly each round of the multiplier cannot take place with infinite speed, and consequently, although the volume of saving will be tending towards the value of investment, at any point in time the two will be unequal; saving will be deficient in relation to the level of investment, except at the final round of the multiplier process. Only where the marginal propensity to save is equal to unity will the increase in saving equal the increment in investment in the same round of the multiplier process. The smaller the marginal propensity to consume, the smaller is the deficiency of saving to investment at each round of the multiplier process. Given this interpretation of the *General Theory*, even by a strong Keynesian, Robertson had grounds on which to launch his attack on the multiplier.

Robertson agreed that without the period of transition from one equilibrium to the next: 'We can declare the problem of the finance of the process of investment to be self-solving'.[25] But if he could show that time lags exist in the multiplier process and that the period of transition cannot be ignored, then Keynes still had to find a source of finance for the increment of investment. Robertson's task was not difficult for the arguments against the static multiplier already existed in his pre-1936 writings. In 1926 Robertson had stressed the time lag between receiving income and spending it. Current consumption was not related to current income, but to income in the previous time period. This was central to his exposition of the dynamic multiplier.

What Robertson failed to utilise in his critical comment on the static multiplier was the lag between additional spending and the impact of that spending upon the level of output. A lag of this kind had been expounded in his *Study* in the guise of the gestation period of investment. In this he emphasised the time lag between undertaking the investment decision and the eventual additional production forthcoming on the capital equipment installed. Had Robertson used this lag in the argument against the multiplier it would have strengthened his case for a forced saving process, since a lag in output behind additional spending, and the need to finance that spending through the banks, could only create price rises (given the failure of output to respond immediately as the competition for goods and services increased). This failure by Robertson to employ the output lag was partially compensated for by a questioning of the operation of the multiplier where supply was less than perfectly elastic. In this situation Robertson argued that prices would have to rise in the face of increased spending, and that the multiplier became a 'somewhat treacherous guide to policy once we leave conditions of extreme depression'.[26]

Therefore, the only operational lag in the multiplier process not to be found in Robertsonian analysis is that associated with Lundberg; this is the lag between additional output and the addition to factor incomes created by that output. But one lag was sufficient to make the fundamental point that instantaneous saving would not be created to finance the investment. As a consequence Robertson highlighted the impact of a change in investment upon the creation of new money in his dynamic interpretation of the multiplier process.[27]

Robertson did not dispute that voluntary saving would eventually be yielded by the multiplier process. In the meantime investment needed financing; but there was a further problem. Robertson saw no guarantee that the saving generated by the multiplier would eventually go towards the financing of the original increment in investment.[28] The multiplier process might set in operation forces leading to the creation of further investment, which again would need financing. The main source of this additional investment was to be found in the additional consumer demand brought about by the multiplier; that is, Robertson believed that the accelerator would be set in motion. Increased consumer demand would create more investment, which would compete for the saving created by the original increment in investment. There would be an even greater deficiency in voluntary saving.[29] Furthermore he cited Kalecki[30] who argued that the induced saving of the multiplier might generate investment of its own. Robertson recognised in this a partial return to the classical view that saving determines investment, not vice versa. Indeed, given that voluntary saving was not automatically forthcoming, Keynes could no longer claim that the search for finance for investment would leave the rate of interest untouched; unless he foresaw a substantial change in liquidity preference.

In the post-*General Theory* debate Keynes introduces the concept of 'finance',[31] whilst still denying that forced saving provides for an increase in investment, he adopts a position which is compatible with a dynamic version of the multiplier process. The increment in investment is in need of financing, and instantaneous voluntary saving is not forthcoming through the multiplier. Finance is required to cover the period between the planning of investment and its execution: 'well in advance of the actual process of investment'.[32] This finance is not supplied from ex-ante saving, but from the entrepreneurs' cash reserves or from the money market. This represents a movement by Keynes towards Robertson's argument against the static multiplier, but the consequences for price movements, and its relation with forced saving, are not fully explored in the debate; only its implications for the liquidity preference versus loanable funds debate are explored in detail.[33]

In the face of the arguments of this section there seems to be a strong case in the post-*General Theory* debate for a reinstatement of the forced saving thesis; that there will always be sufficient ex-post investment is not the point at issue. The fundamental question is how investment can be financed in the absence of voluntary saving.

Robertson's criticism of the static multiplier is indicative of this general approach to economic theory. He never supported a disposition by economists, notably Keynes, to analyse dynamic problems by using comparative statics. He regarded positions of disequilibria as being more worthy of attention than positions of equilibria, and as a consequence could not accept the neglect of the process of adjustment from one equilibrium to another. Disequilibrium is a more normal state of affairs, and, although there may be a tendency to move towards equilibrium, it may never be reached as parameters change and consequently equilibria change. Such comparative statics therefore cannot do justice to the study of economic problems. The static multiplier was a good example of this deficiency. It totally excluded any consideration of how investment might be financed, dismissing a body of doctrine relating to the question of forced saving, and banking policy, which had been handed down and developed from the early nineteenth century; it did this simply by proposing an instantaneous adjustment mechanism from one equilibrium of the equality of saving and investment to the next.

A dynamic treatment of the multiplier does more than bring into question the means by which investment is financed; on the policy side it highlights the necessity for the careful timing of fiscal changes; static analysis simply dismisses the crucial problem. One of the major drawbacks in post-war fiscal policy in the U.K. has been that taxation or expenditure changes have been applied either too early or too late with the result that such policy has been destabilising rather than stabilising. Robertson, perhaps more than any other economist, deserves the credit for drawing attention to the dynamic aspects of fiscal policy.

3. THE STABILITY OF THE PROPENSITY TO SPEND

Central to an explanation of the multiplier process and to its useful application to economic policy is the building block within the *General Theory* that current, real consumption is a stable function of current, real income.[34] From this one can conclude that, knowing the value of the stable propensity to consume, there exists a predictable effect of a given change in autonomous expenditure upon the level of output and income, and in turn upon the level of employment. Policy becomes a fairly straightforward matter of estimating this propensity.

Again, it is clear that Robertson would find it difficult to accept that the propensity to spend out of income was stable. Indeed, although at any point in time it may be fairly stable, Robertson was not able to accept that it would remain stable over the full course of the multiplier process.[35] He did not deny that there was a strong relationship between consumption and income, albeit a lagged relationship; but there were additional factors which were important in determining consumption out of income. Keynes had recognised that objective factors in exceptional circumstances might disturb the propensity to spend;[36] but he was not prepared to concede to their importance. Robertson emphasised the influence which the rate of interest exercised upon saving and consumption. Keynes would not accept the strength of this relationship. In this case to have done so would not only have diminished the usefulness and precision of the multiplier, but it would also have required a modifying, if not a complete rebuilding, of Keynes' theory of interest; where the speculative demand for money was seen as the most important influence upon the rate of interest.

Later, in *Lectures*,[37] Robertson was able to point to the more complex relation that had been found between consumption and income in the work of Duesenberry.[38] In this it can be observed that the propensity to spend out of current income is not constant, but that it varies over the cycle. The marginal propensity to consume is low in the downswing of the cycle and relatively high where income moves above its previous peak level. Furthermore Robertson suggested that the operation of the multiplier may itself bring a change in the propensity to spend by changing the distribution of income between those with low and high propensities. If the entrepreneurial class gain real income as investment increases, so the overall propensity to spend may diminish, if this class represents the relatively rich, low propensity income group.[39] In the 1948 edition of *Money* Robertson saw the propensity to spend as depending upon wealth: 'especially perhaps on the proportion of capital wealth which is ready to hand and easy to spend',[40] a point which was reiterated in *Lectures*.[41]

There is a further argument which Robertson failed to raise against the stability of the propensity to spend, but one which is to be found in earlier Robertsonian analysis. If investment does increase, and if prices rise, induced and automatic lacking must take place. This brings about a further change in the propensity to spend.[42]

Hence as a result of this instability of spending propensities the: 'consumer may take a good deal of whistling back into his neat little theoretical cage'[43] (i.e. the cage built around the static multiplier).

SOME CONCLUSIONS ON THE MULTIPLIER

The foregoing discussion leads to two major criticisms of the multiplier process. Firstly, because it cannot be realistically interpreted in a static manner, voluntary savings will not flow from the process such that finance is provided for the original increment of investment. The saving which does transpire may in any case find its way into other investment projects. This means that the question of how additional investment may be financed is still very relevant and one which the multiplier fails to solve. In other words the forced saving thesis cannot be quickly dismissed because of the recognition of the multiplier. The search for finance for investment may still yield a 'classical' link between investment and saving via the rate of interest. Secondly, the multiplier process does not yield a precise relationship between the increment of investment and the change in output generated. The propensity to spend may not be constant whilst the multiplier process is working itself out; time lags will interfere with its operation, and the fact that: 'Dogs wag tails as well as tails dogs',[44] that is that the changes in consumer demand brought about by the multiplier may induce further changes of investment — reduces the multiplier to a very complex and unpredictable process. So much so that it is no more than a: 'potentially useful little brick'.[45] Certainly not the firm foundation of a *General Theory* of employment, interest and money.[46]

11 Robertson and the Liquidity Preference Theory of Interest

The final stage in the saving/investment debate in the inter-war period was the introduction by Keynes of the liquidity preference theory of interest. If saving and investment were no longer to act together in the determination of the rate of interest, as in the so called 'classical' system, but were to marry themselves through changes in the level of income, how was Keynes to explain the determination of the rate of interest? If he supported the Robertsonian theory of interest,[1] his precise theory of the multiplier would be substantially weakened by the influence of saving and investment upon the rate of interest. Of necessity he had to provide in the *General Theory* a new approach to interest rate determination.

This chapter begins by outlining Keynes' new theory; it then concentrates upon a number of major issues which were subsequently raised by Robertson and Keynes in the aftermath of the *General Theory*. The main issues to be discussed in this and the following chapter are:

i) the role of productivity and thrift in the determination of the interest rate,
ii) the validity of the liquidity preference argument in the *General Theory* and the existence of the liquidity trap,
iii) Keynes' concept of 'finance', and its bearing upon the interest rate controversy,
iv) the rate of interest in the trade cycle.

The theme linking these discussions will be the *central* issue in the debate. This is the role of productivity and thrift in affecting the rate of interest.

From this one can gain a clear picture of the extent to which Robertson was convinced by Keynes, and of the similarities between the Robertsonian and Keynes' theories. Although the approach adopted here focuses upon specific issues raised particularly by Robertson in the aftermath of the *General Theory*, it does provide answers to the fundamental questions raised by the liquidity preference versus loanable funds debate. The major question is whether the two theories are substantially different. The liquidity preference theory looks at the demand for, and supply of, money, whilst Robertsonian theory considers the demand for, and supply of, loanable funds. The former is a static theory involving stock concepts, the latter a dynamic theory concerned with flows of loanable funds. Do such differences make the theories radically opposed? An answer to this question must depend also upon a number of other considerations. The justification for utilising a particular theory is a function of its realism, in this case the extent to which it portrays the true operation of the 'money' market. The debate over the role of productivity and thrift, and the meaningfulness of the speculative motive, is particularly relevant in assessing the realism of the liquidity preference theory. One also needs to examine the consequences of each theory for economic policy. Totally different approaches are capable of reaching the same conclusions when questions of policy action are considered. A discussion of the connections between changes in the supply of money, prices and the rate of interest is particularly relevant here. Finally, but by no means of least importance, one needs to compare the usefulness of each theory as a tool of economic analysis; how far each fits into the general body of economic doctrine. An objective answer to this question unfortunately is difficult to attain since one has to recognise to which body one wishes to fit the arm of interest theory. Is it that of a typical classical 'strawman', or the younger trunk of the Keynesian, 'general equilibrium' man?

THE LIQUIDITY PREFERENCE THEORY OF INTEREST — A BRIEF OUTLINE

The proliferation of modern macroeconomic textbooks surveying Keynes' *General Theory* makes a detailed analysis of the liquidity preference theory unnecessary.[2] It is sufficient in this section merely to bring out the main features of the theory, especially insofar as they relate to the loanable funds versus liquidity preference debate. The revolutionary nature of Keynes' theory is determined in particular by three characteristics:

i) there is no causal influence of the marginal efficiency of capital upon the level of interest rates. In Robertsonian language this means that the demand for loanable funds for investment purposes cannot determine the rate of interest. The function of the marginal efficiency of capital curve is to portray the amount of investment that will take place at an already determined rate of interest,[3]

ii) saving is not interest elastic as in classical theory, but is determined by the level of income; this follows from Keynes' view that the rate of interest: 'cannot be a return for saving or waiting' and that instead it is 'the reward for parting with liquidity for a specified period'.[4] To have argued that the rate of interest has some influence upon saving and consumption would weaken the impact of the consumption function and multiplier process within the *General Theory*.

iii) the third characteristic follows from the first two. The rate of interest is the 'price which equilibriates the desire to hold wealth in the form of cash with the available quantity of cash'.[5] The role of the rate of interest is to determine whether savings are to be held in idle cash balances or in non-liquid securities — not to equate the 'demand for resources to invest with the readiness to abstain from present consumption'.[6]

Keynes' theory therefore is reduced to a discussion of the forces acting upon the demand for, and supply of, cash (not of loanable funds), and is thus a purely monetary theory of interest. It is a stock theory, examining the demand for, and supply of, cash at a point in time, and not a flow theory examining the market for loanable funds over a specified time period.[7] It also, as such, takes on the appearance of static analysis, consistent with the rest of the *General Theory*, and fails to explore, again in contrast to Robertsonian theory, the dynamic nature of the loanable funds market.

The supply of cash is considered to be relatively straightforward, determined by the operations of the central bank and commercial banks. The demand for cash is more complex. Keynes first had to investigate the motives for holding cash, and then to establish their interest rate sensitivity. Two of the motives for liquidity preference, the transactionary and precautionary demands, are considered to be reluctant to change with the rate of interest.[8] The third motive for holding cash, the speculative motive, guarantees a sensitivity of demand to changes in the rate of interest, especially in the liquidity trap region where the demand for money becomes perfectly elastic. The major implication of this is that there is a *minimum* rate of interest. Therefore it is this third motive which occupies an elevated position in the determination of interest rates. This is the motive which gives to money its function as a store of value, in addition to its function as a medium of exchange.[9]

The speculative demand results from Keynes' assertion that the future is uncertain and that this uncertainty breeds varying expectations as to which way the rate of interest is going to move. This uncertainty then makes the speculative demand a logical proposition, for, given that wealth holders have only a choice between holding cash and buying bonds, the disposition to anticipate an increase in the rate of interest will encourage the wealth holder to hold cash in preference to buying bonds. If an increase in the rate of interest ensues, the price of existing bonds will fall and a capital loss will accrue to bond holders. On the other hand, if a fall in the rate of interest is anticipated, it is more profitable for the wealth holder to buy bonds in preference to holding cash. A fall in the rate of interest will increase bond prices and reward the bond holder with a capital gain. This situation works so as to increase the aggregate speculative demand for money as the rate of interest falls. The lower the rate of interest the greater is the expectation in the economy that any further change in the rate will be in an upwards direction — therefore the greater will be the speculative demand for money. In this respect Keynes accepts the existence of a safe, future rate of interest[10] which is having a fundamental influence upon the wealth holder's speculative demand for money, and therefore upon the *actual* level of the rate of interest. However, Keynes fails to enquire as to the factors determining the individual's conception of the safe future rate of interest; this represents a deficiency in his theory, since its determination is crucial to where the actual rate will stand.

There is a second reason why a lower rate of interest will

yield a greater speculative demand for money in a state of given expectations. This was given less emphasis by Keynes, and has disappeared from much of the contemporary interpretation of the *General Theory*. Keynes writes: 'every fall in R reduces the current earnings from illiquidity, which are available as a sort of insurance premium to offset the risk of loss on capital account'.[11] This reason is more classical in nature in that the marginal utility of holding cash is seen to increase with a fall in the rate of interest — the reward foregone by holding cash. It does not rely upon the existence of uncertainty, and expectations; but is undoubtedly less important since uncertainty as to the future movement in interest rates is regarded by Keynes as the 'sole intelligible explanation'[12] of the speculative market for liquidity.

This is where the story ends in the *General Theory* but in the ensuing debate Keynes was to introduce a second interest-elastic motive for holding cash. This is to be found in his concept of 'finance' which appeared for the first time in 1937,[13] and which is Keynes' answer to Robertson's questioning of the sources of finance for investment in the absence of voluntary saving.

PRODUCTIVITY, THRIFT AND THE RATE OF INTEREST

The differences between the interest theories of Robertson and Keynes were much more than the methodological difference of static versus dynamic analysis, or stock versus flow theories. Robertson was critical of the *General Theory* for its neglect of the 'classical' forces of productivity and thrift acting upon the rate of interest,[14] and for its consequent over-emphasis upon the monetary factors determining the rate of interest — the state of liquidity preference, and the quantity of money. Monetary and non-monetary forces[15] work side by side in Robertson's theory, productivity and thrift exerting a long-run influence upon the rate of interest, through their determination of the quasi-natural rate which pulls the market rate of interest towards it. Monetary factors, newly created money, and changes in hoards, help to determine the market rate of interest, but also affect the long-run interest rate by acting upon the quasi-natural rate through their repercussions on thrift. Robertson accuses Keynes of two crimes, firstly of denying that an increase in the productivity of investment (in the Keynesian form represented by a change in the marginal efficiency of capital) can increase the rate of interest, and secondly, of denying that an increase in thrift can lower the rate of interest.

But what is the significance of this possible neglect of productivity and thrift by Keynes upon the rate of interest? The answer is to be found in our earlier discussion of the savings/investment debate, and in the role of productivity and thrift which Keynes recognises; for Keynes, changes in thrift and productivity, and hence changes in saving and investment, will not move the rate of interest, but will act upon the levels of output and employment. An increase in the productivity of investment will, through the multiplier process, generate more income and output, and in turn more consumption (and an equivalent increase in saving). There is no need for the rate of interest to change. If the propensity to save increases, the rate of interest will not decline as in Robertsonian theory, but the level of output and employment will decrease as the value of the multiplier declines. The level of saving depends upon the level of real income, not the rate of interest. This yields a different supply of savings curve in relation to the rate of interest for *every level of income*. This is a strong argument against classical interest theory; since investment determines income through the multiplier, the supply of savings and the investment demand curve are not independent, and therefore the loanable funds theory of interest cannot yield an equilibrium rate of interest.

This deficiency was not recognised by classical writers, but it was acknowledged by Robertson in his dynamic theory of interest.[16] His theory was adjusted accordingly. The theoretical significance is clear; Keynes would dispute the operation of the rate of interest in the cycle as portrayed by Robertson,[17] as well as the existence of automatic and induced lacking, and the underlying movements in the price level in Robertson's cycle theory. The total significance of the neglect of productivity and thrift upon the interest rate, and the substitution of its role in determining output and employment is heightened, when one contemplates the policy implications of Keynes' alternative theory. From the new found relation between investment and savings the belief in fiscal policy results. The encouragement of thrift is no longer a virtue but a vice in a depressed economy; an increase in the propensity to save out of total income, imposed, for example, through an increase in income taxation, reduces the value of the multiplier, yielding less output from a given level of investment, and more unemployment. It does not bring a lowering of the rate of interest and a subsequent encouragement to invest.[18]

The importance of the repercussions of the neglect of productivity and thrift on the interest rate justifies a deeper excursion into the subject. As a beginning one can enquire as to whether Keynes was completely neglectful of the forces of productivity and thrift, and, if so, was he justifiably neglectful? The strength of Robertson's attack upon Keynes in this respect rests upon two pronouncements by Keynes in the *General Theory*. In the first, Keynes declines to offer a shift in the marginal efficiency of capital any effect upon the rate of interest. An increase merely leads to more investment taking place at a given, otherwise determined, rate of interest.[19] In the second, Keynes discredits the view that a decline in the propensity to spend will lower the rate of interest.[20] Equally, however, one can find statements in the *General Theory* which would support the view that Keynes did believe that productivity and thrift, and hence saving and investment, would exert pressures upon the rate of interest.[21]

This conflict in evidence is firmly resolved in favour of Robertson's accusation by recourse to supporting arguments in the *General Theory*, and to the correspondence between Keynes and others. Although it must be stressed that it is important to make a definite distinction between the view of Keynes in the *General Theory* and that which he held shortly after the *General Theory* appeared.[22] The correspondence between Keynes and Robertson, Robinson and Hawtrey[23] is very illuminating in this respect. Robertson proposed that any rightward movement in the expected marginal productivity of loanable funds curve would tend to increase the rate of interest by increasing the competition for loanable funds. Keynes replied that within the *General Theory*: 'It is precisely this proposition which I am denying'.[24] Similarly, to Hawtrey he wrote: 'When the schedule of the marginal efficiency of capital rises the rate of investment is pushed up so as to keep the actual marginal efficiency of capital in equilibrium with the conventional rate of interest'.[25] And on the influence on thrift he wrote: 'one of my main points is precisely that changes in the propensity to spend are in themselves ... wholly and of logical necessity irrelevant to liquidity preference'.[26] *There can be no disputing therefore that it was Keynes' intention to exclude the forces of productivity and thrift from any major part in deciding the level of the rate of interest.*

But how could Keynes justify his neglect of productivity and thrift? His justification appears to come totally from the multiplier process.[27] An increase in investment resulting from an increase in the marginal efficiency of capital will generate its own finance in the form of voluntary saving, through the static multiplier. Interpreting this in terms of the loanable funds theory, the shift in the demand for loanable funds is fully compensated for by an equal shift in the supply of loanable funds or vice versa, leaving the rate of interest untouched by any change in either the productivity of investment or in thrift.

Whether or not sufficient voluntary saving is generated to maintain the rate of interest at its existing level has already occupied our attention in the discussion of the multiplier.[28] If one accepts Keynes' static approach then it is instantaneously provided. If one seeks a dynamic interpretation, as Robertson and others did, then voluntary saving may need to be reinforced by an increase in the money supply, and a resulting change in the rate of interest. But there is a second problem which did not occur to Keynes in writing the *General Theory*. Having given wealth holders a choice between buying securities and holding cash, it would be necessary for Keynes to investigate what wealth holders would do with the additional saving of the multiplier process. It may not necessarily all flow into investment willingly *without* an increase in the rate of interest; that is, to persuade savers to part with liquidity, and to take up the increased supply of securities resulting from additional investment, an increase in the rate of interest may be required. Unless, of course, one can argue that the demand for speculative money balances is *perfectly elastic* in relation to the rate of interest, in which case a reduction in speculative balances can transpire without the rate of interest moving. It is not sufficient to assume, as Keynes did, that the speculative demand for money will remain constant as a change in productivity or thrift occurs; especially when it is clear that, with a given money supply, speculative demand will respond to a movement in real income which affects the demand for active money balances.[29] Robertson saw this difficulty in Keynes' theory and was very critical of it. It is worthwhile quoting at length Robertson's reaction: 'Surely this simple formulation (that "the schedule of the marginal efficiency of capital may be said to govern the terms on which loanable funds are demanded for the purpose of new investment, while the rate of interest governs the terms on which funds are being currently supplied") would only be valid on one of two assumptions; a) that the liquidity schedule proper is perfectly elastic (the curve representing it a horizontal straight line), or b) that the monetary authority not only possesses but is constantly exercising complete power to hold the rate of interest down to some assigned figure in face of upward movements of the productivity schedule'.[30] It is clear, however, as Robertson points out,[31] that outside the liquidity trap region Keynes did not believe speculative demand to be perfectly elastic. The liquidity trap region[32] in any case, according to Keynes, is an extreme situation.[33]

One other lifeline which one could hopefully throw to Keynes in his attempt to escape from the forces of productivity and thrift in interest rate determination is to argue that his theory is a short-run theory, and in the short-run monetary factors are exclusive determinants of the rate of interest. Robertson might have had some sympathy with this argument, since we have already observed that in his own theory newly created money, or changes in hoards, can have some considerable say in the determination of the current market rate of interest; whereas productivity and thrift will exert a long-run influence upon the rate of interest. Unfortunately this is not the answer, for Keynes' liquidity preference theory contains a villain of the peace, the safe, future rate of interest (which is usually labelled the 'normal' rate of interest). This is the measuring rod against which the actual rate of interest is placed when the individual makes his choice between idle cash balances and buying securities. It is the villain of the peace, for as Robertson correctly argues,[34] it is left undetermined by Keynes, yet it is responsible for the level attained by the market rate of interest.[35] Had Keynes enquired as to what determines this normal rate, he would, according to Robertson, have been led straight back to the long-run forces of productivity and thrift. This is an issue to which we will return in a later exploration of the relationship between short-run and long-run rates of interest.[36]

But alas this is not where the story ends. Keynes effectively changed his view upon the role that productivity and thrift played in interest rate determination after 1936.[37] He became less adamant in denying them any say in interest theory, and moved a good distance back towards Robertson's position and the classical theory which he was so keen to oppose in the *General Theory*. It is this Keynesian approach, developed in the heat of the battle of the Keynesian revolution, which had provided an answer to Robertson's charge that the *General Theory* mistakenly failed to offer non-monetary factors any part in interest theory. To this we now turn.

12 Loanable Funds Versus Liquidity Preference — The Hicks-Hansen Framework

Two developments evident from published articles and from correspondence particularly between Keynes and Hicks,[1] indicate that Keynes moved a substantial way back to Robertsonian, and classical, interest theory after 1936, such that he no longer neglected the influence of productivity and thrift upon the interest rate. These were:

i) Keynes' general acceptance of the IS–LM framework put forward by J. Hicks (and later by A. Hansen),[2]
ii) The introduction of the concept of 'finance' in discussing the financial provision for the increment in investment in the multiplier process.

In this section we concentrate upon the former by examining the consequences of the Hicks-Hansen framework upon the role of productivity and thrift in affecting output, employment and the rate of interest. The concept of finance is a subject of a later section.

Keynes' attack upon the classical theory of interest was based upon its indeterminateness. If saving is dependent upon the level of real income, there must be a different savings/rate of interest curve for every level of income. The level of income must be determined before saving can be ascertained; but, according to Keynes, the level of income is determined by the level of investment through the multiplier process), and the level of investment will be affected by the level of interest rates. It appears that the classical theory had reached an impasse. The rate of interest could not be determined without knowing the level of income, nor the level of income without knowing the rate of interest. What Keynes failed to appreciate in the *General Theory* was that his alternative theory was also indeterminate. The transactionary demand for money depends upon the level of income. Thus a total demand for money schedule, giving demand at each rate of interest, will shift rightward for every increase in the level of income. This indeterminateness was resolved by the introduction of the IS/LM framework,[3] and, as the following discussion will show, this justified Robertson's insistence that Keynes inadequately represented productivity and thrift in determining interest rates. Indeed it will be seen that Hicksian analysis took Keynesian economics further back to classical theory than undoubtedly the Keynes of the *General Theory* would have desired.

If prices and wages are assumed to be constant, a stable economy will exist where both monetary and real market equilibrium are attained at a specific level of interest rate and real income. Combinations of the rate of interest and level of real income which yield real market equilibrium ($S = I$) are shown in the IS curve, whilst combinations yielding equilibrium in the money market are shown in the LM curve. As each curve slopes in the opposing directions, there is only one combination of the rate of interest and the level of real income which satisfies equilibrium in both markets. This will be r_0 and Y_0 in the diagram on p. 188. The elasticity of the IS curve is determined by the relation between saving and income, that is by the propensity to save, and by the sensitivity of the level of investment to changes in the rate of interest, that is by the marginal efficiency of capital schedule in Keynes' analysis. Hence the position of the IS curve will be changed by either a change in the propensity to spend/save, or by a shift in the marginal efficiency of capital schedule. The elasticity of the LM curve depends upon the relation between transactionary and precautionary demands for money (M_1) and the level of real income, and the sensitivity of the speculative demand for money (M_2) to changes in the rate of interest. Hence, where the speculative demand curve becomes perfectly elastic (the liquidity trap), the corresponding region of the LM curve is also perfectly elastic; where speculative demand is absent, the LM curve becomes totally inelastic; at this point the constant money supply is being fully

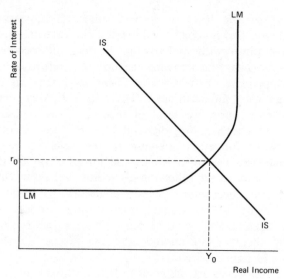

FIG.   IS/LM equilibrium

utilised for transactionary and precautionary purposes. A shift in the LM curve will result from a shift in any of the individual demand for money curves, or from a change in the money supply.

It is now possible to analyse the impact of changes in both productivity and thrift upon both the rate of interest and the level of real income. If the productivity of investment increases, the marginal efficiency of capital curve will be displaced to the right. More investment will be undertaken at each rate of interest. Hence at our equilibrium rate of interest (r_0), more investment will now take place. This will create more income through the multiplier process, which, in turn, will generate an increase in saving equivalent to the initial increase in investment. The IS curve will have been displaced to the right; our previous equilibrium rate of interest (r_0), if it is to bring about the equality of saving and investment (real market equilibrium), must now be associated with a higher level of real income.

But will the equilibrium rate of interest remain at r_0 or will the change in productivity bring, indirectly through its effects upon the level of real income, a change in the rate of interest? The answer to this crucial question depends upon the point of intersection of the two curves (diagram on p. 189). If we take a point of intersection in the range BC of the LM curve, then the equilibrium rate

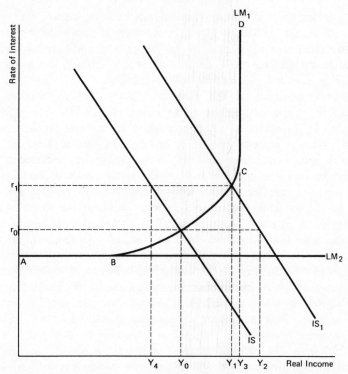

Fig.   Movements in real income and the rate of interest

of interest will change. The transmission mechanism will be as follows: the increase in investment will raise the level of real income at less than full employment and saving will respond equally to the change in investment; but there will be a monetary repercussion of the change in real income. A higher real income necessitates a greater transactionary demand for money (assuming prices are constant). This greater transactionary demand can only come about if, with a given money supply, cash balances are released from the speculative motive for holding money. In this region (BC), the release of speculative balances can only be achieved through an increase in the rate of interest; this increase in the rate of interest will, in turn, diminish the level of investment, dampening the change in income that occurs from Y2 to Y1. The more inelastic the LM curve the more the rate of interest will rise as a result of an increase in the productivity of investment, and the less will be the change in real income. The extreme situation arises if the IS and LM curves intersect in the region CD. Here the rise in the productivity of investment is completely offset in its effects upon real income by an increase in the rate of interest. Equilibrium income will remain at Y3 whatever the extent of the change in the productivity of investment.

Keynes' position in the *General Theory* can clearly be seen if we take a perfectly elastic LM curve (LM2). In this case any increase in productivity will not result in an increase in the equilibrium rate of interest, but in a higher equilibrium level of real income, and hence employment. An increase in investment here brings an equal increase in saving, the higher level of real income will create a greater transactionary demand for money, but this can be drawn from speculative balances without the need to raise the rate of interest. This is what is called the 'liquidity trap' region, where a minimum rate of interest is achieved, that is where no holders of cash feel that the rate of interest will decline in future. A decrease in speculative balances provides for the necessary increase in transactionary balances, without the need for wealth holders to sell bonds and for the rate of interest to increase. This argument is consistent with Keynes' view in the *General Theory* that changes in productivity and thrift would not influence the rate of interest, but at the same time Keynes failed in the *General Theory* to propose conditions which would make the LM curve elastic; indeed the LM curve in the above diagram (LM1) is indicative of Keynes' views in the *General Theory* on the elasticity of liquidity preference relative to the rate of interest.

It is unnecessary as a result of the above arguments to dwell for too long on the influence of changes in thrift upon the rate of interest within the IS/LM framework. An increase in thrift will, through the multiplier process, lead to less real income being generated by a given level of investment. If the equality of saving and investment is to be maintained the IS curve will need to shift to the left (e.g. IS_1 to IS) indicating that at each rate of interest a lower level of real income is required for real market equilibrium. In region BC an increase in thrift will therefore lower the rate of interest. Less income is generated through the multiplier process as a result of the increase in thrift; less income requires a lower transactionary demand for money, leaving a greater proportion of the fixed money supply available for speculative purposes; this will increase speculative demand and lower the rate of interest. The fall in the rate of interest will prevent income falling to the level it otherwise would have attained (Y4), by offsetting, to some extent, the fall in investment. Again this reaches an extreme situation in the region CD, where the fall in the rate of interest, accompanying the increase in thrift, neutralises the effect upon real income of an increase in thrift, by increasing the level of investment. The acceptance of this interpretation of the *General Theory* would therefore considerably modify Keynes' earlier pronouncements on productivity, thrift and the rate of interest; in particular, it highlights the relevance of the elasticity of the liquidity preference curve to deciding whether or not changes in productivity and thrift will affect the rate of interest, real income (and employment) or both. Consequently, it is very important in a consideration of the policy implications of Keynesian analysis. This is an issue to which we will return later.[4]

Bearing in mind the importance of changes in productivity and thrift in classical and Robertsonian theory, and the extent to which Keynes'went in the *General Theory* to divorce himself from these forces in his theory of interest, his reaction to IS/LM curves was somewhat surprising; he was evidently over-awed by Hick's constructive interpretation of his theory, incorporating productivity and thrift within a Keynesian framework. Keynes offered no fundamental criticism of Hick's important article,[5] except that he doubted an increase in the inducement to investment would always raise the rate of interest. In terms of the above analysis, Keynes argued that a rightward shift in the IS curve could be offset by a rightward movement in the LM curve, through an increase in the money supply; this would keep the rate of interest constant.[6] This was an argument which Robertson would not dispute, but one which Keynes thought the 'classicals' might object to.[7] Keynes also declared in 1937[8] that it had been his intention in the *General Theory* to show the propensity to save and the rate of interest as moving in opposite directions. Therefore, it is only in the extreme case of the liquidity trap region that changes in productivity and thrift do not exert some influence upon the rate of interest. In general such changes would bring both a movement in the rate of interest and in output and employment in the Keynesian system.

The Hicksian analysis had demonstrated that it was possible, as Robertson had argued, to bring the classical forces of productivity and thrift: 'under the liquidity hat'.[9] It was an *alternative* approach to that developed in his 1934 article,[10] where monetary forces, hoarding and newly created money, were incorporated in a loanable funds framework.[11]

A RECONCILIATION BETWEEN KEYNES AND ROBERTSON
IN INTEREST THEORY?

If Keynes now accepted the role of productivity and thrift outside
of the liquidity trap region, superficially there appears no longer
to be a fundamental difference between Robertson and Keynes
over the determination of the interest rate. But such a conclusion
disguises a number of important areas of debate, and possible
conflict:

1) Is there agreement on the transmission mechanism linking
   productivity and thrift to the rate of interest?
2) What is the meaning of liquidity preference, and how elastic
   is the liquidity preference function?
3) How does the rate of interest behave in the trade cycle?
4) Is there any connection between short-run and long-run rates
   of interest?

A final conclusion is therefore delayed until these issues have
been resolved.

1. THE TRANSMISSION MECHANISM LINKING
   PRODUCTIVITY, THRIFT AND THE RATE OF INTEREST

In the above Keynesian analysis an increase in the productivity
of investment shifts the IS curve to the right, raising the rate
of interest. The more responsive is the demand for money to
changes in the rate of interest, that is the more elastic the LM
curve, the lower is the change in the interest rate. Compare this
with Robertsonian analysis in which it was also found that an
increase in productivity would shift the demand for loanable funds
curve to the right, raising the rate of interest. The extent of
the rise in interest rate here would depend upon the elasticity
of the supply of loanable funds curve; the more inelastic is the
supply, the greater is the increase in interest rate. If banks respond
to a greater demand for loanable funds by creating additional
credit, the rise in the interest rate may be dampened; this is
exactly the same conclusion as that of Keynesian analysis where
an increase in the money supply would shift the LM curve to
the right, limiting the rise in interest. Similarly with a change

in thrift, in the Keynesian system an increase in thrift lowers the rate of interest (except in the liquidity trap region), by shifting the IS curve to the left; whereas in the loanable funds theory, the supply curve is displaced to the right, reducing the rate of interest providing the demand curve is not perfectly elastic. Although not strictly comparable because of the differing methodologies of the two theories, it is apparent that whether or not Robertsonian and Keynesian theories will bring like movements in the interest rate depends very much upon the elasticities of the LM curve and the loanable funds curves. It does not follow that when the LM curve is elastic, the supply of, or demand for, loanable funds curves will also be elastic; the factors determining each are independent.

However, the transmission mechanism, whereby a change in either productivity or thrift culminates in a change in the interest rate, is substantially different in the respective theories. Robertson was critical of the Keynesian view that there is an indirect link between productivity, thrift and the rate of interest, through their effects upon real income,[12] and that this indirect link will fail to operate in the liquidity trap region. To Robertson, a change in thrift or productivity will work directly upon the demand for, and supply of, securities, directly affecting the rate of interest. If, for example, thrift increases, the demand for securities will increase, and the rate of interest will fall, without there being any change in output; but any change in interest rate may induce a change in income and output by stimulating a change in 'K', the proportion of income which people wish to hold in the form of cash balances. (i.e. a change in hoarding habits). In our example, if thrift increases, the rate of interest falls and 'K' will increase, bringing a decline in income. If the rate of interest falls, the volume of hoards will increase: 'so that the money put onto the securities market by the increase in thrift does not all find its way out again in the form of increased investments; investment is less than saving and income falls as a result'.[13] Therefore, Robertson chose to emphasise the impact of a change in interest rates upon income, and not vice-versa as in the Keynesian system.[14] But again, it is important to note the coincidence of movements in interest rates and economic activity in the two theories. In both theories, lower interest rates (caused by either diminished productivity of investment or increased thrift) are associated with a lower level of income, and vice versa.

It is evident from this, and more so from earlier discussion,[15] that Robertson did *not* assume a fully employed economy, such that changes in the rate of interest might take place without interfering with a constant level of output and employment, as the 'classical' economists are accused of doing. The level of economic activity can fluctuate alongside the rate of interest, but the rate of interest is not a cause of this fluctuation, merely a means of transmitting the underlying cause responsible for the interest rate movement to output. This underlying cause in most cases is a change in the productivity of investment.

2. THE MEANING OF LIQUIDITY PREFERENCE AND ITS SENSITIVITY TO CHANGES IN THE RATE OF INTEREST

One obvious conclusion from the analysis so far is that the similarity between Robertsonian and Keynesian theories on the effects of productivity and thrift upon economic activity and the rate of interest is strongly dependent upon the elasticity of the LM curve. This elasticity is determined by the responsiveness of Keynes' demands for money to interest rate changes. Consequently it is not surprising that Robertson devoted a good deal of his comment upon the liquidity preference theory to this particular question. But, before this is examined, we need to go one step further back in the debate — to ascertain Robertson's reaction to Keynes' concept of liquidity preference.

THE THREE-FOLD MARGIN

The difference between the theory of interest in the *General Theory* and that found in Robertsonian literature has its origins in the roles attached to the rate of interest in the respective theories. Keynes' emphasis upon liquidity preference stems from his view of the rate of interest as: 'the reward for parting with liquidity for a specified period',[16] or: 'the reward of not hoarding'.[17] Contrast this with the classical role of the rate of interest, as the reward for not spending; as such it is: 'the price of time',[18] the reward for going without current consumption.

The *General Theory* neglected the influence of the decision to save or spend (out of income) upon the rate of interest, but this is not to say that Keynes was unaware of the classical approach.[19] Indeed he regarded the accepted theories of interest to 1936 as concentrating *entirely* upon the decision to save or spend out of income, to the neglect of the second decision which the saver makes. This was the decision as to the form in which to save — by holding idle balances or by buying bonds. He concluded: 'It is this neglect which we must endeavour to repair'.[20] In doing so he left himself open to the criticism of giving scant regard to productivity and thrift in the determination of the interest rate. Robertson, for example, felt that Keynes failed to take account of the demand side of the market for loanable funds, and of concentrating instead, through the liquidity preference theory, upon the rate of interest as the supply price of loanable funds.[21]

There was no reason why, as correctly emphasised by Robertson,[22] the view of the interest rate as a reward for not spending should be inconsistent with the rate being a reward for not hoarding.[23] If income is to be used to earn interest, not only must that income not be spent, it must also not be hoarded in a form where no reward is offered. This latter point recognises that hoarding takes place if income is deposited in interest bearing accounts (at, for example, commercial banks),[24] in which case it is incorrect to argue, as Keynes did, that it is the reward for not hoarding. In fact one can argue that the rate of interest upon bank deposits is a reward for hoarding, not dishoarding. Approached in this manner it is the difference between interest on money dishoarded, and that hoarded in interest bearing accounts, which is the true reward for dishoarding.

Robertson believed[25] that saving could be related to the rate of interest as well as liquidity preference. There is a threefold, not a twofold, margin. In Keynes' theory the marginal convenience of holding money is equated with the rate of interest; in classical theory the marginal inconvenience of going without consumption is equated with the interest rate. Why should not all three be equated in equilibrium? If we reflect on Robertson's theory of interest,[26] the prospective hoarder and consumer make both deci- sions — to save, to hoard — with reference to the rate of interest. The interest rate can perform both functions at the same time. As Robertson remarked: 'such phrases as that interest is not the reward of not-spending but the reward of not-hoarding seem to indicate a curious inhibition against visualising more than two margins at once. A small boy at school is told that if he wins a race he may have either an apple or an orange: he wins the race and chooses the orange. When his mother asks him how he got it, must he reply "I got it for not eating an apple?" May he not say proudly "I got it for not losing a race?" '[27] The fact that saving might be related to the rate of interest therefore does not put an end to a possible relation between hoarding and the rate of interest.[28]

Johnson has interpreted Keynes in a different manner.[29] He argues that Keynes was aware of the classical relation between saving and the interest rate at the micro level; that is each individual will decide upon his level of saving out of a given level of income by reference to the rate of interest. At the macro level he suggests that Keynes regarded this relation as being unimportant, for, at any given level of income in the economy, aggregate saving will be insensitive to changes in the rate of interest. Thus Keynes was able to concentrate fully upon the relation between saving and income without reference to the interest rate interfering with the relation between saving and investment. One can accept the macro level argument, but there is no convincing evidence in the *General Theory* to support the view that Keynes recognised the threefold margin.

Robertson regarded this as a grave omission from the *General Theory*. He believed that, as a consequence, a *positive* rate of interest could only come about in Keynes' theory if uncertainty as to the future course of interest rates existed. If this uncertainty was absent, and the actual rate was taken to be equivalent to the expected future rate, Robertson argued that the two rates must be equal to zero in Keynes' theory (as the speculative demand for money disappears).[30] If the marginal convenience of holding money is zero, the rate of interest must become zero. Intuition, and empirical fact, tell us that even in a perfect world the money rate of interest must be positive.[31] Although there is nothing to prevent the real rate from being negative as in recent years in Britain.

In fairness to Keynes the presence of certainty, and the absence of the speculative demand, need not prevent the possibility of a *positive* money rate of interest. It may simply mean that the rate of interest is indeterminate. Alternatively, if the transactionary demand is interest elastic, there may still be a determinate positive rate.[32]

THE SPECULATIVE DEMAND FOR MONEY

The major Robertsonian criticism of 'liquidity preference proper', that is the Keynesian speculative demand for money, is the narrowness of its conception. Keynes visualised the individual as having a straightforward choice between buying bonds or holding idle money balances. This was the crucial decision in deciding the level of the interest rate.[33] Robertson saw the choice as being much wider than this.[34] Keynes' theory was to Robertson a 'College Bursar's theory', requiring a few wealthy individuals to choose between bonds and idle balances on the basis of their conception of the difference between the actual and normal rates of interest.

What other choices are available to the individual? Robertson believed that the individual might prefer to hold a wide variety of real capital assets instead of cash or bonds. He would do this in an attempt to guard against the uncertainty associated with business life.[35] Real capital assets would include: 'both fixed capital and stocks of goods at all stages'.[36] The final choice depended upon the economic conditions of the economy, particularly the movement in the price level and the state of business confidence.[37] The significance of this wider choice for our earlier analysis,[38] is that it makes the speculative demand schedule very unstable over time; as a consequence the LM curve will dance along the IS curve bringing continuous changes in the rate of interest and the level of economic activity. In terms of our earlier discussion of productivity and thrift, the implication of this criticism is that it is not the IS curve alone which moves as the marginal efficiency of capital, or the propensity to save, change; the LM curve will shift under the influence of a change in business confidence or a movement in prices (which in Robertsonian theory can occur at less than full employment). It will also be sensitive to changes in the rate of return on real capital assets, which is also reflected in movements in the IS curve. For example, if the rate of return on assets increases, (i.e. the IS curve moving to the right) the demand for speculative balances may fall in response to the increased attractiveness of holding such assets and the LM curve will move to the right.

It is in this respect that Robertson talked of a revival of interest in the use of 'V', and 'K' (of the quantity theory and Cambridge Equation respectively) in economic analysis;[39] the shift in the LM curve would reflect a change in 'K' and therefore 'V'. If, for example, the productivity of investment increases, the IS curve shifts to the right raising the rate of interest and increasing the level of real output (in the intermediate range of the LM curve). The rise in the rate of interest will induce a change in 'K' and the increase in economic activity may bring a change in business confidence and a further change in 'K'; the change in 'K' will, in turn, influence prices, with again further possible repercussions on business confidence and 'K'. Bearing this in mind, it was logical for Robertson to believe that the variability of 'K', in a dynamic Keynesian system, and the subsequent movements in the LM curve which it brings, is much more worthy of attention than the consideration of movements along a stationary LM curve and the emphasis upon the elasticity of that curve which this creates.[40]

But the above criticism is an attack upon a *dynamic* Keynesian system used in the analysis of cyclical fluctuations.[41] The *General Theory* involves static analysis, with prices and business confidence remaining constant at any particular time; thus the LM curve is correctly portrayed as invariant. Undoubtedly, over time the value of 'K' and the LM curve would move, as productivity and thrift change. How much of the eventual change in economic activity or the rate of interest could be attributed to changes in liquidity preference, or to shifts in the IS curve, is largely a question of deciding the elasticities of both IS and LM curves. For example, if the IS curve is perfectly elastic, any amount of movement in the LM curve will not influence the rate of interest, only the level of real output. Conversely, if the LM curve is perfectly elastic, a movement in the IS curve cannot change the rate of interest. The elasticity of the IS curve depends largely upon the sensitivity of investment to changes in the interest rate. Robertson's views upon this have been explored elsewhere.[42] This leaves us with the question of the elasticity of the LM curve.

HOW ELASTIC IS THE LIQUIDITY PREFERENCE FUNCTION?

When one attempts to apply the *General Theory* to a particular economic problem, it invariably involves stepping out of carpet slippers into running shoes. There are obvious dangers in using static analysis to yield answers to questions involving economic dynamics. This is typified by the post-Keynes application of IS/LM analysis to economic policy. Fiscal and monetary policy changes result in shifts in either IS or LM curves or both, and one has to analyse the whole complex jungle of relationships taking the economy from one equilibrium to the next. This is the dilemma in which Robertson found himself when commenting upon Keynesian theory. He did not see the relevance of 'taking on' Keynesian economists in the static field, when all the important questions were dynamic in nature. The criticisms which we have seen so far of Keynesian economics display Robertson's disposition to highlight the dynamic consequences and limitations of the *General Theory*. His comments upon liquidity preference, as we have seen above, are not an exception to this general rule.

In this respect it may prove to be a great pity, since the relevance of the elasticity of the static LM curve has been stressed, and one really needs to determine Robertson's view of this elasticity. Robertson's earlier defence of his lack of consideration of a static liquidity preference function was that liquidity preference is: 'bulging with dynamics, and that if used as an instrument of "comparative statics" it gives precisely the wrong result.'[43] He was content to elaborate the reasons why the liquidity preference function would not be stable, due to changes in economic variables which Keynes had assumed constant in his static analysis.

But this anti-climax is avoided on two counts. Firstly, the influence of changes in productivity and thrift upon the rate of interest will be to change the interest rate through a shift in the IS curve (unless the LM curve is elastic). This is contrary to the *General Theory*; yet it is to the *General Theory* that we can look for the discovery of the less than perfectly elastic liquidity preference function[44] which validates this statement. Keynes believed that at a minimum rate of interest the liquidity preference function is perfectly elastic, but at interest rates above this minimum it becomes more inelastic. Furthermore, Keynes disputed the relevance of the perfectly elastic portion of the curve to modern day economies in that he could find no previous example of an economy operating in the liquidity trap region.[45] Robertson need not lay claim to discovering an inelastic LM curve, it was already there in the *General Theory*. Secondly, in *Lectures*, one finds that Robertson has a change of heart, whilst still concentrating upon dynamic analysis, he does put one foot into the static field and gives an insight into his view on the elasticity of the liquidity preference function.

Taking a wider definition of liquidity preference proper, to include the precautionary motive, and recognising the wider choice available to the saver, Robertson's ultimate conclusion is that: 'the existence of the liquidity trap is much less likely than it has lately been fashionable to suppose'.[46] Hence, even in a static, Keynesian system, Robertson believed that changes in productivity and thrift must result in a change in interest rate, as liquidity preference is affected by real income changes which raise or lower the proportion of the money supply being used for transactionary purposes.

THE CONCEPT OF FINANCE

The conclusion has been reached that by supporting Hicks' interpretation of his theory, Keynes went a good way back towards the Robertsonian view that productivity and thrift help determine the rate of interest. The fundamental difference between Keynes' and Robertsonian theories that remains is observed in the transmission mechanism linking productivity and thrift and the rate of interest; for Robertson, productivity and thrift work directly upon the interest rate by affecting the demand for, and supply of, loanable funds; for Keynes and Keynesians, they work indirectly by creating changes in real income, which in turn, affect the demand for money and interest rates. A further development in the debate however leads one to suspect that even this difference between the two theories can be removed, and that Keynes' interest theory, in its eventual form, is not dissimilar to Robertson's theory.[47]

In 1937 Keynes introduced the concept of 'finance' into his formulation of the various demands for money.[48] This introduction is an illustration of the kind of confusion which can result from attempting to give a static theory a dynamic interpretation. In relation to the *General Theory* it has been argued[49] that Keynes, because of the instantaneous adjustment of voluntary saving to an increment of investment, did not regard the financing of investment as a particular problem. The additional voluntary saving of the multiplier process would automatically finance investment, without there being a need for forced saving. Once Keynes recognised that the multiplier process was not a static but a dynamic process, the problem of financing investment became more important in his theoretical structure. If instantaneous additional saving is not forthcoming, there is a need for 'finance' to facilitate investment until the act of saving is performed. Keynes now argued: 'Planned investment . . . may have to secure its "financial provision" before the investment takes place; that is to say, before the corresponding saving has taken place . . . this service may be provided either by the new issue market or by the banks . . . if he (the entrepreneur) accumulates a cash balance beforehand (i.e. before investment occurs) then an accumulation of unexecuted or incompletely executed investment decisions may occasion for the time being an extra special demand for cash . . . let us call this advance provision of cash the "finance required by the current decisions to invest"'.[50] This represents the birth of a further demand for money in Keynes' theory of interest.

How far this new concept provides a further reconciliation of Robertsonian and Keynesian theories of interest depends upon two issues. Firstly, it must be determined how changes in the productivity of investment influence the demand for finance, and secondly, how the demand for finance relates to the interest rate. The first is easily resolved. Keynes would not dispute that the demand for finance is related to the productivity of investment. If this productivity increases, the demand for finance will also increase. It is the second issue which is more difficult to resolve. Keynes believed that, if the rate of investment was constant, the demand for finance would also be constant;[51] more important, in these circumstances, the same finance would be used over and over again as part of a revolving fund. The finance used by one entrepreneur is recovered once the investment is undertaken. It is recovered through the creation of additional income and saving which act so as to release the original finance to entrepreneurs just embarking on the investment process. Therefore, if the rate of investment is constant, this constant revolving fund, according to Keynes, will have little impact upon the rate of interest; that is the current demand for money arising from this source will be equally met by the recovery from current actual investment of the finance utilised in a previous period, and will have a neutral effect upon interest.[52]

However, the rate of interest is not left unaffected if the rate of investment is changing from one period to the next. If, for example, the rate increases, Keynes argues that the increased demand for money will force up the rate of interest;[53] that is, unless the additional finance required is provided by the banking system through an increase in the money supply without the imposition of an increase in the rate of interest. There is therefore an admission here by Keynes that changes in the productivity of investment, by influencing the demand for finance, do affect the rate of interest. What is more, there is no indication that this is an *indirect* relationship: if the productivity of investment increases, this directly raises the rate of interest by working upon the demand for finance; it does not require a movement in income to occur before the interest rate will move.

This, in itself, is a major about turn. It is true that Robertson was unhappy with Keynes' discussion of finance and together with E. Shaw[54] was responsible for clearing up a good deal of its confusion, particularly in relation to the mechanism by which the revolving fund came to be replenished.[55] But this new Keynesian argument would fit easily into the Robertsonian framework already outlined. It has been shown[56] that Robertson believed that economic progress, because of the nature of capital, cannot be smooth. Industrial fluctuation is an inevitable feature of a capitalist economy. The prime feature of the cycle is the variability in the productivity of investment; therefore the demand for finance would be sometimes expanding, other times contracting. It could not be regarded as a constant revolving fund. Its variability, in turn, would influence the course of interest rates over the cycle.

In the end therefore there was what amounted to be a fairly substantial recantation by Keynes of his position in the *General Theory*.[57] In the concept of finance one has the force of a change in the productivity of investment having a direct role in the determination of the level of interest rates. What is disappointing about this particular debate on finance is the failure by Robertson to bring the discussion around to the forced saving thesis of *Banking*, and especially to exclude any consideration of possible price changes in the provision of finance for planned investment.

THE RATE OF INTEREST IN THE TRADE CYCLE

Although Robertson did not regard the Keynesian theory of interest as being dissimilar to his own, he did argue that it presented an inaccurate account of the course of interest rates through the trade cycle.[58] In this respect Robertson has misinterpreted the *General Theory*, although not the ensuing Keynesian analysis. This section will show that again there is little difference between Keynesian and Robertsonian theories on this question.

Robertson's misinterpretation of the *General Theory* here arises from a failure to distinguish between short-run and long-run analysis. This can be examined by considering the relation between the money supply and the rate of interest over the cycle. The Robertsonian argument stresses that during the upswing of the cycle the quasi-natural rate of interest will rise under the influence of the increasing productivity of investment.[59] An expansion in the money supply will take place in response to the increased demand for loans (bringing forced saving). This expansion will prevent the market rate of interest rising immediately to the new quasi-natural rate, but the general movement in the rate of interest will be in an upwards direction. Therefore, during the upswing of the cycle an increase in the money supply is associated with an increase in the rate of interest.

Robertson accuses Keynes, and Keynesians, of accepting the *reverse* association during the upswing (of an increase in the money supply occurring alongside a decline in the rate of interest). This accusation is strongly supported if one takes at face value the passages from the *General Theory*, and from Mrs. Robinson's work,[60] used by Robertson to uphold his criticism. Keynes argues that an increase in the quantity of cash will create a decline in the interest rate except where the liquidity preference curve becomes perfectly elastic. Mrs. Robinson argues that during a phase of monetary expansion, the rate of interest will initially fall, but subsequently rise. It will not however rise beyond the level at which it stood at the beginning of the expansion.

Both statements are taken by Robertson to refer to periods of cumulative expansion,[61] in Mrs. Robinson's case this is correct, but it is doubtful that Keynes was looking beyond a short-run, or momentary position. The only fundamental difference between the Robertsonian and Keynesian (and Keynes') views on this issue is brought about by a difference in assumption. Robertson begins his process of cumulative expansion with an increase in the productivity of investment. The Keynesian argument assumes that the marginal efficiency of capital remains constant; for Mrs. Robinson an increase in the money supply will lower the rate of interest; this in turn will raise the level of investment. At and beyond full employment the increase in effective demand will raise prices, increasing the transactionary demand for money at each level of real output, lowering the speculative demand for money and hence increasing the rate of interest. This is more easily interpreted by using IS/LM curves:[62]

Illustration of the upswing.

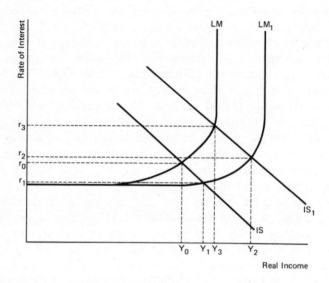

Initially equilibrium exists at r_0/Y_0. If the money supply increases with the IS curve stationary, the equilibrium rate of interest falls to r_1, and the level of real income rises to Y_1 under the influence of additional investment brought about by the lowering of the interest rate. If Y_0 is a full employment level of income, an increase in the money supply will only succeed eventually in raising prices and not real income; the LM curve, initially displaced to LM_1 will return towards LM, restoring the interest rate to the level existing before monetary expansion took place.[63] There is nothing in this argument which is inconsistent with the Robertsonian approach, except in the transmission mechanism which connects the rate of interest and economic activity; for Robertson, if the money supply increases, the supply of loanable funds increases at each rate of interest, and the market rate of interest will fall (if the demand for loanable funds curve is not displaced). Once this monetary disturbance has disappeared, the market rate of interest will return to the higher initial quasi-natural rate of interest (*ceteris paribus*).

Equally one could slightly modify Mrs. Robinson's argument to bring a strong similarity with Robertson's thesis. Had she accepted that initially the productivity of investment increased, the IS curve would have been displaced to the right (IS_1), an increase in the money supply would then only succeed in limiting the rise in the interest rate to r_2 (if Y_2 is a less than full employment level of income, prices will remain constant in the Keynesian model). If however full employment initially existed at Y_0, the rightward shift in both IS and LM curves would raise prices, and return the LM curve to its initial position (LM); the rate of interest would therefore rise further (to r_3) because of the change in the productivity of investment, and the increase in money supply, than it would do at less than full employment levels of income. There is little difference between the argument at full employment here, in the Keynesian system, and Robertson's argument at less than full employment. The increase in the money supply acts so as to keep the market rate of interest below a new, higher quasi-natural rate brought about by the increase in the productivity of investment. However, in the long run there will be a tendency for the market rate to move towards a quasi-natural rate.

But why should the productivity of investment increase in the cumulative expansion? In our earlier Robertsonian analysis[64] the change in productivity was taken to be unrelated to the change in the money supply. In his criticism of Mrs. Robinson's argument the implication is that it is raised by the change in the money supply. The banks, by expanding their willingness to lend, create a rise in prices or real output which, in turn, shifts the demand for investible funds to the right—raising the rate of interest.[65] But how this particular mechanism operates is left unexplained by Robertson. Neither is it clarified by his reference to Marshall's work.[66] One suspects, though it is only a suspicion, that the mechanism is produced by a lag in wages behind any increase in prices as the money supply expands; this raises the rate of return on investment, and redistributes income in favour of entrepreneurs; alternatively where real output increases and not prices, Robertson may be thinking in terms of the increase in demand created by greater income, working through the accelerator upon investment. Either way it would be a surprising thesis for Robertson to advocate, since monetary forces now appear able to cause the cycle, not merely to exaggerate it.[67]

Robertson's criticism of Keynes and Robinson regarding their view of the behaviour of the rate of interest through the course of the cycle, and, in particular, their view of the impact of monetary changes upon the interest rate, disappears once an increase in the productivity of investment is grafted on to the Keynesian picture of the upswing (and a decrease in the downswing). Mrs. Robinson's argument is only contentious on the grounds that it fails to recognise the movement in the productivity of investment through the trade cycle; but clearly this, as we have seen, is central to the Robertsonian thesis. Again the Robertsonian and Keynesian conclusions amount to the same thing in the end — although the differences in the causal chain still persist.[68]

THE CONNECTION BETWEEN THE LONG-TERM AND SHORT-TERM RATE OF INTEREST

It appears that we are on the road to a more total reconciliation between the Robertsonian and Keynesian theories of interest; although each is using a different means of transport, both appear to be getting to the same place in the end. However, there is still one collision along the way which has not yet been directly mentioned. This is the differing view as to the link between the short-term and long-term rate of interest.

Interest theories usually proceed by assuming one market rate of interest; the theories we have seen have not been exceptions to this. In reality there exists both a short-term rate of interest — the rate for short period loans, indicated by the Treasury Bill rate, — and a long-term rate, indicated by the rate on government bonds. In a free enterprise economy Robertson believed that both rates would influence each other,[69] but the stronger influence would be exerted by the long rate upon the short rate. This again brings Robertson back to the forces of productivity and thrift. If, for example, there is an increase in the productivity of investment, new issues will take place in the market for long loans and the long rate will tend to rise. Speculators will be attracted away from the short-loan to the long-loan market; thus the short rate is affected by movements in the long rate.[70] This is the dominant influence, since Robertson argues that the monetary authorities will not, in the long run, wish to go against the underlying conditions operative in the market for loanable funds (determined largely by productivity and thrift).

Contrast this argument with that of N. Kaldor.[71] He would

agree with Robertson that there is a gap between the normal long rate and the normal short rate, and that this gap reflects the additional uncertainty in keeping bonds rather than assets closer to money[72] and the greater liquidity of the latter. Secondly, both agree that it is discount which determines the amount of speculation in both markets.[73] Where they fail to agree is on the determinants of this gap. Kaldor believes that productivity and thrift will exert only a negligible influence upon the long rate, because of the influence of speculators upon the market. The long rate is influenced by the expected future short-term rates of interest over a long period; uncertainty as to future movements in interest can only lead to the long rate being higher than the short rate. Any change in productivity or thrift will not bring any considerable change in the long rate in this theory, since it will not succeed in altering the average expected short rate, which determines the actions of the speculator, and in turn the long rate.

This is a largely irreconcilable issue — but it does demonstrate the difference which still persisted between the manner in which Robertson and Keynesians thought about problems within interest theory. Robertson continued to emphasise the importance of productivity and thrift; Keynesians concentrated upon liquidity preference, and the role of uncertainty and expectations in interest rate determination.

To an objective bystander there is no reason why both arguments should not be correct on the connection between short and long rates. Why should not the long rate be influenced by, for example, a change in productivity which alters the demand for loanable funds, and by a change in expectation as to the future course of the short rate? Both are not mutually exclusive.

THE DEFENCE OF THE CAMBRIDGE ECONOMISTS

Critical comment by Robertson upon Keynes' liquidity preference theory was not directed solely as a defence of his own theory of interest. Robertson took upon himself the task of defending Cambridge economists — past (Marshall and Lavington) and present (notably Pigou) — from the Keynesian attack. This defence is exhibited primarily in Robertson's attempt, eventually successful, to persuade Keynesians of the importance of productivity and thrift in determining the rate of interest — an argument which was central to the interest theory of his fellow Cambridge economists.[74]

But the defence was more than this. Keynes portrayed his interest theory as a monetary theory, neglecting real forces; it was shown as a total contrast to the real theories of the earlier classical and Cambridge economists. Robertson felt this treatment of the Cambridge economists in particular to be vastly unfair.[75] They too had recognised the importance of monetary forces acting upon the rate of interest and, according to Robertson, had been much more realistic and meaningful in their treatment of liquidity preference than Keynes had himself. But Keynes failed to acknowledge sufficiently this earlier work on liquidity preference.[76] It will be wise to dwell upon this defence a little longer since it highlights much of the source of Robertson's counterattack upon the liquidity preference theory. The discussion will proceed in two parts. Firstly, there is a need to decide whether or not the Cambridge economists did in fact recognise liquidity preference and its influence upon the interest rate. Secondly, it must be decided whether their treatment of it was more convincing than that of Keynes.

The recognition of liquidity preference, although not necessarily in the form propounded in the *General Theory*, would be confirmed, if Robertson could show that the Cambridge economists had accepted the existence of hoarding and its impact upon the rate of interest. As a beginning one must remember that the Cambridge economists, from Marshall onwards, had considered money sitting, rather than money on the wing in their approach to monetary theory; that is they had argued in terms of the forces governing the demand for money, as well as in terms of the velocity of circulation of money.[77] It was a logical extension of this approach to consider the breakdown of the demand for money. The confirmation however is contained in the Cambridge economists' preoccupation with the threefold margin. The interest rate did not only influence the decision to save or spend, it also affected the decision to hoard or dishoard.[78]

How similar the concepts of liquidity preference contained within the Cambridge school, and in the *General Theory* are, is a matter of interpretation. Marshall, Pigou and Lavington[79] each wrote not only of the influence of productivity and thrift upon the interest rate, but also of the effect of uncertainty and hence expectations upon the rate.[80] The latter was central to Keynes' theory of interest. But did they recognise the speculative demand for money as it appeared in the *General Theory*? This is a point of contention. Robertson argued that Pigou and Lavington were kinder to speculative demand, giving it a much wider definition than that of Keynes. They did not concentrate upon the choice between bonds and cash and the influence of expectations upon this choice. As with Robertson, the choice was much wider than this; in addition they sought to bring the precautionary demand for money into a direct relation with the rate of interest. Marshall too had included a discussion of the speculative motive in his analysis by considering the actions of bulls and bears on the stock exchange.[81]

Therefore, the fundamental difference between the Cambridge school and Keynes' liquidity preference theory is largely a matter of emphasis. The Cambridge economists were not totally neglectful of monetary forces in determining interest, but such forces did not occupy the degree of importance displayed in Keynes' theory. Keynes chose to exaggerate the role of speculative demand and, in so doing, heightened the role played by uncertainty and expectations and consequently the role of psychological factors in determining interest. The Cambridge economist chose to concentrate, but not exclusively, upon the forces of productivity and thrift in interest theory.

CONCLUSIONS — LOANABLE FUNDS VERSUS LIQUIDITY PREFERENCE

The first, and most obvious, conclusion arising from this chapter is that the interest theories of Keynes and Robertson are not as radically opposed as Keynes thought them to be.[82] In the *General Theory* Keynes sought to weaken the forces of productivity and thrift acting upon the rate of interest to the benefit of liquidity preference and the supply of money; as such, his theory was opposed to that of Robertson; but it has been one of the purposes of this chapter to show that Keynes' position changed substantially in the period after 1936. With Hicks' formulation of the Keynesian system, perhaps also persuaded by Robertson's critical comment, and with Keynes' introduction of the concept of finance, Keynes was no longer able to ignore the role of productivity and thrift in interest rate theory — although he was still able to maintain an emphasis upon liquidity preference and, in particular, the speculative motive.

Not only did the Keynesian system eventually recognise the role of productivity and thrift, but the role was very similar to that displayed in Robertson's theory; an increase in the productivity of investment would tend to raise the rate of interest; the only exception to this being in the liquidity trap region; a fall in productivity would lower the rate of interest. Outside the liquidity trap, an increase in thrift would lower the rate and a decrease would raise it. Only in the extreme case of the liquidity trap region were the conclusions of both theories incompatible. However, one substantial difference did remain. This is to be found in the transmission mechanism linking such changes to the rate of interest; for Robertson, it was a direct relation, with changes working directly upon the demand for, and supply of, securities and therefore the rate of interest. For Keynes and Keynesians, it was an indirect relation with changing productivity and thrift affecting the level of real income through the multiplier process and this in turn influencing the demand for money and the rate of interest.

There is a second question which this chapter has gone some way to answering. This is the question of the revolutionary nature of Keynes' theory of interest when compared with the Robertsonian theory. The following observations in this chapter suggest that Keynes did not alter drastically the theory of interest:

1) Keynes' recantation of the role of productivity and thrift after 1936, which took him much of the way back towards Robertson's theory.

2) The recognition that the influence of liquidity preference, and of monetary forces in general, upon interest was not new to theory. It had not been a feature of classical economics, but it had its origins in the work of Marshall, Pigou and Lavington, as well as in the writings of Robertson. These economists had acknowledged the role of uncertainty and expectations in interest determination. What was different about Keynes' theory was his formulation of the speculative motive and his concentration upon the choice between bonds and cash. This took pride of place over and above the non-monetary forces acting upon interest. Expectations played a central role, unlike that found in neo-classical interest theory. Robertson's discussion of liquidity preference — found in his formulation of hoarding — was less sophisticated than that of Lavington,

in particular, who, with Pigou, accepted a much wider approach to speculative demand (and arguably more realistic) than that of Keynes. The revolution is not to be found with respect to liquidity preference.

3) Crucial to the classical theory of interest is the causal link between saving and the rate of interest. Keynes replaced this link with that between saving and the level of income and this gave rise to the multiplier process. It is this innovation which is generally regarded as revolutionising monetary theory.[83] The implication of this innovation is that there will be a different supply of savings curve (in relation to the rate of interest) for every level of income. Classical theory is invalidated as soon as income is taken to be variable. There can no longer be a stable equilibrium where the curves of the supply of saving and the demand for saving for investment purposes intersect; so long as income is changing, the supply curve will be shifting. Similarly, theories of interest which recognise the difference between natural and market rates of interest are invalidated; the natural rate can no longer be regarded as a stable or equilibrium rate. But Keynes moved from one extreme to the other; having found a connection between saving and income he then proceeded to ignore the influence of the rate of interest upon saving. This was remedied in Hicks' IS/LM curve analysis which introduced the indirect relationship between the two, via the level of income. But had it not been remedied before in Robertson's dynamic theory of interest?[84] Robertson argued that both interest rates and the level of disposable income would influence the level of saving. Neither income nor the rate of interest were assumed constant.[85] Both were free to fluctuate in his dynamic theory and to influence the level of saving. There was not a stable natural rate of interest in his theory, but a continually changing quasi-natural rate;[86] this was continually changing due to changes in productivity and thrift, and also monetary changes influencing the distribution of income. In other words, the demand for, and supply of, loanable funds curves were continuously moving over time, such that a stable equilibrium could never be reached.

The meaningfulness of the liquidity preference theory of interest therefore depended very much upon the strength of the relationship

Keynes thought he had found between saving and income and consequently upon the strength of the multiplier process. This strength, as Robertson pointed out, would be mainly affected by the stability of the propensity to consume out of income. If this propensity varied (through interest rate changes), even though income might remain constant, the precision of the multiplier would be lost and the liquidity preference theory of interest would be in need of rebuilding to incorporate the link between saving and interest.

It will be difficult, if not impossible, to convince Keynesians that this chapter has not been unduly pessimistic regarding Keynes' contribution to interest theory. Our conclusion at this stage is that Keynes merely chose a different way of telling the same story that Robertson had told two years earlier.[87] It was different because of its static, not dynamic, approach and of its use of stocks rather than flows. But was it a more interesting, a more useful, way of saying the same thing? Robertson believed not for the following reasons:

1) His own theory could be regarded as a branch of the general theory of pricing and therefore was consistent with the conventional classical approach.[88] The loanable funds theory was integrated within the Robertsonian system. Given a change in the productivity of investment, the forced saving process helped explain not only how prices and output might change, but also how the rate of interest would be affected. The theory of interest in the *General Theory* was not integrated with the other theories it contained. In particular there was little attempt by Keynes, to relate the theory of interest to the theory of output and employment. Only later, under the influence of Hicks, are the two brought together, and the influences of the effects of changes in the productivity of investment upon both interest rates, and real income explored. It is then possible for Keynesians to argue that the liquidity preference theory is more compatible with general equilibrium analysis;[89] and that this theory would fit within the Keynesian framework. Which interest rate theory is more worthwhile therefore depends upon the resolution of the broader issue of the Keynes versus classical framework of analysis.

2) The liquidity preference approach gave an *exaggerated* picture of the importance of the role of monetary factors in interest

rate determination. It dwelt too long upon speculative demand and too little upon productivity and thrift.

3) However, above all other reasons, it is the advantages of dynamic analysis and of flow rather than stock arguments which convince Robertson of the superior strength of his theory. Two advantages dominate. Firstly the loanable funds theory accords more with the manner in which businessmen and speculators actually think. They think in terms of flows rather than stocks. As B. Tew has forcibly remarked,[90] having found himself teaching a liquidity preference theory to his students: 'when I leave the classroom and proceed to the Bursar's office to chat about stock market prospects, all my arguments seem to present themselves in terms of flows: I talk about such things as the volume and probable destination of the new money flowing onto the market, the volume and composition of the new issues which the market will be called upon to digest . . .'[91]

Secondly, and more important, when one attempts to apply static analysis it invariably involves re-interpreting it in a dynamic fashion. Equilibria are never reached. It is the process of change which is important — the growth or fluctuation of a number of economic variables, — in particular prices, wages, output, employment and interest. Similarly, economic policy considerations are dynamic — one needs to examine the impact of policy over time. Since Robertson was primarily concerned with industrial fluctuation the dynamic approach to interest theory was more meaningful and could be more directly related to other trade cycle analysis. What is more, the dynamic re-interpretation of a static theory does not always yield the same conclusions as static analysis. We have two very good examples of this in relation to interest theory. Once Keynes recognised that additional saving would not be automatically and instantaneously generated to finance the investment of the multiplier process, he had to introduce the concept of finance into his analysis. This, in turn, involved a total re-examination of the role of the banking sector in the economic system. Secondly, Keynes, by ignoring the adjustment process, was free in the *General Theory* to imply that the supply of goods would be perfectly elastic at less than full employment and that prices need not increase as investment expands. In the Robertsonian system the time period under consideration determines the elasticity of supply; in the very short period, an increase in investment will succeed in raising prices, until additional output is forthcoming.

The misleading nature of Keynesian static analysis has persisted right through to the present day. It is common ground for most economists (including the author) to examine economic policy action in an IS/LM framework. Fiscal policy is viewed by shifting the IS curve, monetary policy by moving the LM curve. It is precisely this kind of analysis which Robertson was fighting against. What Robertson believed — and it is also evident that Keynes thought the same way to some extent[92] — was that the LM curve was inherently unstable as V and hence K varied as the level of output changed. The corollary of this is that it is impossible to reach any firm conclusions on the influences of economic policy by using IS/LM analysis, except by using very restrictive assumptions.

The choice of approaches therefore depends upon the problem which is to be solved. Robertson's preoccupation with the trade cycle justifies continued faith in the loanable funds theory. The Keynesian disposition to investigate the conditions necessary for equilibrium equally justified the maintenance of the liquidity-preference theory. But the final comment of this section rests with Robertson: 'the rate of interest — that central mystery about the importance or unimportance of which it is so hard to keep pace with the vagaries of high-brow opinion, though I find that, if one stands fairly firmly in the same place, high-brow opinion, like a hunted hare, has a way of coming round in circles. Wicksell, Fisher and Marshall had taught us that the actual market rate of interest can be influenced by those who have it in their power to create or destroy money. It needed emphasising that it can be influenced too by those who have it in their power to use or not to use existing pools of money; and Keynes, with his immense intuitive understanding of the speculative markets, was the person destined to emphasise it. But it is a far cry from this to a "purely monetary theory of interest", or rather to an analysis which passes off as a theory of interest what is really only a theory of the divergences of the rate of interest from some normal level left unexplained. I feel sure we are on the eve here of some retreat and re-integration towards which perhaps Lange above all has shown the way. In some recent writings, such as Lerner's and I think Pigou's, there are lying about the *disjecta membra* of different theories of interest — productivity theories, abstinence theories, liquidity theories — which do not seem to have been remoulded into an intelligible whole'.[93] This brings together a good deal of what has been said here!

THE STAGNATION THESIS

Much of the Robertsonian criticism of the last two chapters can be seen in relation to the 'stagnation thesis'. This thesis is based upon two propositions — the richer a community becomes:

1)   the more it will save out of real aggregate income. This stems at the micro level from Keynes' tentative assertion[94] that the greater a person's real income, the lower is his marginal propensity to consume.

2)   The fewer will be the profitable investment opportunities available; that is the marginal efficiency of capital will decline over time, as the most profitable investment outlets are used up first.

Initially Robertson had some sympathy with this thesis in relation to the inter-war period,[95] but later he was to attack the validity of both propositions. We have seen this attack in two features of the Robertsonian criticisms of Keynes. Firstly, Robertson argued that real income was not the sole determinant of consumption; any decline in the marginal propensity to consume, as real income rose, could be counteracted by a change in one or several of the other factors influencing consumption. Later he was able to use Duesenberry's hypothesis, based upon the empirical evidence on the consumption function, that in the long run the propensity was fairly stable and equal to the average propensity to consume to support his view.[96] Secondly, Robertson argued that periodically invention and innovation acted so as to increase the marginal productivity of further investment.[97] In other words, what the stagnation thesis was proposing was that the demand for loanable funds curve would shift continually to the left whilst the supply of loanable funds would move to the right as an economy progresses. Robertson's response to this was that both supply and demand may move in the opposite direction to that indicated by the stagnation thesis — and thus there is no long-term tendency for the rate of interest to decline.

13 Some Observations upon the Similarity of Keynes' and Robertson's Work

The last two chapters have emphasised Robertson's critical reaction to the *General Theory*, in particular his response to the static analysis of the multiplier and the liquidity preference theory. It would be wrong to leave the reader with the impression that the Robertsonian and Keynesian theories are totally opposed to one another; indeed it is the purpose here to throw some light on the statement by T. Wilson that: 'the polemical literature, both Keynesian and Robertsonian, leaves an exaggerated impression of the differences between their respective theories'.[1] I offer the contents of this chapter as food for thought.

The most important theoretical conclusion which came from the *General Theory* was that an equilibrium level of employment could exist at less than full employment. This will arise where the level of aggregate spending in the economy is insufficient to support the aggregate level of the supply of goods and services which is capable of employing all available resources. As a direct result of this conclusion, the U.K. and other Western economies have seen fit to regulate aggregate demand in the post-war period in order to achieve higher employment levels. This concern with effective demand is in marked contrast with early classical economics, where, on the basis of Say's law, the very action of production is seen to generate the demand necessary to purchase it. But this concern is not alien to Robertsonian economics. The major cause of a depression is the 'temporary gluttability of wants', the *saturation* of the economy with capital goods. The only difference here between Keynes and Robertson is the Robertsonian emphasis upon the lack of demand for capital goods as the cause of unemployment, rather than the deficiency of demand for goods in general, or consumption goods in particular. Robertsonian and Keynesian remedies for unemployment are very similar — both especially advocate an artificial stimulation of the demand for capital goods by the introduction of public works policies.[2] A policy of wage reduction as a cure for unemployment is not a feature of Robertsonian economics. As Robertson himself admits,[3] he had no exaggerated respect even before 1936 for Say's Law and for the belief in an automatic movement towards full employment. He was not, in his early publications, preoccupied with the theory of price determination, but with an explanation of the movements of output and employment, as well as prices, through the course of the trade cycle. This has been borne out by earlier chapters.[4] For Robertson, the inherent nature of capitalist economies, with their reliance upon the price mechanism and the investment process, means that fluctuation in all macro-economic variables is inevitable; if economic progress is to take place, unemployment is inevitable and indeed justifiable, to some extent.[5] Keynes saw the cause of the crisis as a downturn in the marginal efficiency of capital during the boom, exactly the cause emphasised by Robertson. Keynes suspected[6] that where he differed from the Robertsonian over-investment thesis was in his recommendation as to how to prevent the downturn.[7]

Both theories lay stress upon the significance of investment. In the *General Theory*, it is the level of investment which, through the multiplier process, determines the final level of total demand in the economy, and consequently the level of real output and employment. The emphasis here is upon the role of investment in creating total effective demand, not upon its second role as the major determinant of the level of productive capacity within the economy. Both roles are evident in the Robertsonian system, although the former role was not as developed as in Keynes' multiplier theory; indeed Robertson would choose to highlight the reverse relationship to that found in the multiplier, that is the influence of a change in consumer demand upon the level of investment.[8] Subsequent Keynesian analysis has also examined the dual role of investment and not specifically the demand side.[9]

Robertson's claim to have found the multiplier process in the work of Marshall and Lescure is not convincing;[10] what is more convincing however is his argument that the multiplier is not unique in its determination of the level of income. What Keynes failed to appreciate was the instability of the propensity to spend out of income created by influences other than income upon consumption and saving, the interference into the operation of the multiplier imposed by the acceleration principle and the dynamic, not static, nature of the multiplier process. This made the financing of investment a crucial issue to be resolved — crucial in that whether or not finance was forthcoming, and the extent to which it was forthcoming, determined, through the forced saving process, the resulting change in the price level and the interest rate brought about by an increment in investment.

The multiplier is little more than an oversimplification of the Robertsonian system. It only exists in the form described by Keynes where the following assumptions are made:

1) there is an instantaneous adjustment of saving to the change in investment, such that the availability of finance for investment is not a problem; in other words it has to remain a *static* and not a *dynamic* theory. Once this static analysis is disposed of, the multiplier process is no longer an adequate answer to the forced saving thesis. There is no guarantee that the additional investment can be financed by a reduction in speculative money balances without a rise in either prices or the rate of interest.

2) the supply of goods is perfectly elastic such that any increase in demand created by additional investment does not raise prices at less than the full employment level. This assumption, implied in the *General Theory*, stems from a use of static analysis; output is seen instantaneously to adjust to an alteration in demand without there first having to be a period of price adjustment.

3) the acceleration principle does not operate; otherwise a change in consumer demand, caused by a change in investment, would in turn create further investment. This further investment would compete for the savings created by the original increment in investment, and lead to additional (to (1) above) difficulties in the financing of investment.

4) current income is the sole determinant of current, real consumption. Once the other Robertsonian influences upon consumption and saving are introduced the stability of the marginal propensity to consume disappears and the multiplier is left in disarray.

Once these assumptions are taken from the *General Theory* — that is once the theory is made to accord more with the true features of the economic system, one would suspect that the *General Theory* would move back a considerable way towards *Banking*.

Finally, in the last chapter, it was observed that within two years of the publication of the *General Theory*, Keynes' position on interest theory had moved some considerable way towards that associated with the loanable funds theorist. It was Keynes purpose to deny a major influence of productivity and thrift upon interest — this was to be the revolutionary nature of his interest theory.[11] But he was unable to maintain this argument, since any change in productivity and thrift would lead to a change in income (through the multiplier) which would change speculative demand (given a constant supply of money) and alter the rate of interest. He could neither convincingly assume that transactionary or speculative demand would remain constant as income changed, or that the economy was permanently operating within the liquidity trap region. Hence, although Robertson and Keynes differed over the transmission mechanism operating within the theory of interest, they did eventually agree that both real and monetary forces acted in the determination of the level of interest rates. Although Keynes regarded his theory as a revolution in relation to early classical theory — it was clearly not a revolution alongside the Robertsonian version of the loanable funds theory.

If the *General Theory* is no more than a simplification of the earlier Robertsonian system, why did not the revolution in economic theory come with the publication of *Banking* in 1926? There are two possible explanations of this fact which dominate all others. Firstly, in presenting economic analysis, Robertson treated his theories as a *development* of the work of earlier Cambridge economists. Keynes was keen, as Robertson was anxious to point out, that his theory differed substantially from that of earlier economists. In fact, it has been observed in the last two chapters, that the differences were not so extreme as Keynes would have wished everyone to believe. The *General Theory* was written with the objective of creating a revolution in economic theory; none of Robertson's major works had been regarded by the author in this manner. This leads on to the second explanation, and one of possibly greater conjecture. Robertson's writings before 1936 are extremely difficult to understand. He avoids simplifying assumptions to the same degree that the majority of economists are anxious to shelter under their wings. The terminology which

he uses is also complex and difficult to keep in the mind.[12]
He is very much concerned with the detailed analysis — as is
ably demonstrated by his response to the *General Theory*.[13] He
is never worried about the complexity of the picture of the economic
system he is painting — so long as it is an accurate picture. Simplifying assumptions for Robertson do nothing but smudge the colours,
distorting the final impressions created. As a consequence, as Keynes
suspected of *Banking*, very few economists ever really understood
what Robertson was getting at — hardly the makings of a revolution.
In addition, Robertson did not bring together all branches of
his theory under one cover. The real theory is to be found in
the 1915 study, the monetary theory in the books published in
1922 and 1926, and the bulk of interest theory in the 1934 article.
Therefore there is nowhere, in one source, a comprehensive guide
to *his* general theory.

These deficiencies in the prerequisites of a revolution in economics
were admirably remedied by Keynes. A *General Theory* was presented within one book. What is more it was presented in a
fashion in which fellow economists could begin to digest — not
always successfully judging from the various interpretations of it
which resulted and still abound today. Keynes was a populariser
of economic theory, successfully reaching a wide audience; Robertson, particularly in *Banking* and later work, was an academic's
economist, consequently he did not reach such a wide audience.
The danger of being a populariser in this case is that it involved,
as we have seen through Robertson's comments upon it, a good
deal of over-simplification of the economic system. One is reminded
of Hicks' comment[14] that the effect of the *General Theory* upon
his mind had been profound, but that through the *General Theory*
he had been led back to Robertson's work. How much this is
true of post-war economics in the Western world. Post-*General
Theory* developments have largely been such that the simplifications
of Keynes' work have been eliminated one by one leading us
progressively towards a Robertsonian way of doing things. Let
me offer four examples. The static approach has been replaced
by the dynamic analysis of growth models and mathematical models
of the trade cycle and inflation. These recognise the acceleration
principle and the consequences of time lags upon achieving ultimate
equilibria. Secondly, empirical evidence has demonstrated the complex nature of the determinants of consumption and given rise
to the theories of Duesenberry, Friedman, Smithies, Ando and

Modiglianni on the relation between consumption and present, past and future income, and has isolated the other factors determining consumption. The liquidity preference theory has led to a wider interpretation of speculative demand, to the theory of portfolio behaviour. Finally, the current popularity of 'monetarism', a recognition that prices can rise at less than full employment, and the disposition to return to an examination of the variability of V and K, is again a return to Robertsonian analysis, as well as to that associated with I. Fisher and R. G. Hawtrey.

Perhaps surprisingly Robertson did not respond to the challenge to write a comprehensive theoretical work in the postwar period. His response to T. Wilson's encouragement to do so explains this apparent failure: 'I am too old and too lazy! But even if I were young and less lazy, I think history has made it impossible. I believe that, once Keynes had made up his mind to go the way he did, it was my particular function to go for the "dammed (jessant) dots" and to go on pegging away at them (as is still necessary). It will not be easy for *anyone* for another twenty years to produce a positive and constructive work which isn't in large measure a commentary on Keynes, — that is the measure of his triumph. For me, it would now be psychologically impossible, and the attempt is not worth making'.[15]

14 The Value of Money

The major omission from the Robertsonian analysis so far is the failure to enquire as to the determination of the price level. It has been seen that price changes are an integral part of the forced saving process — and by now there should be no necessity to elaborate the importance of this process both for the theory of industrial fluctuation, and for the Keynes/Robertson debate on the multiplier and interest theories; but the theory of how the aggregate price level is determined is not part of the latter debate. The *General Theory* is principally a theory of employment, not an explanation of inflation; for Robertson prices are free to vary even where unemployed resources exist. This chapter takes as its theme the Robertsonian explanation of price movements, but the objective is wider than this. In addition it will show the integration found between the theories of interest and prices, the extent to which the Robertsonian theory of prices followed in the Marshallian tradition, and the reaction of Robertson to Patinkin's interpretation of the neo-classical theory of absolute prices.[1]

The development of the theory of price determination can be seen by summarising three of the major works, *Money*, *Banking* and *Lectures*; by adopting this approach it is possible to contrast the simplicity of Robertson's work in 1922 with its sophistication and penetration in 1926, and also to illustrate the consistency of *Lectures* with the earlier work despite the intervening Keynesian revolution.

1) MONEY (1922)

It was the intention of this first work on monetary theory by Robertson to lay stress upon monetary theory 'as a special case of the general theory of value'.[2] As such the value of money[3] is determined in much the same way as the value of any of other commodity, that is in this case by the interaction of the demand for, and supply of, money.[4] The demand for money is conditioned by the taste and habits of the community, and, given these conditions, the value of money must depend upon its supply.

But the demand for money is distinct from the demand for any other commodity in two respects.[5] If an individual looses a unit of money, the total utility of the community is not necessarily diminished, as it would be if that individual lost a commodity. The individual, through his loss of money, is transferring purchasing power to the rest of the community by the subsequent increase in the real value of their money holdings. Secondly, if the supply of money is diminished, the value of the remaining units of money will be proportionately increased.[6] It is this characteristic of money which Robertson claimed gave rise to the 'quantity theory of money'. This theory he viewed as neither asserting that the value of money will always change proportionately with the supply of money (since the conditions of demand might change as a result of the change in the supply of money), nor that a change in the supply of money need be the only cause of the change in value (conditions of demand might change independently of the supply of money). Additionally, and equally important, the theory tells us nothing of cause and effect, but merely demonstrates the association of a change in the money supply with changes in the value of money.[7] The 'quantity theory' does no more than emphasise the peculiarities of money, it does not provide any answers to the possible transmission mechanisms leading from the money supply to prices or vice versa.[8]

As a result of discovering 'more of the truth about the theory of money',[9] the third edition of *Money* appeared in a very modified form in 1928. The changes were largely of approach, and detail, than fundamental changes in relation to the theory of money expressed. To a limited extent the sophisticated analysis of *Banking* (1926) was included; the main exclusion being the detailed examination of induced lacking in the latter, and its influence upon the proportional relationship between the money supply and the price level.[10]

The major difference in approach was the introduction and emphasis upon the Cambridge equation in discussing the value of money, and the demotion of the quantity theory as a tool of analysis. A distinction is made between the stock and flow of money; the Cambridge equation considers the former by looking at 'money sitting'; the quantity theory is derived from an examination of 'money on the wing'. The two approaches are contrasted in the following equations:

1(a) $P = \dfrac{M}{KR}$

(b) $P_1 = \dfrac{M}{K_1 T}$

2(a) $P = \dfrac{MV}{R}$

(b) $P_1 = \dfrac{MV_1}{T}$

R = real national income,
T = real national volume of transactions,
M = quantity of money in existence,
K = proportion of R which people wish to have enough money on hand to purchase,
K_1 = proportion of T which people wish to have enough money on hand to conduct,
V = average velocity of circulation of money against the constituents of real income,
V_1 = average velocity of circulation of money against the constituents of real transactions,
P = income price-level,
P_1 = transaction price level.

1(a)(b) refer to alternative statements of the Cambridge equation showing the distinction made by Robertson between K_1 and K, the proportions of real income and real transactions which people wish to hold on hand in the form of money over the period. Similarly 2(a)(b) make a distinction between transactions and incomes velocity in the formulation of the Fisher equation of exchange, reflecting the expression of the value of money in terms of its 'transactions value' and 'income value'.

The real balance approach of the Cambridge equation enabled the attention to be focused upon the motives for holding the stock of money. The demand for money, and hence the value of K and K_1: 'depends on the one hand ... on the convenience and sense of security derived from the possession of a pool of money, and on the other, on the strength of the alternative attractions of increased consumption, or lucrative investment in trade capital or in Government or industrial stocks, against which these advantages have to be weighed up. Thus the magnitude of the demand for money, like that of the demand for bread, turns out to be the result of a process of individual weighing up of competing advantages *at the margin*'.[11] But this approach does not have advantages over its 'money on the wing' counterpart in all respects. Robertson was keen to point out that the 'money balance' approach, utilising the velocity of circulation of money, is more useful in aiding the working out of the manner in which actual prices change in real life, whilst the real balance method aids the understanding of the psychological forces acting upon the value of money.[12]

Robertson did not claim any originality for his theory of money; in 1922 he expressed his indebtedness to the writings of Pigou, Cassel, Fisher, Hawtrey and Withers, and to the oral tradition at Cambridge which had been handed down from Marshall to him through Pigou and Keynes.[13] Eshag has exhaustively documented the influence of Marshall upon his pupils.[14] Both approaches to monetary theory utilised by Robertson have their origins in the work of Marshall, which, in turn, can be traced back to his classical predecessors.[15] Indeed, Robertson had not in 1922 adopted the real balance approach despite its appearance already in both equation and verbal form in the work of A. C. Pigou.[16] By the time it first appeared in Robertsonian literature (1926), Keynes also had made use of it.[17] The determination of the individual's demand for money by a balancing of alternative uses of money at the margin, was also a common feature of the Cambridge literature by 1928, having been seen in the work of Pigou, Lavington and Keynes[18]; this also can be regarded as directly descending from the work of Marshall.[19]

THE TRANSMISSION MECHANISM LINKING MONEY WITH
PRICES AND THE 'PROPORTIONAL RELATIONSHIP'

The Robertsonian presentation of monetary theory was, however, much more than a simple comparison of positions of equilibria. The disposition to analyse the process of adjustment rather than to stop at comparative statics has already been observed, and the theory discussed here is no exception to this; but the transmission mechanism linking a change in the money supply to prices in both early editions of *Money* is considerably less developed than that found in *Banking*.

In the 1922 edition this transmission mechanism is married to the forced saving thesis.[20] This demonstrates clearly the intention to integrate monetary theory, as displayed by the development of the Cambridge and quantity theories, and the theory of interest (as more thoroughly developed later in terms of saving-investment analysis). The two theories are not expressed as competing, incompatible approaches. Let us take as an example an increase in the money supply which results from an increase in the productivity of investment. If productivity increases, businessmen, due to the shortage of voluntary saving, make calls upon the banks for additional loans. Given excessive liquidity, banks respond; the resulting loans are utilised to increase the demand for current production which is unable instantaneously to respond to the increased demand for it. As a consequence prices rise. Forced saving is imposed on those with fixed money incomes, who find themselves unable to undertake their previous level of consumption. This monetary expansion, in turn, has the effect in this case of holding down the market rate of interest in relation to its quasi-natural level.[21]

One question of obvious importance is the predictability of the association between changes in the money supply and prices. This depends upon the constancy of K in the Cambridge equation.[22] In some respects there is an apparent inconsistency in the 1922 and the 1928 editions of *Money* which leaves the Robertsonian view of this question in dispute. One reconciliation of this inconsistency, would be, as far as *Money* is concerned, (but not for *Banking*) to suggest that Robertson had both a short-run and a long-run view of price determination; one might then suggest that K is variable in the former and constant in the latter. But there is no convincing evidence to assist this conclusion. In the earlier edition we find the argument that the proportional relationship may not exist because of the changing conditions in the demand for money, or because of the lack of independence of the demand for money from the supply.[23] Yet in the 1928 edition one can observe a real balance effect in operation which acts to restore the initial level of real balances existing at the beginning of the forced saving process. As prices rise, individuals find the real value of their money balances diminished, and respond by diminishing their consumption in order to re-establish this real value (i.e. restore the original value of K). Hence Robertson concludes that, at the end of a forced saving process: 'the volume of bank loans has permanently increased by, let us say, 10% and so has the volume of money in the hands of the public. But since prices have risen by 10%, the aggregate real value of the public's money supply is no greater than it was before'.[24]

A clue to the unravelling of this inconsistency rests in the discussion of the hyper-inflation in Germany (1922–23).[25] It is only in extreme circumstances that K will change; one such extreme is where the expansion of the money supply leads to expectations of further price rises, and brings a diminution in the desired level of real balances. This, in turn, creates further inflation, and further expectations of price rises; for a clarification of this one needs to go on to *Banking*.

2) BANKING POLICY AND THE PRICE LEVEL (1926) (*BANKING*)

Money is an undergraduate textbook, and the treatment of the theory of money within it reflects this fact. *Banking* is much more rigorous in its content, and it contains analysis, which, although relevant, is not included in the later edition of *Money*.[26] In its pages there is a much more thorough attempt to integrate saving analysis and the theory of price determination.[27] Indeed in a letter to Patinkin,[28] Robertson expressed a hope that the omissions of *Money* will be excused on the basis of the elaborate account contained in *Banking* of the process of induced lacking, and the real balance effect.

In *Banking* it is the Cambridge equation which is favoured in the analysis of cyclical fluctuations.[29] The introduction of induced lacking, as well as the automatic lacking recognised (under forced saving) in *Money*, allows a detailed examination of the behaviour of K over the course of the cycle. It is clear that Robertson upholds the proportional relationship between the money supply and the price level. Proportionality is assumed to exist in the mathematical exercise to show the process of adjustment to a new equilibrium level as a result of the injection of new money by the government.[30] The justification of this assumption is that during periods of either moderate inflation, or deflation, characterised by monetary change, there will be a desire on the part of those individuals whose real balance level may have been disturbed by the injection or withdrawal of money (and the resulting change in prices) to restore their original real balance level. In this case induced lacking, which is voluntary and designed unlike automatic lacking, leads the individual to adjust his expenditure on real goods so as to restore the level of real balances existing before the process of mild inflation or deflation commenced. The proportionality of the money supply and the price level, assuming real income to be constant, can only exist once the equilibrium position has been reached; during the process of change, K is moving back to the equilibrium level which maintains this proportional relationship. At any point in time therefore it is unlikely that this proportional relationship exists. But there is more than this in *Banking*; under the strong influence of Keynes,[31] Robertson argues that in certain circumstances K may not remain constant for each successive equilibrium;[32] that is, there are forces creating induced lacking which take the individual to a level of real balances which did not exist at the outset of the forced saving (or dissaving) process, and therefore leads to a new equilibrium level of K being established. Such forces are believed to be operative in a period of 'rapid and violent inflation',[33] and one might logically assume also in a period of rapid and violent depression. In the former K will fall and in the latter it will rise.

The reasons for this instability of K have been seen before,[34] and need only be summarised here. Initially in a forced saving process, as prices rise, the individual's level of real balances falls; his immediate reaction is to restore this real level, by curtailing consumption. This is the first form of induced lacking. But the individual consumer may alter his view of the *appropriate* level of his real balances as a consequence of the price rise. He may feel that further price rises are to follow, and will rush his purchases of goods, reducing his real hoarding in relation to his level of real income, reducing K; for the entrepreneur there will also be an 'expectations' effect in that, if prices are expected to continue rising, he will increase his preference for keeping resources in goods rather than in the form of money, again reducing K.[35] By this action again we get an addition to the inflationary pressure of the initial monetary injection of the forced saving process; but there is a second reason why Robertson believed that K would change, and it is apparent that, had *Banking* been revised, it would have commanded more weight.[36] The underlying assumption of the analysis of chapter 5 in which K is taken to be constant, is that the economy is made up of a group of small entrepreneurs, such that incomes quickly respond to price changes and hence real incomes are maintained. In this circumstance the redistribution effect of forced saving upon incomes is negligible, and less important in its effects on K than the expectations effect. Later on this assumption is relaxed, and the inflationary process is seen to redistribute income away from the rentier and salaried classes, who respond by dishoarding to maintain their consumption level; this has the effect of reducing K. According to Robertson: 'their action may have a marked effect on the price level'.[37] It is apparent from his own admission however,[38] that he had not fully thought through the consequence upon prices of the redistribution effect for an economy where the incomes of entre-preneurs are flexible, whilst the incomes of most of the factors of production are relatively fixed. Yet the lag of some incomes behind prices is crucial to the operation of the forced saving process.[39]

There are two further reasons which would reinforce the view that Robertson did not see the proportional relationship persisting over time. Firstly, in the Robertsonian theory of interest, it has been demonstrated that real hoarding by the individual would vary with the rate of interest; fluctuations in the rate of interest have been shown to be a feature of industrial fluctuation, and the forced saving process. During an expansionary phase[40] therefore, the rate of interest will tend to rise, and this rise will:

a) diminish the desire to dishoard;
b) encourage entrepreneurs to finance purchases out of windfall gains, rather than by borrowing from the banks;
c) diminish the level of demand for circulating capital which has to be financed through the banks.[41]

Each will create a change in the proportion of real income that money balances command; that is the elasticity of the demand for money with respect to interest rates is not zero. Secondly, the proportional relationship depends not only on the constancy of K, but also upon the constancy of T or R. Again it is clear from earlier sections, that Robertson did not believe that an assump-tion of full employment, or an automatic tendency of the economy to move towards full employment, was justifiable.[42] In *Banking* he was not concerned with presenting a theory of prices, but with an examination of the role of money in the cyclical process, that is its role in exaggerating the underlying real forces which cause fluctuations in output. A feature of any cyclical process is forced saving or dissaving, which brings with it price movements; but output, and hence R and T, would be continually changing over the cycle. In the forced saving process we have seen that the effects of monetary changes are not only upon prices, but also upon output.[43] Thus the values taken by R, T and K are not independent from P or M.

One would suspect that the view of the meaningfulness of the simple 'quantity theory of money', and its judgement that the price level and the money supply remain proportional, did not change from the view expressed in *Money* (1922): 'no longer either a triumphant *credo* or a pestilant *heresy*, the "quantity theory of money" remains a dowdy but serviceable platitude'.[44] The complexity of the determination of the aggregate price level found in Robertsonian literature reflects a differing approach to economic analysis than that portrayed by the quantity theory. Robertson uses period analysis suitable to the discussion of cyclical movements, considering the process of adjustment of prices from one level to the next; the usual expression of the quantity theory is in the form of a comparison of long-run equilibria, in which proportionality attains. Whether or not Robertson would subscribe to the long-run view of the determination of prices, depends upon the permanency of the expectations and redistribution effects on the desired real value of money balances. On this question unfortunately there is no evidence to offer in Robertsonian literature.

3) LECTURES ON ECONOMIC PRINCIPLES
(3 VOLS. 1957–59) (*LECTURES*)

The notable feature of this work is its consistency with the theory of the value of money expressed in *Banking* 30 years earlier. Robertson continues to maintain a faith in the Cambridge equation, that 'ancient ceremony' which 'makes the exchange value of money, considered as a special case of the general theory of value, the centre of the picture, and sets out the factors for discussion in a very simple and modest array of symbols'.[45] Cumulative processes are then to be examined in terms of the variability of K, R,

P and M (definitions of these terms are on p. 224). The Keynesian approach, focusing attention upon saving and investment, and upon income and expenditure, is not to Robertson a better, more worthwhile, method of looking at the cycle; indeed there is no reason why both approaches cannot be utilised side by side, which is exactly what Robertson attempts to do in the inter-war period, and continues to do in *Lectures*. Keynesians would argue that the stability of the propensity to spend justifies the use of the income-expenditure approach. The implicit conclusion of *Lectures* is that this propensity is no more stable than the propensity to hoard, and therefore is no more useful a tool of analysis.

This is not to argue that Robertson believed K to be any more stable than he had suggested in *Banking*. K, the 'Prince of Denmark in the Hamlet of the Cambridge equation',[46] is determined by five factors in a stable economy; these factors relate to business habits, the structure of industry, social and business life, the state of development of the markets for existing capital goods, and the rate of return on employing resources and alternative uses to holding money. If the supply of money is changed it is doubted that the elasticity of demand for money with respect to its value $(1 \div p)$ will be unity, such that the price level will move in proportion to the money supply. The conclusion is reached that it is likely to be less than unity; if, for example, the money supply is expanding, the individual is likely to diminish his stock of money in order to increase monetary expenditure in the face of a price rise, but not to such an extent that his initial level of real balances is restored. In the more extreme circumstances (described in *Banking* as rapid inflation or deflation), Robertson continues to witness the interference of the expectations and redistribution effects on the value of K, but the latter now appears to carry more weight.[47] The demand for money is neither independent of its supply, nor supply independent of demand.[48] What is not contained in *Banking* is the recognition that the existence of administered prices would tend to create a greater effect of a change in the money stream upon real income, rather than prices. The previous section has also illustrated the dependence of K upon the rate of interest, which Robertson again developed from *Banking* and from the proddings of the Keynesian debate.

Again therefore we have a demonstration of the consistency of Robertsonian economic analysis over the years. He remained unchanged in his analysis of economic problems despite the Keyne-

sian revolution, and continued to support period analysis, and
his attempted integration of the theories of interest and prices
through the forced saving thesis. His faith in the Cambridge
approach was not dispelled by Mrs. Robinson's accusation that
'we have been telling the equation what is happening, it has
not been telling us'.[49] In fact this was to Robertson the attraction
of the approach; 'its complete generality' enabled the ordering
of 'our thoughts about a great number of different sequences
of events, some of them starting at one point of the causal chain
and some at another — in some of them the rate of interest playing
a prominent part and in others not'.[50]

THE PATINKIN PARADOX

By way of comment and conclusion upon the treatment of the
monetary theory it is relevant to examine Robertson's reaction
to the issues relating to classical monetary theory raised by Professor
Patinkin.[51] It is not proposed that the debate begun by Patinkin
is surveyed through to its current state; it has not yet reached
a conclusion, and perhaps never will whilst disagreement persists
on the interpretation of the 'classical economics'; this survey in
any case exists in extensive form elsewhere.[52]

The central issue in the debate relates to the classical dichotomy.
Given that the classical economist accepts Say's law,[53] that the
act of supplying commodities constitutes also a demand for commodities, the aggregate money demand for commodities in a period
must be equal to the aggregate supply, such that the net demand
for money is zero. This is the 'homogeneity postulate'. It will
be zero at any particular collection of relative prices, irrespective
of the level of absolute prices. The holding of money therefore
on the real side of the classical system, in the determination
of the demand for commodities, yields no utility. The dichotomy
arises where, in presenting a theory of prices in the form of
the quantity theory of money, the classical economists present
money as yielding utility, and consequently consistency between
the real and monetary theories would require that the demand
for commodities be determined by absolute as well as relative
prices.

Predictably, the reaction of Robertson to this criticism, which
was levied also at the neo-classical writers, was to come to the

defence of Marshall, and Marshallian economics. This is most evident in correspondence between Robertson and Patinkin. Robertson writes: 'in the Cambridge tradition, the desire to hold command over resources in the form of money being a desire for a real source of utility, peoples' consumption programme will depend on absolute as well as relative prices'.[54] But this was not the point at issue. Patinkin did not deny that in the theory of money the neo-classical writers recognised the real balance effect; his criticism was directed at their failure to utilise this argument in their examination of the real sector of the economy. This is illustrated by his reply: 'it is clear that in the discussion of the real sector of the economy it was assumed that behaviour was independent of the absolute price level and dependent only on relative prices'.[55] Robertson was still not convinced, however, of the inconsistency of the neo-classical theory, the correspondence proceeded to debate, inconclusively, the classical disposition to include the absolute price level as one of the determinants of the demand for commodities in value theory.

What is more relevant here, is the weight of the Patinkin criticism in relation to Robertsonian economics. Archibald and Lipsey[56] have dismissed the validity of the classical dichotomy on the grounds that the real balance effect is irelevant to comparative static analysis which involves a comparison of long-run equilibria (utilising the quantity theory). The effect demonstrates what happens in disequilibrium and therefore is not needed in comparative statics; but the irrelevance of the real balance effect would not be the Robertsonian answer to the suggested dichotomy. He did not utilise comparative statics in his theory of money, and was very much concerned with the disequilibria adjustments. The real balance effect, from which Patinkin provides the integration of monetary and value theory, was very much a part of the Robertsonian theory of money. If prices rise, the fall in the real value of money balances will stimulate a response by consumers to lower their consumption, and to restore the real balance to an appropriate level. The change in the absolute price level is affecting consumption through this real balance effect. This argument, as we have seen, was given in Robertsonian literature from *Money* through to *Lectures*.

But then Patinkin did not deny that the neo-classical economists, including Robertson, had recognised the real balance effect. What he did deny was that they utilised it to provide 'stability analysis'.[57]

It is here where any reconciliation of the dispute meets an obstacle. What does Patinkin mean by 'stability analysis'? A logical definition would see such analysis as yielding the mechanism by which the price level will move to its new equilibrium level. Robertson clearly thought that the analysis of *Banking*, in particular, constituted both the real balance effect and stability analysis. He wrote: 'I don't regard the failure to perform a little stability exercise in a book of the character of "Money" . . . as any evidence against either me or my teachers! Personally, I should have hoped that there might have been accounted to me for righteousness the elaborate account in "Banking Policy and the Price Level" (p. 49 and Appendix I, recapitulated in 'Saving and Hoarding', reprinted in 'Essays in Monetary Theory', p. 78) of how the public in an inflation performs "Induced lacking" *to the extent necessary to restore the equilibrium level of its real balances*'.[58] Patinkin was not so convinced that the Robertsonian analysis qualified as 'stability analysis'; although he did concede that the appendix to *Banking* 'might be used in this way'.[59] Taking the above definition of 'stability analysis', the appendix does qualify. Until we have a clear agreement on what constitutes such analysis this would appear to be an irreconcilable issue.

The subjection of Robertsonian economics to the classical dichotomy charge can therefore be counteracted by the observation of the extensive use of the real balance effect, and its possible use in performing stability analysis. But the analysis of previous chapters enables a stronger defence of Robertsonian economics to be made. Firstly, Robertson did not uphold Say's law, and therefore, in theory relating to the real sector of the economy, he did not assume that the net demand for money would be zero. Money indeed does have utility — money balances are held for their own sake in the Robertsonian system — as the discussion of the three-fold margin indicated.[60] The level of real balances held has also been seen to vary with the rate of interest. Secondly, Robertson does not argue that money is neutral in its effect upon economic activity. Changes in the money supply not only affect prices in the long run, but also the rate of interest,[61] and the level of output. An increase in the flow of money may initially raise prices and not output. Output cannot respond immediately to additional monetary demand even if unemployed resources exist. The ultimate movement in the price level depends upon the speed with which output is able to react to a monetary stimulus.[62]

The forced saving thesis outlined earlier also, not only demonstrates that money works upon economic activity by affecting cash balances, but that it could, since unemployed resources exist, affect the level of output. The non-neutrality of money is therefore not only guaranteed by the real balance effect, but by the much wider discussion by Robertson of the links between lacking, in its various forms, and the level of demand, and output.

The foregoing chapters indicate that it is not implicit in Robertsonian literature that any change in the money supply brings a proportionate change in prices.[63] The arguments relating to the forced saving process[64] do not support the conclusion that relative prices, and real balances, remain untouched by any monetary change. The only reasonable conclusion must be that Robertson is not guilty of the charge directed by Patinkin against classics and neo-classics.

PART III
Theory and Policy —
Some Conclusions

1 Economic Policy and the Trade Cycle

'I may say that by comparison with my own extremely libertarian position, Robertson seemed to me nearly as much an interventionist as did Keynes. Robertson clearly had a great belief in individualism, but so did Keynes. And when it came to economic intervention, . . . Robertson had a good deal of tolerance for it'. — M. Friedman.[1]

We have concentrated upon Robertsonian macroeconomics in a closed economy; in particular the development of, and influences upon, the theory of industrial fluctuation has been examined. By way of conclusion, these last two chapters consider the policy implications of the theoretical analysis. Again we will find, as with theory, a remarkable consistency in Robertson's economic policy recommendations throughout his lifetime. He stood resolute against the 'Treasury view' in his early publications,[2] and against what he saw as a Keynesian devaluation of the role of monetary policy during a period of demand pressure after 1945. His approach to economic policy is 'many-sided'.[3] Monetary and fiscal policy both had roles to play in alleviating the problems created by the trade cycle.

ECONOMIC OBJECTIVES

Robertson never claimed too much for his policy recommendations. He not only doubted that economic objectives could be attained, but also that these objectives could themselves be accurately defined.[4]

239

This reflects his view of the capitalist economy. Economic fluctuation is an inevitable feature of economic progress where that progress is to be founded upon private enterprise, and, in particular, upon the investment decision remaining largely in the hands of the private individual. All that policy should attempt to do is to get rid of the undesirable fluctuation, as Robertson so aptly says: 'to limit the turbulence without destroying the vitality'.[5] There is no precise measuring rod available to discover when the fluctuation is desirable and undesirable. The indivisibility of investment, its longevity, its intractability, all impose an uneven distribution of investment over time and create unavoidable instability. In the interest of economic progress this may be desirable. What must be avoided are the additional stimuli given to fluctuation by the psychological forces of errors of optimism and pessimism, the monetary over expansion or contraction which may accompany bursts or deficiencies of investment, and the gestation period of investment which disguises the capital equipment under construction and increases the uncertainty of the business environment. The very nature of these forces does not allow an indisputable rule for judging where an expansion or contraction of output, employment or prices goes too far and requires remedial action by the government.

This lack of precise economic targets does not mean that the government should be complacent in avoiding inflation, or allowing unemployment to spread. There is a justification for government interference in the private sector in regulating the cycle. Robertson tended to focus attention upon the problem of inflation throughout his writing, but at the same time he did not neglect the problem of unemployment. This emphasis upon curing inflation was founded on the belief that: 'if this (inflation) could be avoided, there was good hope that the worst evils of trade depression could thereby be averted'.[6] That is, the boom creates its own destruction; guard the boom from its eventual excesses and the depression can be prevented; undesirable unemployment need never arise.[7] It will be apparent however from what has gone before that Robertson did not disregard unemployment before or after Keynes' *General Theory*. His theoretical analysis did not assume full employment and he was adamant that the government must do something about unemployment and 'all that it means of suffering and demoralisation'.[8] He was to remark much later: 'it is now generally recognised that this evil of complete and prolonged unemployment consists not only in loss of income but in loss of *status*, and the feeling of being unwanted, — an evil which is not removable either by doles or the provision of obviously "made" work'.[9] He was somewhat distressed by Keynes' attempts to 'outbid the rest of us'[10] as an advocate of government policy to alleviate unemployment, and by Lord Beveridge's attempt to outbid Keynes as an advocate of high and stable employment in 1944; He proudly indicated the attention which he had paid to unemployment in 1915.

What did worry Robertson was the disposition by economists to encourage employment to reach too high a level. He did not, as Samuelson claims,[11] argue that the state need not do too much about unemployment, although he did suggest reserves of unemployment to cope with any unexpected demand in the economy.[12] Robertson warned of the inflationary dangers of low unemployment long before the Phillips Curve depicted the strong inverse, empirical relation between the rate change of money wage rates and the level of unemployment. In 1957 he welcomed the abatement of rising employment, conscious of the pressures it was placing upon the stability of the general price level, and declared: 'If we want to prevent the continuance or recrudescence of inflation we should not try to work our industrial system with such a small margin of unemployment of this kind (transitional unemployment) as we have been doing in recent years'.[13] Similarly, as a member of the Cohen Council, he expressed no alarm at the level of unemployment going beyond the 1.8 per cent of January 1958,[14] in the interests of controlling inflation caused by excessive monetary demand.

POLICIES FOR REGULATING THE LEVELS OF OUTPUT AND EMPLOYMENT

The obvious starting point for building up the Robertsonian cure for cyclical unemployment is to consider what is the underlying cause of this type of unemployment in Robertsonian theory. Part I laid the blame for unemployment upon the deficiency of demand for capital goods brought about by over-investment in the boom, and a consequent devaluation in the marginal utility of capital goods. This deficiency in demand prompted a laying off of labour in these industries. In evidence to the Macmillan Committee, Robertson called for 'the temporary gluttability of wants'[15] to be remedied by an 'elevation in the demand for constructional goods'.[16] Clearly in his early writings it is a deficiency in demand for capital goods which needs to be made good; His later found faith in the acceleration principle[17] indicates that the deficiency could be put right in two ways, either by working directly upon the demand for capital goods, or indirectly upon it by changing the demand for consumer goods which in turn would have an accelerator impact upon the demand for capital goods.[18] In this section we examine the Robertsonian recommendations for governmental regulation of the level of demand.

THE USE OF MONETARY POLICY

Three aspects of Robertsonian theory presented in the foregoing analysis reveal the degree of effectiveness which Robertson attached to monetary policy in depression and over-expansion. We have witnessed a continual stress upon *real* factors as the cause of cyclical fluctuations and the passive role of monetary factors in the cycle. Monetary factors could only exaggerate the amplitude of the cycle, and were not responsible for instigating fluctuation.[19] The successfulness of monetary policy therefore depended upon the ability of monetary factors to interfere with the real forces affecting the cycle. In 1922 Robertson had declared that: 'Money is afterall a fundamentally unimportant subject',[20] and even after the more rigorous analysis of *Banking* money is still regarded as a 'subject of secondary importance in the sense that neither the most revolutionary nor the soundest monetary policy can be expected to provide a remedy for those strains 'and disharmonies whose roots lie deep in the present structure of industry and perhaps in the very nature of man himself'.[21]

But this rather pessimistic role for monetary policy is offset by two further aspects of Robertsonian theory which demonstrate the mechanism by which a monetary change can influence the level of spending. The first was encountered in relation to the loanable funds theory of interest.[22] Newly created money entered into the supply of loanable funds and brought with it the possibility of an inequality between the Robertsonian quasi-natural rate of interest and the actual market rate of interest for loanable funds. The gap between the two rates had repercussions upon the amount of investment taking place in a given period. This indirect transmission mechanism from money to investment through the rate of interest is usually described as Keynesian; although it did appear in Robertsonian writings, and elsewhere, before the *General Theory* was published. Secondly, in the last chapter we have seen a second, more direct, monetary transmission mechanism in operation in Robertsonian theory. The Robertsonian statement of the quantity theory rendered also a direct relationship between the change in the money supply and the amount of spending undertaken in the economy; a change in the money supply need not necessarily work only upon the price level but also upon output and employment through the level of spending. The automatic and induced lacking created by a monetary expansion will have repercussions upon both consumption and investment. Automatic lacking diminishes the real consumption of the fixed income groups, redistributes income, and therefore affects aggregate spending. Similarly induced lacking, and a consequent change in spending, may occur as consumers alter their hoards of money in response to expectations of further inflation, or to changes in the real value of their existing assets. Here we have a more direct link, as in monetarism, between changes in the money supply and spending. These then are the theoretical clues as to the role of monetary policy.

If the Robertsonian theory of interest is strictly applied, a monetary expansion should be able to depress the market rate of interest below the quasi-natural level and so stimulate investment and employment. However, Robertson did not always feel that this was a realistic policy for promoting recovery. The market rate of interest may not be able to sink low enough to encourage an increase in investment. This was the message strongly given in *Money*,[23] and in several later writings.[24] This particular view was perhaps determined by Robertson's own experience of the great depression. In his evidence to the Macmillan Committee he stated: 'I think that no purely monetary policy could have kept industrial activity at the level of the 1920s'.[25] He conflicts with Keynes[26] on this very point who argues that at a very low rate of interest there *do* exist investments which businessmen are prepared to undertake. Robertson, on the contrary, argued that, even at such low rates of interest, businessmen may not feel confident enough to employ loanable funds in the purchase of capital goods. If the cheap money policy was to be introduced too early in a depression, and if businessmen did respond, there was always the danger that the saturated investment outlets would be further burdened, and the depression intensified.[27]

Although monetary policy was regarded as a 'blunt and clumsy weapon'[28] in a period of acute depression, where businessmen are unwilling to borrow whatever the cost of finance, it may not be so impotent in a more moderate state of depression. Robertson remained convinced that investment was sensitive to changes in the rate of interest. He criticised J. M. Keynes and A. Hansen for wrongly concluding that the opposite was true,[29] and consequently believing that monetary policy would be ineffective. Similarly, he attacked the neo-Keynesians for being too pessimistic on the contribution which interest rate policy can make to regulating investment.[30] He supported the Radcliffe Report findings that the investment plans of larger companies may be insensitive to changes in the interest rate, but still maintained that there was a wide margin of transactions which could be affected by a movement in interest rates.[31] His final pronouncement on monetary policy to the Canadian Royal Commission on Banking and Finance confirmed his earlier views on its effectiveness; credit easing could stimulate investment under normal conditions; where business confidence was absent it could do very little to increase spending.[32] Monetary policy was therefore no panacea in times of depression, it had a positive contribution to make to recovery, but it needed the strong assistance of other policies.[33]

It may not be possible to make the business horse drink from the money pool if it has no thirst in a depression, but it is possible to prevent it quenching its excessive thirst by turning off the money tap during the boom. Robertson was a strong advocate of restrictive monetary policy during periods of over-expansion and was very critical of postwar sceptics of the deflationary powers of higher interest rates. This is most forcibly illustrated by his comment upon both the early postwar cheap money policy and the findings of the Radcliffe Report.[34] He was very critical of the cheap money policy at a time when there was heavy demand pressure in the U.K. He attributed such a policy to the Keynesian view that monetary policy would have little success in a period of over-expansion,[35] and called for an increase in the interest rate and restrictions on credit expansion (such a policy was in fact adopted in 1951–52). He disagreed with the conclusions of the Radcliffe Report, which he saw as being too pessimistic on the potential success of monetary policy in an inflationary period. True, monetary policy had been ineffective in the 1950s, but this was a fault of the type of monetary policy implemented rather than a permanent condemnation of all shades of such policy. Robertson doubted that a situation of rising prices and profits, as existed in the 1950s, could be remedied by moderate changes in bank rate; what was required were larger movements in interest rates.[36] In periods of inflation, when the prospects of a high rate of return on investment predominate, businessmen are not too put off by a rise in interest rate of 1 or 2 per cent; in a period of continued inflation some large firms find themselves with large cash reserves and are therefore not dependent upon external finance. Add to this the fact that in the 1950s a large proportion of investment was in the hands of the public sector, and as such was not determined by interest rate considerations, one would not expect a moderate change in bank rate to have significant repercussions on gross investment.[37]

The role of monetary policy will be encountered again in the discussion of inflation.[38] What can be concluded from this section is that Robertson neither completely condemned a monetary policy, nor gave it unqualified support. The success of monetary policy depended upon the extent of the depression and the mood of businessmen, and the severity with which monetary measures were imposed. But it was not a policy which could function alone in regulating the cycle; it needed the support of, in particular, fiscal policy in an acute depression. As a final comment it is interesting to observe in the climate of current controversies between monetarists and Keynesians that Robertson was an advocate of *discretionary* monetary policy; he viewed the economic system as being too complex to warrant any mechanistic kind of monetary policy of the type frequently associated with Professor M. Friedman.[39] But he was aware of the limitations of such discretionary policy. By the time it had been introduced and its effects felt, it could well be too late.[40] The beauty of having a mechanistic policy, if it were practicable, was that it could *prevent* the ravages of the cycle, rather than attempt to cure them once they had appeared. Later comment will also demonstrate this *theoretical* support for monetarist policies, combined with an awareness of the impracticability of such policies.[41]

FISCAL POLICY AND UNEMPLOYMENT

One of the most encouraged of Keynesian myths is the belief that in 1936 Keynes was the first economist to advocate fiscal measures as a cure for unemployment.[42] The emphasis which Keynes placed upon the importance of effective demand led to his strong recommendation of fiscal action; but we have already emphasised the Robertsonian disposition to stress the importance of a deficiency of demand in bringing about the crisis; it was not unnatural therefore for Robertson also to call for fiscal action as a cure for unemployment, long before the *General Theory* appeared. (Although this was not reinforced by the recognition of the multiplier process as it was for Keynes).

Robertson was one of the first economists to strongly recommend public works policies in the U.K. In 1915 he called for increased government spending to bring about: 'an artificial elevation of the demand for constructional goods'[43] in times of crisis; this would be necessary until private investment recovered. This support for fiscal action was not only consistent with his view of the causes of the crisis, but a confirmation of his agreement with the minority report of the Poor Law Commissioners, which had proposed the tendering of government contracts during times of bad trade. By 1926 Robertson was able to write of the: 'once heretical but now perhaps over-respectable policy of "public works"'.[44] Clearly Robertson may have been one of the first to propose public works policies before 1936, but he was certainly not the only advocate of such policies.

His most thorough early analysis of fiscal action came in his evidence to the Macmillan Committee.[45] This demonstrated a number of Robertsonian policy beliefs in the pre-1936 period. Firstly, since the crisis was invariably caused by a temporary saturation of demand for capital goods, the solution available to the government was to temporarily raise the level of public investment. Government action therefore was to take place on the spending, rather than the taxation, side of its budget; there was no suggestion to reduce taxation as a stimulant to demand. Secondly, increased government spending should be concentrated on building such things as roads and bridges; but, in particular, there was a very emphatic advocacy of a programme of housebuilding from the mid-1920s to the early 1930s.[46] Thirdly, it was not necessary to insist on higher rates of return on investment in the public sector.[47] Finally, fiscal policy should not be subservient to monetary policy, although it should be planned in conjunction with monetary action.

Economists have continuously debated, for the greater part of this century, the relationship existing between possible monetary and fiscal measures. More recently this debate has focused upon the 'crowding out' effect.[48] Robertson was always aware that fiscal action would have monetary repercussions. However, in the 1920s he was the foremost critic of the 'Treasury view' that government expenditure, by utilising savings, would be withdrawing funds from the money market which would otherwise have gone into private investment. This criticism was again most obvious in his evidence to the Macmillan Committee. In this he argued: 'the doctrine of temporary gluttability which I have tried to outline above is in direct conflict, not only with the so-called 'Treasury view' that such a policy of promoting public works absorbs resources which would otherwise anyhow be employed by private enterprise, but also with a doctrine which has been maintained, for instance, by Mr. Hawtrey, that public works are: "a mere piece of ritual" achieving nothing which could not equally be achieved by the banking system acting alone, through a sufficiently great alteration in its terms of lending'.[49]

Robertson believed that during a depression savings would not be otherwise employed in the private sector and therefore were available to be productively engaged by the government to stimulate employment. Public works policies had to be organised at times when they did not compete with the private sector for resources. In this respect he was critical of the housing programme introduced at the end of the first world war. It was justifiable on social grounds, but not from an economic stability standpoint.[50]

The 'crowding out' effect can be best illustrated by utilising the IS/LM framework.[51] If the economy is operating in region A (diagram on p. 248), an expansionary fiscal policy which shifts the IS curve to the right (IS_0 to IS_1) will not succeed in raising the level of real output (Y_0). If public investment has been increased, the rise in the rate of interest (r_0 to r_1) is sufficient to dampen private investment to the full extent of the increased public investment. The Keynesian mechanism operating is as follows: increased public investment, in the absence of a monetary restraint, will increase output and employment through the multiplier process. However, if the money supply is fixed, any additional investment has to be financed in region

The Crowding Out Effect

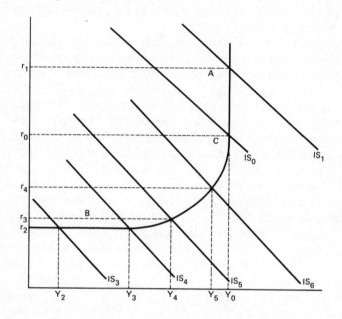

A (where the speculative demand is zero), by the sale of government bonds. This raises the rate of interest and dampens the level of private investment. In region B, the Keynesian liquidity trap region, there is no monetary restraint on fiscal policy and increased public investment can be met by a reduction in the speculative demand for money without an increase in the rate of interest. In region C we have an intermediate situation in which there is a dampening of the multiplier caused by the monetary repercussions of fiscal policy in the absence of an expansion in the money supply (which would shift the LM curve to the right).

The relevant question here seems to be how far Robertson recognised the monetary repercussions of a *real* change in the economy in the 1930s. An objective interpretation on the basis of the material contained in Part II seems to be that Robertson was very much aware of the 'crowding out' effect. In terms of the loanable funds theory, increased public investment would shift the demand curve to the right; the rate of interest would increase, and the level of total investment would consequently be lower than it would otherwise be. If the government supported its public investment policy with an expansionary monetary policy, then the monetary restraint on fiscal policy would be prevented. The supply curve for loanable funds would shift to the right as the money supply is expanded and the increase in the market rate of interest would be avoided. This, in Keynesian analysis, would be the equivalent of a rightward shift in the LM curve. The implications of Robertsonian analysis are therefore that the strength of fiscal action depends upon the elasticity of the LM curve (or alternatively the elasticity of the supply of loanable funds curve), and upon the behaviour of the money supply as fiscal policy is implemented. We have already seen Robertson's views on the elasticity of the liquidity preference function.[52] In addition we have also witnessed the Robertsonian belief that the LM curve is prone to instability.

Indeed in an expansionary situation with the IS curve shifting to the right, Robertson would support the argument that the LM curve must be moving to the left (if the money supply is fixed). As output expands so too will the price level in Robertsonian analysis. Transactionary demand will increase for each level of real output, speculative demand will decline and a higher rate of interest will be needed to equate the demand for, and supply of, money. This would lead to even further monetary restraints upon the effectiveness of expansionary fiscal policy. This is shown in the diagram on p. 250. Taking the intermediate case, if prices are constant (as they are assumed to be in Keynesian analysis) income will increase from Y_4 to Y_5 with an expansionary fiscal policy (IS_5 to IS_6). If the velocity of circulation of money and prices change along with output (as Robertson believed), the LM curve will shift to the left as a consequence of expansionary policy, and income in this case would contract from Y_4 to Y_7 under the influence of an increase in the rate of interest (r_6). It seems to be indisputable therefore that Robertson was very familiar with the limitations which *may* be imposed upon the effectiveness of fiscal policy in curing unemployment by the monetary repercussions of that policy in the absence of compatible monetary measures.

After the publication of the *General Theory*, Robertson saw a dangerous reversal of economic policy away from monetary measures to a concentration upon fiscal action. Although he did not believe fiscal policy should be subservient to monetary measures, equally he did not feel that it should dominate such measures. This may have stemmed partly from his view of the monetary limitations of fiscal action, but his post-war writings indicate that

Movements in IS/LM curves

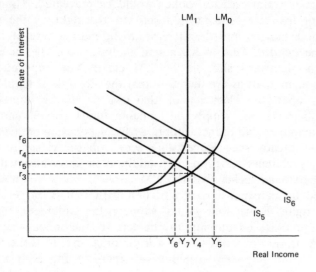

he chose to emphasise the other limitations; the major limitation was to be found in the time lags inherent in fiscal policy. Robertson remarked: 'fiscal policy is by its nature a somewhat cumbrous and unwieldy one, working with a pronounced lag and difficult to set moving ... more than once or at most twice a year'.[53] In his evidence to the Canadian Royal Commission on banking and finance he proposed that there should be scope for changing taxes more frequently to avoid the delayed, and possibly adverse, effects of tax changes.[54] Robertson continued to favour expenditure changes rather than tax changes in fiscal policy. Tax changes he regarded as being unhealthy. They needed to be administered with fairness and consistency. In any case, they were needed to support other objectives of policy other than the objective of economic stabilisation. Tax changes might bring disincentive effects to work. In addition to all this, Robertson saw frailties in politicians; very few were capable of handling tax changes successfully.[55]

His view on taxation and stability changed very little in the postwar period. Even in his evidence to the Canadian Royal Commission, although he suggested: 'it ought to be possible to move rates of taxation, direct or indirect, upward or downward, according to circumstances'.[56] He proceeded to enlarge upon its limitations,

and concluded: 'it is well I think, thus to stake out a claim
for Public Finance as a serious subject in its own right, with
a philosophy and experience of its own, and incapable of being
pushed around, in the interests of stability, beyond a certain point
without damaging consequences'.[57]

WAGE FLEXIBILITY AND FULL EMPLOYMENT

The Keynesian myth relating to the absence of support for fiscal
policy in the pre-1936 period has been reinforced by the argument
that the typical classical economist had great faith in wage manipula-
tion as a cure for unemployment. The demand for labour is
seen to vary inversely with the marginal product of labour; a
fall in the real wage paid to labour will increase the volume
of labour that it will be profitable to employ. Unemployment
must therefore be the consequence of too high a level of real
wages. Such an argument was tailor-made for Keynesian criticism.
It failed to explore the repercussions of wage reduction upon
effective demand. A policy designed to lower wages would be
impotent in its effects upon employment if it did not promote
an enlargement of effective demand; from the preceding section
it is apparent that Robertson could not be branded a typical
classical economist, for he was conscious of the need to affect
demand if employment was to be raised. But how did a reduction
in real wages affect employment in Robertsonian analysis?

It is crucial in Robertsonian literature to distinguish between
micro- and macro- economic analysis, and between theory and
policy. At the micro level Robertson continued throughout his
writings to base his discussion of the labour market upon the
marginal productivity theory of wages. In 1930 he defended what
he called the 'orthodox' theory of wages against its critics.[58] In
Lectures he upheld the relationship between the marginal productivity
of labour and the demand for labour found in classical literature;[59]
But it is incorrect to suggest that support for the marginal productivity doctrine implies that one is in favour of a policy of wage
reductions to cure unemployment. On questions of macroeconomic
policy Robertson always stressed that the effect of wage reductions
upon demand was the key to the suitability of wages policy.
In his evidence to the Macmillan Committee he emphasised that,
if crises were caused by the saturation of demand, the demand

for labour would be inelastic; Even if wages fell, employment would not improve since there would not be any additional demand for goods and services coming forward. He used the depression in the shipbuilding industry to illustrate this point; no matter what the level of wages might be there would be no recover in the shipbuilding industry as the volume of shipping tonnage was already too excessive. In 1931 he was less certain on this question. Wage reductions should not always be resisted since they need not always be damaging to purchasing power; however, there was still an emphasis upon the link between wage level changes and effective demand.[60]

This emphasis prevailed into *Lectures* where Robertson was even less pessimistic as to the damage wage reductions may do to the volume of spending.[61] Indeed Robertson puts forward two arguments which may lead to increased effective demand as wages fall. The first is to be expected from the earlier discussion of induced lacking. A decline in wages which is accompanied by a fall in prices will bring an increase in the real value of the existing stock of money. People may be induced to spend more in order to restore the real value of their money stock to its original level. This argument is normally associated with A. C. Pigou,[62] although we have witnessed its existence in *Banking*.[63] Secondly, if a lag exists between wage reductions and any subsequent movement in prices or sales volume, businessmen may be encouraged to invest by an increase in the marginal efficiency of investment. In such a situation a wages policy may be more fruitful in promoting investment than would be a policy of cheap money.[64]

Although in the end Robertson grew less averse to the theoretical case for wage reductions, he did not regard such a policy as a practicable possibility.[65] What was more significant as an answer to Keynesian criticism was the disposition of Robertson, even before 1936, to judge wages policy in terms of its repercussions upon effective demand. Certainly not the disposition attributed to a classical economist by Keynesians!

INVESTMENT PLANNING

It would be remiss to leave this chapter without a brief indication of the Robertsonian view of economic planning. Again we can look for clues in the theoretical sections earlier in this book.

The extremes of the cycle are to be seen in the wide fluctuations in output present in the capital good industries. Over-investment is the cause of the crisis, and this is primarily the result of uncertainty in the business environment.[66] But this did not lead Robertson to propose a totally planned economy, or indeed a total state responsibility for investment. He was brought up within Cambridge to think in terms of 'tinkering at the systems of private property and economic freedom',[67] not in terms of replacing the market by state control.

But he did see the need for some form of indicative planning even in 1915. One must hasten to add that the purpose of such planning was not that associated with post-war attempts of planning in Britain and France. Its aim was not to foster higher rates of economic growth; on the contrary, Robertson believed that it may involve the sacrifice of higher growth rates on the 'alter of stability',[68] an approach which he favoured even in the 1960s.[69] Investment planning was a means to reducing the vast swings in the level of unemployment through the trade cycle; in other words an attempt to lower the *average* level of unemployment over the cycle.

The form which investment planning might take is described in the following manner in the *Study*: 'the excesses of investment during the boom are admittedly due in no small measure to the prevalence of competition and the ignorance on the part of each individual producer of the scale of the preparations which have been and are being made by his competitors. Combination, by pooling information and prospective markets and so facilitating a common investment policy, may be expected materially to reduce the temptations to over-investment. ... Even, however, without actual combination, a somewhat saner and more centralised investment policy might perhaps be secured by a greater publicity and diffusion of information. It may be suggested that a detailed report of new contracts for structural work or machinery in any trade should be compulsorily submitted to the Board of Trade, who should be obliged to prepare in the *Labour Gazette* or elsewhere a monthly analysis of such reports'.[70] Planning in this context, therefore, is no more than an attempt to educate businessmen as to what is happening in their own and other industries; it is the provision of information on which a sounder investment decision can be undertaken.

As a member of the Cohen Council, Robertson was against

the return of physical controls upon investment in the late 1950s. He saw no reason for controlling *essential* investment. The insurmountable problem as far as Robertson was concerned was the inability to determine any sane criterion for deciding where investment was either essential or not. He could not, therefore, recommend selective controls upon investment.[71]

There were dangers present in any attempt to harmonise the investment plans of the private and public sectors. The gain may be greater stability in investment levels, but at the expense of more collusion between producers which may end 'in some conspiracy against the public or some contrivance to raise prices'.[72] Thus Robertson was anxious that Mr. Lloyd should not take indicative planning too far in the early 1960s.

Robertsonian policy aimed at both prevention and cure in relation to unemployment. The recommendation of investment planning was primarily concerned with preventing the volatility of the capital good industries and consequently preventing the variability of employment in these industries. Doubts on the effectiveness of a cheap money policy in stimulating investment and the recovery of employment led Robertson to suggest that the *artificial* elevation of demand, through fiscal policy, may be more successful. Cheap money may not sufficiently encourage businessmen to become more optimistic with regard to the returns available on investment projects; public investment programmes did not contain the same element of chance in the stimulus provided to increase employment. Monetary and fiscal policies should therefore be combined in seeking the movement out of depression, but the senior partner must be fiscal activity in *severe* depressions.

2 Robertson and the Price Level

Finally attention is turned to the problem of inflation and in particular to two questions. The starting point must be to enquire as to what Robertson believed to be the justifiable behaviour of the price level. Having established this we need to consider the policy proposals which seek to accomplish this justifiable behaviour; this will involve a brief consideration of the cause of the price movements to be found in Robertsonian literature.

HOW SHOULD PRICES BEHAVE?

It would be convenient, if simplistic, to argue that Robertson favoured price stability over the trade cycle. Although, as a compromise, Robertson did support a policy of price stabilisation, he did envisage occasions on which prices should vary either upwards or downwards. In 1928 he wrote: 'the ideal banking policy might be one which was founded on the principle of price stabilisation as a norm, but which was ready to see the fruits of a prolonged and general increase in individual productivity shared in the form of lower prices, and perhaps to acquiesce in moderate price rises in order that advantage might be taken of discontinuous leaps in industrial technique'.[1] This view prevailed into the 1950s, although as a member of the Cohen Council, he did stress the importance of finding some means by which increased economic activity could benefit the community without prices having to rise.[2]

255

Again we can go back to Part II to find the reason why prices might justifiably be allowed to rise in a period of recovery.[3] The major cause of the upturn is the application of invention to industry. This can only come about if the supply of lacking is sufficient to finance the additional demand for capital which the invention creates. The forced saving thesis argues that in order to supplement the voluntary saving taking place, banks must expand their credit creation to accommodate the *desirable* enlargement in the demand for capital. The consequence is a price rise which imposes automatic lacking upon the fixed income groups in the economy, as well as encouraging induced lacking. The price rise is *essential* if the invention is to be fully, and correctly, exploited in the interests of aggregate economic welfare.[4] But the price rise is only of a temporary nature and will eventually be reversed when output expands as a result of the installation of additional capital equipment; at which time the increased productivity generated by the additional investment can be shared by all in reduced prices.

Putting forward this view in the 1920s Robertson found himself arguing against the orthodoxy of the time, and against Keynes.[5] In *Banking* he stressed: 'it seems unreasonable to expect the banking system *both* to ensure that appropriate additions are made to the quantity of Circulating Capital *and* to preserve absolute stability in the price level'.[6] In comments to Keynes he indicated that priority should be given to providing the right quantity of circulating capital — at the expense of price stability.[7] His review of Ropke's work led him to doubt that effective expansion could be carried through without price rises even where excess capacity existed.[8] Even in *Lectures* he remained faithful to some extent to this advocacy of price rises during recovery,[9] — if major inventions were to be usefully exploited. But he concluded, 'I would now hold that the pursuit of monetary equilibrium to be a sufficiently ambitious, and the wiser path.'[10]

He was very much aware of the disadvantages which inflation could inflict upon the community. As early as 1921 he emphasised the detrimental effect of inflation upon fixed income groups in the economy, and the advantage which inflation gave to debtors over creditors. He wrote of the damaging repercussions of inflation upon the Balance of Payments, and recognised the problem which it might create for state finance.[11] As a consequence, in general, he advocated price stability, with price variations only justifiable in certain circumstances. As an author of the Cohen Report he went a good deal further than in the 1920s towards recommending price stability.[12] Forced saving, and the price movements which it creates, was taken to be no longer advantageous in promoting economic expansion.[13] A rise in the price level should only be permitted as a consequence of increases in imported raw material prices, increased rates of indirect taxation, or in order to remedy price distortions.[14]

The advocacy of price stability is complicated somewhat if the level of productivity is assumed to vary. Ideally Robertson believed that the price level of final goods should be allowed to fall with the 'progress of technical efficiency'.[15] The benefits of progress should be found in lower commodity prices,[16] and not in increased money wages, nor in higher profit margins if money wages and prices remain constant as productivity increases.[17] Price stability ought to be achieved in relation to the prices of productive services, not in relation to final prices. The justification for this approach was to be found in the view that everyone should be able to share in the gains of increased productivity, not exclusively those workers who are employed in the higher productivity industries.[18] All can gain from lower final prices, no-one can gain directly from extra income in someone else's pocket. The advantage of allowing prices to fall rather than raising money wages is not only to be found in relation to avoiding the redistributive effects on income of wage rises for specific workers; it is also to be found in preventing the spread of wage increases on grounds of comparability of wages to industries where productivity is not increasing.[19] By the end of the 1950s Robertson recognised the practical limitations of introducing a policy based on falling prices in the wake of increased productivity. At the end of the day the best one could hope for — the ultimate compromise — was to keep prices steady as productivity rose; that is to keep wage increases in line with productivity changes.[20]

HOW TO CONTROL INFLATION

Policy recommendations for controlling inflation must depend upon the *cause* of the continual upward movement of prices. Two previous indications have been made as to where Robertson put the blame for a falling value of money. Firstly, the price rises which created forced saving originated from the willingness of the commercial banks to utilise excess liquidity in satisfying the additional demands for finance caused by the improved productivity of investment.[21] Secondly, Robertson's faith in the Cambridge Equation[22] led him to emphasise the connection between the volume of money and the price level. Therefore it was not surprising that when writing of inflation he should lay the blame upon the monetary *flabbiness* of an economy.[23] However, an excess of money was not the *initial* cause of the disturbance in prices in Robertsonian theory. Inflation had two origins. One was to be found in the forces inherent in the trade cycle, in particular the real forces of invention and innovation. The other was present in an autonomous increase in money wage rates which would have repercussions upon prices.[24] But whatever the initial cause Robertson believed that prices could not continue to rise without the support of an increasing flow of money.[25]

This was most evident in Robertson's policy statements in the 1950s. He saw great danger in the policy of maintaining a high monetary demand in order to keep unemployment at a minimal level. Inflation was caused in the 1950s by the excessive demand for goods and services, not by cost-push elements independent of the state of demand. Trade unions were restricted in their ability to force up wage rates by the state of monetary demand; Robertson argued: 'while under a capitalist system wage claims will always be forthcoming, . . . the scale on which they are pitched, and the force with which they are pressed, depends largely on the resistance which they expect to meet and which they do meet, and this again on the general state of monetary demand it is the business, and which it is ultimately within the power of monetary policy to control'.[26] Not only was a policy of restraint on monetary demand recommended, but this was to be imposed even if it involved a sacrifice in terms of unemployment; Robertson argued that Keynesian policies for full employment in the 1950s had fostered the inflationary process. The cure for one problem had been accomplished at the expense of introducing a further problem. This philosophy even penetrated the Cohen Report, and it was to receive much critical comment for sanctioning increased unemployment in the interests of price stability.[27] Robertson remained firm on this belief and argued: 'extra unemployment, though an evil, would be a lesser evil than allowing the slide of the currency to continue indefinitely'.[28]

But did a control of monetary demand guarantee the *prevention* of the inflationary process? Robertson believed not. The Cambridge Equation demonstrates that inflation can be associated not simply with a change in the money supply, but also with a change in the desire to hold money (a change in K). Although monetary policy could effectively be used to control the money supply, it could not directly effect the value of K. Changes in K can either offset monetary policy or reinforce it. Hence: 'the incalculable K of the public hangs like the sword of Damocles over the head of many amiable and ambitious schemes'.[29] The Cohen Report again emphasised this point: 'Even if the quantity of money is not increased, the stream of monetary demand can be fed',[30] by a change in V or K. It recognised that V had in fact been changing since 1945 and had been adding to the pressure upon the price level.

In evidence to the Canadian Commission, Robertson upheld the belief in monetary policy, but he stressed that monetary management should not be hesitant or indecisive. He praised the monetary control imposed in the U.K. in 1958 which dampened the inflationary pressure, but was critical of the premature relaxation of control in 1959 and 1960 which allowed inflation to accelerate again and brought the introduction of an incomes policy.[31] He stressed the limitations of monetary policy, doubting that increased rates of interest dampened spending; he also suggested that large companies did not borrow to finance their spending but used either retained profits, or extracted credit from their weak customers and suppliers. A monetary restriction might therefore be counteracted by what would show itself in an increase in the velocity of circulation of money. We have seen before that there are a number of forces operating in Robertsonian theory which can alter K. It is not necessary to examine these again, but allow me to emphasise the expectations effect of an initial rise in prices which reduces K. This has its popularity today in the monetarist approach to inflation, but don't let us forget that it appeared in *Banking* in 1926, largely as a result of Keynes' counsel.

In conclusion, therefore, it remained the disposition of Robertson to argue throughout the post-war period of inflation that: 'control over the quantity of money is a *necessary* condition, even though not by itself a *sufficient* condition, for controlling the supply of loanable funds and hence the stream of total demand'.[32]

ALTERNATIVE APPROACHES — FISCAL AND INCOMES POLICIES

Although fiscal policy had advantages over monetary policy as a cure for economic depression, it had not the same merits from Robertson's point of view as a means of stabilising prices. Fiscal policy was a vehicle of demand management, and as such it was relevant to controlling prices, but it was only of secondary importance to monetary policy. The disadvantage of taxation or government expenditure changes was that they represented *cures* for an already existing inflation; how much better it would be to *prevent* inflation occurring in the first place by regulating the money supply. Robertson remarked: 'I do not of course dispute that such taxes may be an indispensable means of mopping up spilt milk; but I do suggest that they are very much in the nature of a *pis aller*, and by no means a perfect substitute for measures designed to prevent the spilling of the milk in the first instance'.[33] It was much wiser to adopt a monetary policy which would avoid price rises accruing through increased taxation which could in turn be used by trade unions as an excuse for raising their members' remuneration.[34] Automatic taxation stabilisers might take some of the sting out of inflation, but they could not be sufficient to yield price stability. Discretionary tax changes designed to regulate demand and prices would also interfere with the other economic objectives to be achieved through taxation.[35]

Robertson was even less enthusiastic in relation to incomes policy. At best such a policy could be a supplement to, but not a substitute for, monetary and fiscal policies. The drive could be taken out of inflation by restricting monetary demand, this would be sufficient to make trade union demands for higher wages less optimistic, and diminish the need for an incomes policy. Robertson warned of the dangers of certain types of incomes policies. If wage rises were to be allowed to match increases in productivity, he believed the net effect may be inflationary; because 'some industries are inherently more susceptible to technological progress than others',[36] wage increases in these industries will exceed the *average* national rate of growth of labour productivity. An incomes policy which permits wage and productivity rises to be equated, and also allows wages to be raised on the basis of comparability, was bound to encounter difficulties. Effective demand would not only be raised by the increase of wages in some industries, but also the inflationary pressure would be heightened by attempts by other industries to emulate wage rises in the high productivity growth industries in order to preserve 'existing relatives in the reward for effort'.[37] Robertson was equally critical of incomes policy which laid down a wage rise 'norm'. He believed that such a 'norm' rather than being an *average* percentage rise, soon would come to be regarded as the *minimum* obtainable rise by trade unions. No-one familiar with incomes policy in the United Kingdom in the 1960s would now doubt the wisdom of Robertson's criticism.

This opposition to incomes policy was not founded on the belief that such a policy could not cure inflation. Robertson recognised possible deficiencies which might be present in an incomes policy, but these could be remedied. It is true that Robertson preferred preventing inflation to curing it and monetary policy offered the best means of doing this; but more important, the underlying reason for Robertson's critical response to incomes policy is that he believed it interfered too much with the working of the free enterprise economy. Relative wages between industries should be the determining force in the distribution of labour. An incomes policy which altered the structure of relative wages stood the danger of damaging the efficient utilisation of the labour force. Hence an incomes policy which could be enforced in the public sector and not in the private sector may curtail the supply of labour in the public sector, and promote an imbalanced economy. Similarly if wage differentials were not maintained on the basis of differences in profitability and productivity between industries, labour may not be redistributed in the most efficient manner. Short and long term growth of the economy may suffer. Not surprisingly, Robertson was also critical of a profits policy which aimed at a uniform rate of profit over all industries. Again this would damage the efficient use of resources between industries.

SOME CONCLUSIONS

Again in this chapter we have seen that the Robertsonian approach to the solution of particular macroeconomic problems, in this case inflation, is determined by the theoretical structure outlined in Parts I and II. In the 1920s he did not categorically support price stability. In the interests of economic progress, if invention was to be fully exploited, prices may need to rise. Price variations of this kind should not be resisted. In the post-1945 period he put more weight on the achievement of price stability as a compromise economic objective given that prices would be reluctant to fall as productivity rose. The only realistic means of maintaining price stability was to be found in monetary policy; but even strict control on the money supply and the rate of interest could not guarantee a tight control of monetary demand. Monetary demand could still escape and ravage the price level if people accelerated the rate at which they got rid of money.

Notes

LIST OF ABBREVIATIONS USED IN THE NOTES

1. Books written by Sir Dennis Holme Robertson:
    SIF — *A Study of Industrial Fluctuation* (1915)
    BPPL — *Banking Policy and the Price Level* (1926)
    EF — *Economic Fragments* (1931)
    EEA — *Economic Essays and Addresses* (with A. C. Pigou, 1931)
    EMT — *Essays in Monetary Theory* (1940)
    UAT — *Utility and All That* (1952)
    EC — *Economic Commentaries* (1956)
    LEP — *Lectures on Economic Principles* (1957-9)
    EMI — *Essays in Money and Interest* (1966)

2. Other major books or journals referred to and abbreviated:
    GT — *The General Theory of Employment, Interest and Money*
        J. M. Keynes (1936)
    CW — *The Collected Writings of John Maynard Keynes* Volumes
        XIII and XIV.
    Principles — *Principles of Economics* A. Marshall (1890)
    EJ — *The Economic Journal* (various issues)
    QJE — *The Quarterly Journal of Economics* (various issues)
    AER — *American Economic Review*

A full bibliography of the works of Sir D. H. Robertson is given on
page 310.

INTRODUCTION

1. A task already undertaken to some extent by Sir J. R. Hicks in *EMI*, pp. 9–22.
2. DHR, *SIF*, (P. S. King and Son Ltd., 1915).
3. The honour of a Fellowship of Eton College was given to him in 1948.
4. Being a member of the A.D.C. and the Marlowe Society.
5. See later, Part II, Ch. 2.
6. He was in fact awarded the Military Cross.
7. Letter to the author, November 1972.
8. JMK, *Tract on Monetary Reform*, (London: Macmillan, 1923).
9. JMK, *Treatise on Money*, (London: Macmillan, 1930).
10. Part II, Ch. 2.
11. See his comment in *UAT*, p. 44.
12. DHR, *EF*, p. 175.
13. Ibid, p. 212.
14. DHR continued to live in Cambridge until his death in 1963.
15. DHR, *LEP*, 3 volumes 1957–9, (London: Staples Press Ltd., Paperback edition, London, 1963) (The Fontana Library).
16. DHR, written and oral evidence to the (Macmillan) Committee on Finance and Industry, on 8–9th May, 1930.
17. The Memorandum which Robertson submitted to this Commission was reprinted in *Essays in International Finance*, No. 42, (May 1963, University of Princeton); oral evidence is contained in Vol. 42, (20th September 1962) pp. 5107–5208.
18. Including *The Control of Industry*, (Cambridge Economic Handbook, 1923) (1960 edition with S. R. Dennison).
19. See bibliography, p. 311.
20. P. Samuelson, 'Sir D. H. Robertson', *QJE*, No. 4 (November 1963) pp. 528–36.
21. DHR, *LEP*, p. 325.
22. W. Fellner, 'The Robertsonian Evolution', *American Economic Review*, Vol. XLII, No. 3 (June 1952) p. 266.
23. L. Robbins, *The Evolution of Modern Economic Theory*, (London: Macmillan) pp. 248–53.
24. JMK, *CW*, Vols. XIII and XIV, edited by D. Moggridge, Macmillan, published for the Royal Economic Society, 1973.
25. See especially DHR, *UAT*.

PART I   THE THEORY OF INDUSTRIAL FLUCTUATION

1: BACKGROUND TO A STUDY OF INDUSTRIAL FLUCTUATION IN 1915

1. DHR, *SIF*, Ch. 1, p. 2.
2. Letter from A. C. Pigou to DHR dated 1913.

3. Letter from A. C. Pigou to DHR 1913. Pigou indicated that he may be biased in putting forward this advice because it reflected his own theoretical approach.
4. T. S. Ashton, 'Industrial Fluctuation' — Review, *Economica*, Vol. 18, No. 71, (August 1951) pp. 298–302.
5. See A. Hansen, *Business Cycles and National Income*, (Norton 1951) pp. 211–217.
6. See especially C. Juglar, *Des Crises Commerciales et de leur retour periodique en France, en Angleterre, et aux Etats-Uns*, (Paris, 1859). For this view see J. Schumpeter, *History of Economic Analysis*, (London: Allen & Unwin, 1954) p. 1124.
7. W. Phillips, *Manual of Political Economy*, 1828.
8. J. Wade, *History and Political Philosophy of the Middle and Working Classes*, (Edinburgh Chambers, 1833). Schumpeter regards this as a fairly comprehensive theory of the commercial cycle (*op cit.* p. 743n).
9. Lord Overstone, then Samuel Jones Loyd, *Reflections Suggested by a Perusal of Mr. J. Horsley Palmer's Pamphlet on the Causes and Consequences of Pressure on the Money Market*, (London, 1837).
10. A. Spiethoff, *Krisen, Handwörterbuch der Staatswissenschaften*, (Lieferung 1923, 29 and 1930) (Bog 1–10 des VI Bandes).
11. See T. Tooke, *A History of Prices and of the State of Circulation from 1792 to 1856*, published in six volumes from 1838 to 1857.
12. W. Mitchell, *Business Cycles*, (New York: Franklin, 1927) p. 3.
13. See DHR, *SIF*, Introduction (1948 edition).
14. W. Mitchell, op. cit., p. 468.
15. See Part 1, Ch. 7 and Part II, Ch. 6.
16. J. Schumpeter, op. cit., p. 742.
17. N. D. Kondratieff, 'Die Langen Wellen der Konjuctur', *Archiv für Sozialwissenschaft und Sozial politik*, (December 1926) (see also abridged translation, *Review of Economics and Statistics*, November 1935). The Long Cycle was also recognised by J. A. Schumpeter, *Business Cycle*, (McGraw-Hill, 1939) and by W. Mitchell, *op cit.*, 1927, amongst others.
18. This is the opinion of J. A. Schumpeter, *op cit.*, p. 1123.
19. A. Hansen, *op cit.*, p. 225, concludes: 'By 1890 ... apart from the work of Juglar ... the work on depressions and cycles had been peripheral and tangential'. For a similar conclusion see J. A. Schumpeter, *op cit.*, p. 1123.
20. M. Friedman, 'The Counter Revolution in Monetary Theory', *Wincott Foundation Lecture*, (Institute of Economic Affairs, 1970) p. 10.
21. See J. B. Say, *Traite d'economie politique*, (Paris, 1803).
22. See DHR, *SIF*, p. 1.
23. W. Persons, 'Theories of Business Fluctuations', *QJE*, Vol. 41, (November 1926) pp. 94–128.
24. Ibid, p. 99.
25. G. Cassel, *Theory of Social Economy*, Rev. Ed. (Harcourt, Brace & Co., 1932).
26. Ibid, the brackets are mine.
27. W. Mitchell, op. cit., p. 25.

28. J. R. Hicks, *A Contribution to the Theory of the Trade Cycle*, (Oxford: Clarendon Press, 1950).
29. For example the 'propagation' and 'impulse' cycles recognised by R. Frisch, in *Economic Essays in Honour of G. Cassel*, (Allen & Unwin, 1933).
30. M. Tugan-Baranowski, *Les Crises Industrielles en Angleterre*, (Paris, 1913).
31. W. Mitchell, op. cit., p. 50. The third grouping corresponds to one group found in Person's Classification discussed above.
32. F. A. von Hayek, *Prices and Production*, (London: Routledge & Son, 1931) and *Monetary Theory and the Trade Cycle*, (London: Cape, 1933).
33. K. Marx, *Das Capital*, (C. Kerr & Co., 1907, originally published in 1867).
34. W. T. Foster and W. Catchings, *Money*, (Boston, 1923).
35. DHR, 'The Monetary Doctrines of Messrs. Foster and Catchings', *QJE*, (May 1929) pp. 413–499.
36. W. Mitchell, *Business Cycles*, (New York: Burt Franklin, 1913) and J. Lescure, *Des Crises générales et periodiques de surproduction*, (Librairie du Recueil Siney, 1907).
37. M. Tugan-Baranowski, op. cit., and A. Aftalion, *Les Crises Periodiques de Surproduction*, (Paris: M. Rivière et Cie, 1913). Both were reviewed by DHR (*EJ*, March 1914, pp. 81–89).
38. G. H. Hull, *Industrial Depressions*, (New York, 1911).
39. R. G. Hawtrey, *Good and Bad Trade*, (London: Constable & Co., 1913). Reviewed by DHR in the *Cambridge Review*, November 27th, 1913.
40. M. Labordère, 'Autour de la crise américaine de 1907' *Revue de Paris*, (1st Feb 1908).

2: THE NATURE OF THE INDUSTRIAL FLUCTUATION AND THE ROBERTSONIAN METHODOLOGICAL APPROACH

1. DHR, *Money*, (1928), p. 156.
2. DHR, *UAT*, p. 193.
3. See especially DHR, *SIF*, Ch. 1.
4. DHR, *BPPL*, p. 6. Similar definitions are also to be found in *Money*, p. 155 and *EF*, p. 130.
5. DHR, *EF*, p. 130.
6. DHR, Review of *Les Crises Periodiques de Surproduction*, *EJ*, (March 1914) pp. 81–89.
7. DHR, *EF*, p. 214.
8. See, for example, DHR, *SIF*, p. 189.
9. DHR, *SIF*, (1948) New Introduction, p. vii.
10. A. C. Pigou, *Wealth and Welfare*, (1912). DHR had also in 1913 complimented A. Aftalion for his discussion of fluctuations in production, (*EJ*, March 1914, p. 85).

11. DHR, *UAT*, p. 193 taken from W. Rostow, *British Economy of the Nineteenth Century*, (Oxford: Clarendon Press, 1948) p. 31.
12. DHR, *SIF*, 1948, p. ix.
13. DHR, *EC*, p. 91.
14. DHR, *SIF*, p. 7.
15. See DHR, *SIF*, p. 1, and *BPPL*, p. 7.
16. DHR, *BPPL*, p. 7.
17. DHR, *SIF*, Preface.
18. Taken from DHR, *UAT*, pp. 14–15.
19. DHR, *EMT*, p. 128.
20. DHR, *LEP*, pp. 23–24. Some would argue (e.g. K. Popper) that the economist must have some preconceived theory to collect facts about; otherwise what facts does he keep and what facts does he reject as irrelevant? DHR's approach follows A. Marshall (see *Principles*, p. 30).
21. See, for example, his first major article, 'Some material for a Study of Trade Fluctuations', *Journal of the Royal Statistical Society*, (January 1914) pp. 159–73.
22. DHR, *SIF*, pp. 9–10.
23. Letter from A. C. Pigou to DHR (1913): see above, p. 9–10.
24. DHR, *EF*, p. 188.
25. DHR, *UAT*, p. 87.
26. DHR, *SIF*, p. 2.
27. See, for example, DHR, *EMT*, p. 137 and p. 105, *SIF*, p. 2.
28. DHR, *SIF*, pp. 1–2.
29. DHR, *EMT*, p. 105.
30. DHR, *SIF*, (1948) p. vii.
31. Except in appendices. See especially the Appendix to DHR, *BPPL*, Ch. 5.
32. DHR, *LEP*, p. 26, 'the science of making figures speak, of getting the most out of crude numerical data by systematic arrangement and treatment'.
33. There are numerous references here. See, in particular DHR *LEP*, p. 418, p. 26 and *EC*, p. 80, p. 174.
34. DHR, *SIF*, p. x.
35. Ibid, pp. xvi–xvii. In an unpublished paper: 'Reflections of an ex-Magus' he is critical of the work of A. Phillips on inflation. He doubts that: 'anything (inflation) so highly elusive, working through so many diverse minds under so many diverse conditions, on the attitude to wage claims in the face of unemployment, can be reduced to a mathematical formula remaining valid for a century'. See also *EC*, p. 174.
36. See, for example, his treatment of the Agricultural Sector in *SIF*.
37. DHR, Review of *Good and Bad Trade*, *Cambridge Review*, (November 27th 1913) p. 163. In this respect DHRs theory is somewhat similar to the later theory of F. A. von Hayek (see chap. 9 'Natural and Market Rates of Interest').
38. See pp. 99–102.
39. See pp. 168–74. But see DHR, *EMT*, p. 138 for a comment upon the usefulness of static analysis.

3: THE ROBERTSONIAN THEORY OF INDUSTRIAL FLUCTUATION — AN OUTLINE

1. On 16th December 1913.
2. DHR, 'Some Material for a Study of Trade Fluctuations', *Journal of the Royal Statistical Society*, (January 1914) pp. 159–173.
3. Ibid, p. 163.
4. Ibid, p. 163.
5. DHR, *EJ*, (March 1914) pp. 81–89, two Reviews.
6. See pp. 59–64.
7. Letter from A. C. Pigou to DHR, 1913.
8. DHR, *SIF*, Part 1. (1948 reprint)
9. Ibid, new introduction, pp. x–xi.
10. Ibid, p. 239.
11. Ibid, p. 157.
12. Ibid, pp. 239–40.
13. Ibid, p. 156. This is not to argue that the demand for consumer goods will be constant. As income varies over the cycle so this demand would change. *BUT* it is the demand for construction goods which is more variable.
14. DHR, *LEP*, p. 416.
15. See, for example, T. Wilson, 'Robertson and Effective Demand and the Trade Cycle', *EJ*, Vol. 63, (September 1953) pp. 553–78.
16. DHR, *SIF*, p. 13, defined as: 'the length of time necessary to construct and prepare for use the requisite instruments of production'.
17. Ibid, p. 14.
18. Ibid, p. 240.
19. Ibid, p. 180.
20. Ibid, p. 165.
21. Ibid, p. 165.
22. Ibid, Part 1, Ch. 11.
23. Ibid, p. 172.
24. This view may have been stimulated by the first crisis which DHR observed in 1907–8, which he did attribute to a shortage of saving.
25. These explanations are given more detailed treatment in Part II, Chap. 3.
26. DHR, *SIF*, p. 254. Robertson used the expressions desirable and undesirable, appropriate and inappropriate in relation to fluctuation.
27. This thesis is repeated on several occasions including *LEP*. See, for example, DHR, Review of *Crises and Cycles*, *Economica*, (November 1936) pp. 476–8.

    In 1931 he wrote: 'I think these slumps are a very natural feature of a world which is making very rapid advances in the technique of production and which sets great store by material progress', *EEA*, p. 209.

    See also DHR, 'Is Another Slump Coming', *The Listener*, (28th July) 1937; *EMT*, p. 136; *UAT*, p. 203.

28. DHR, *BPPL*. Preface to 1949 edition p. VIII.
29. *Cf.* K. Wicksell, *Lectures on Political Economy*, Vol. II, (London: Routledge & Kegan Paul, 1935) p. 209, and G. Cassel, *op cit.*, Ch. XIX, p. 80.
    See also DHR, *BPPL*, p. 2.
30. DHR, written evidence to the Macmillan Committee on Finance and Industry, 8th May 1930 Minutes of Evidence Section 1, Para. 11, p. 323.
31. DHR believed that crises would result irrespective of the kind of government, 'good or bad, left or right' — even if business confidence were to be inspired more by one kind of government than another. See DHR, 'Is Another Slump Coming', *The Listener*, (July 28th) 1937.
32. DHR, *BPPL*, p. 1.
33. DHR, *BPPL*, p. 39, also see later DHR, *LEP*, pp. 412–4.
34. DHR, *SIF*, pp. 239–40.
35. That is, he does eventually witness the acceleration principle having a key role to play in the trade cycle. Hence the marginal utility of consumer goods is more variable than he had previously envisaged. One must remember, however, that constancy of the marginal utility of consumer goods does not necessarily mean that the *demand* for consumer goods is constant. In fact, if the level of purchasing power (as judged by real income levels) varies over the cycle then one must admit to the variability in the demand for consumer goods.
36. A phrase used by DHR in various sections of his evidence to the Macmillan Committee.

4: THE CAUSES OF THE UPTURN

1. For Robertson's comments upon the transmission of fluctuation in one industry to others see chapter 7, see also *SIF*, New Introduction (1948), p. xii.
2. See Chap. 5 'The Theory of Crisis — From Boom to Recession'.
3. e.g. DHR, *SIF*, p. 46.
4. See Part I: Chap. 7. para: 'Robertson and the Marshallian tradition.' See also J. N. Wolfe, 'Marshall and the Trade Cycle', (*Oxford Economic Papers*, Vol. 8, Feb. 1956) pp. 90–101, and M. Friedman, *Essays in Positive Economics*, (Chicago Univ. Press, 1953) pp. 65–68.
5. DHR, *SIF*, Part 1, Ch. III.
6. DHR, *BPPL*, p. 8ff.
7. DHR also observed that where two industries were competing for a common raw material (composite demand), when one industry prospered, the other was in a depressed state. He gave the boot trade depression (1913) as an example of this, caused by prosperity in the leather goods trade (*SIF*, pp. 51–2).

8. DHR, *SIF*, pp. 53–4.
9. Ibid, p. 55ff.
10. Ibid, pp. 56–60, see also DHR, *EF*, p. 121.
11. DHR, *SIF*, p. 64.
12. Ibid, p. 66ff.
13. Where 'industry is in the hands of a group of equal co-partners' (see *BPPL*, p. 7, and *SIF*, p. 126). This analysis was applied to a barter economy, but DHR also thought it valid for a monetary economy.
14. DHR mentions also the effects of change in tariffs and taxes upon demand. See *SIF*, p. 72.
15. DHR, *BPPL*, p. 11.
16. DHR, *SIF*, p. 70, *BPPL*, pp. 10–11.
17. DHR, *SIF*, p. 126, *BPPL*, p. 8ff.
18. Provided the elasticity of demand for the commodities offered in exchange is greater than unity. (See this Chap. pp. 41–6 below).
19. DHR, *BPPL*, p. 14.
20. See pp. 41–6.
21. DHR, *BPPL*, pp. 16–17.
22. This depends upon the effort elasticity of demand for agricultural produce (see pp. 41–6). More will be said about the role of agricultural forces in the cycle in Chapter 6.
23. DHR, *SIF*, p. 239.
24. DHR uses the expression 'instruments' of production. See *BPPL*, p. 12.
25. DHR, *BPPL*, p. 9.
26. See DHR, *SIF*, pp. 183–4.
27. Ibid, p. 157.
28. Ibid, pp. 183–7 and *BPPL*, p. 11.
29. DHR, *SIF*, p. 157.
30. Ibid, p. 127. See also pp. 41–6.
31. DHR, *LEP*, pp. 410ff. DHR does not commit himself fully on their relevance for fluctuation in the 20th century.
32. See especially DHR, *EMT*, p. 134.
33. See DHR, *LEP*, p. 416. See also pp. 59–61.
34. A. C. Pigou, *Wealth and Welfare*, (London: Macmillan, 1912) p. 447. See also *SIF*, New Introd. p. ix.
35. Letter from A. C. Pigou to DHR, 1916.
36. A. C. Pigou, *Industrial Fluctuations*, 2nd ed. (London: Macmillan, 1929) p. 56.
37. DHR, review of *Good and Bad Trade* by R. G. Hawtrey, *Cambridge Review*, (Nov 27th 1913).
38. A paper titled 'How Far are Bankers Responsible for the Alternations of Crisis and Depression?' presented to the Political Economy Club at the Hotel Cecil in 1913. See JMK, *CW*, Vol. XIII, pp. 2–14.
39. DHR, *EC*, p. 89.
40. See Part I: Chap. 3. Introduction paras.
41. He was adamantly opposed to agricultural explanations of the trade cycle.
42. See Part II: Chap. 9 'Natural and Market Rates of Interest and the Trade Cycle'.

43. See, for example, A. Aftalion, 'Le Rhythme de la Vie economique', *Revue de Metaphysique et de Morale*, (1921) p. 278.

44. For A. Spiethoff's early ideas see: 'Vorbemerkungen zu einer Theorie der Uberprodktion', *Jahrbuch für Gesetzgebung*, (Verwaltung und Volkswirtschaft 1902).

45. G. Cassel, *Theory of Social Economy*, Rev. Ed. (New York: Harcourt, Brace & Co., 1932) (orig. pub. in 1918).

46. J. A. Schumpeter, 'Die Wellenbewegung des Wirtschaftslebeus', *Archiv fur Sozia wissenschaft. und Socialpolitik*, Vol. 39 (1914) pp. 1–32, and *Business Cycles*, (New York: McGraw-Hill, 1939) Vols. 1 & 11.

47. DHR, by 1914, had read W. Mitchell's *Business Cycles* (New York: Burt Franklin, 1913) which included a very brief summary of Spiethoff's 'shortage of saving' theory (pp. 8–9). Mitchell did not cover the work of Schumpeter in this book.

48. DHR, *BPPL*, Introduction.

49. The first reference to the work of Schumpeter is contained in the second edition of *Money* (1928) p. 156. Schumpeter had published an article on 'The Explanation of Business Cycles' in *Economica*, (Dec 1927).

50. See A. Spiethoff, *Krisen*, (*op cit.*) p. 82, 'the "normal" is neither expansion nor depression, nor, needless to say, crisis. The normal of the free, money using capitalist market is the cycle of fluctuations'.

51. M. Tugan-Baranowski, *op cit.*

52. See A. Hansen, *op cit.*, p. 300.

53. Particularly G. Cassel, *Theory of Social Economy*, 1st Ed. (1918) (but ready for print in 1914). Published in English in 1924 (New York: Harcourt, Brace and World Inc.).

54. Ibid, (later editions).

55. Value in Cassel's analysis appears to relate to the rate of return on capital goods.

56. See Part II. Chap. 11 'Robertson and the Liquidity Preference Theory of Interest'.

57. J. Schumpeter, *Business Cycles*, (op cit.) p. 1.

58. Ibid, pp. 87–8.

59. Schumpeter in fact saw this, not as a move out of depression, but as a move towards equilibrium, which lies between the lower and upper turning points. His analysis takes the form of explaining movements towards/from equilibrium. See G. Haberler, *Prosperity and Depression*, 4th Ed. (Allen & Unwin, 1958) pp. 81–82n.

60. J. Schumpeter, *Theory of Economic Development*, (U.S.A. Harvard Univ. Press, 1934) p. 224. (first edition in German published in 1911).

61. DHR, *SIF*, p. 39.

62. Ibid, p. 39, see also Part I, Ch. III.

63. DHR, *BPPL*, pp. 12–3, *SIF*, pp. 204–5, pp. 132–3.

64. DHR, *BPPL*, p. 7. This assumption avoids the complications imposed by making a distinction between employers and employees, between the interests of capitalists and wage-earners.

65. For a clarification of this term see L. Robbins, 'On the Elasticity of Demand for Income in terms of Effort', *Economica*, (June 1930) pp. 123–9.

66. See DHR, *SIF*, p. 132, pp. 205ff.
67. Consider the innovating industries:

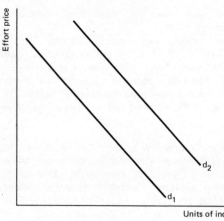

A revision of d_1 to d_2 means that more units of effort are offered for each unit of income (in terms of capital goods) gained.

68. DHR, *SIF*, p. 127.
69. H. Dalton, *Principles of Public Finance*, 9th Ed. (London: Routledge and Kegan Paul Ltd., 1936) pp. 100–8.
70. A. C. Pigou, *Industrial Fluctuations*, pp. 41–42, and especially Ch. V.
71. A. C. Pigou, *Economics of Welfare*, (London: Macmillan, 1920) p. 818.
72. See G. Haberler, op cit., pp. 157–8.
73. DHR, *BPPL*, Ch. 3.
74. Especially in the construction·good industries.

5: THE THEORY OF CRISIS — FROM BOOM TO RECESSION

1. M. Tugan-Baranowski, op cit.
2. M. Labordère op cit., A. Spiethoff, op cit.
3. A. Aftalion, op cit.
4. See DHR, *SIF*, p. 240. Also *BPPL*, p. 95n.
5. DHR, Evidence to the Macmillan Committee, Section II, p. 323.
6. See Part II: Chap. 3. 'Saving in the Cycle . . .'
7. A. Aftalion, op cit.
8. DHR, Review of A. Aftalion, op cit., *EJ*, March 1914, pp. 81–9.
9. Ibid, p. 85; but without further elucidation he contends that this is 'an aspect of that doctrine of quasi-rent long familiar to English readers'.

10. DHR, 'Some Material for the Study of Trade Fluctuations', *Journal of the Royal Statistical Society*, January 1914.
11. DHR, *SIF*, p. 15.
12. See JMK, *CW*, Vol. XIII, p. 4ff.
13. DHR, *SIF*, pp. 15–18.
14. DHR, *EF*, p. 113. He suggests that the gestation period may be exaggerated by government interference in relation to shipbuilding. (See *SIF*, p. 82, also JRSS (1914) p. 162).
15. DHR, *SIF*, p. 178.
16. DHR, Review of A. Aftalion, op cit., *EJ*, (March 1914) p. 88.
17. A. Aftalion, 'The theory of Economic Cycles based on the Capitalistic Technique of Production'. *Review of Economic Statistics*, (October, 1927). Similar emphasis was made in his earlier work with which DHR was familiar.
18. See G. Haberler, op cit., p. 136.
19. See Part I: Chap. 7 'Robertson and Alternative Theories . . .'.
20. K. Marx, *Das Capital*, vol. ii, part ii, ch. 9. Eng. Ed. (London: Allen & Unwin, 1938) vi, p. 211 see DHR, 'Some Material for the Study of Trade Fluctuations', *Journal of the Royal Statistical Society*, (January 1914) p. 165.
21. DHR, ibid, pp. 165ff.
22. DHR, *SIF*, Part I, Ch. 2.
23. Ibid, p. 31.
24. In other words, it is of no use building a railway part of the way from A to B, if passengers wish to be carried all the way to B.
25. DHR, *SIF*, pp. 32–36.

6: AGRICULTURAL FORCES IN THE TRADE CYCLE

1. The work of both A. Aftalion and M. Tugan-Baranowski is a good example of this.
2. T. S. Ashton, 'Industrial Fluctuation', *Economica*, Vol. 18, No. 71, (August 1951) pp. 298–302.
3. He had read the work of the Jevons and also that of Piatt Andrew. Each is referred to in *SIF*.
4. W. S. Jevons, *Investigations in Currency and Finance*, (London: Macmillan, 1884).
   H. S. Jevons, 'The Sun's Heat and Trade Activity', *Contemporary Review*, (August 1909).
   H. L. Moore, *Economic Cycles: their law and causes*, (New York: Macmillan, 1914).
   Each of these authors also suggested other causes of the cycle.
5. W. S. Jevons, op cit., p. 215.
6. H. S. Jevons, op cit., p. 8.
7. Ibid, p. 8.

8. H. L. Moore, op cit., p. 149. See the review of this book by R. A. Lehfeldt, *EJ*, (September 1915) pp. 409–11.
9. H. L. Moore, *Generating Economic Cycles*, (New York: Macmillan, 1923).
10. Ibid.
11. Ibid.
12. See especially A. Piatt Andrew, 'The Influence of the Crops upon business in America', *QJE*, Vol. XX, (1906) pp. 322–55.
13. DHR, *SIF*, Part 1, Ch. 5. It is interesting to note that this is an argument utilised by JMK (see *GT*, pp. 330–1).
14. DHR, ibid, pp. 89–90. Here DHR is arguing against G. Hull, op cit., p. 46.
15. DHR, ibid, p. 75. Robertson also argues that increased farm incomes may exert a psychological influence, increasing the level of investment (pp. 91–2).
16. Accounting for 40 per cent of British exports in this period.
17. See the statistical evidence, *SIF*, pp. 106–120.
18. DHR, *SIF*, pp. 110–20.
19. DHR does go to considerable length nevertheless to defend the sunspot theory, *SIF*, pp. 144–8.
20. DHR cites J. Hobson and G. Hull. A later version of this argument appears in G. Haberler, op cit., pp. 153ff.
21. See Part I: Chap. 4. paras. subheaded 'The theoretical framework — the elasticity of demand . . .'.
22. DHR himself was critical of writers who supported an active role of agricultural change in the industrial cycle without recognising that more than a redistribution of income might take place. See his treatment of A. C. Pigou, *SIF*, p. 137.
23. DHR, *SIF*, p. 137.
24. Again G. Hull was regarded by DHR as one of the main proponents of this.
25. Ibid, pp. 141–3.
26. Where, because of the existence of several sources of supply, fluctuations in supply from one source may be offset by opposite fluctuations in other sources.
27. DHR, *SIF*, p. 145.
28. The exceptions being the slumps of 1921–4 and 1929–32. The latter slump he viewed, in his preface to the 1948 edition of *SIF* (p. xi), as partly the result of a glut of agricultural products; but at the same time this depressive influence was counteracted by a stimulus to house-building brought about by low food prices. House-building was affected largely by the level of wheat prices; although the causation is obscure Robertson (*SIF* pp. 118–120) concluded, on the basis of statistical evidence, that lower wheat prices meant lower expenditure on wheat, and increased spending by families on shelter. House-building as a consequence was stimulated.
29. DHR, *BPPL*, pp. 14ff.
30. DHR, *LEP*, p. 409.
31. JMK, *GT*, Ch. 22.

32. A comment made by W. Beveridge in *Full Employment in A Free Society*, (London: Allen & Unwin, 1944) p. 305. It is indeed a surprising comment since Beveridge himself had researched on this topic in the 1920s. (See his 'Weather and Harvest Cycles', *EJ*, Vol. 31, (December 1921) pp. 429–452). See also DHR, *SIF*, (1948), p. x.

7: ROBERTSON AND THE ALTERNATIVE THEORIES OF INDUSTRIAL FLUCTUATION

1. The discussion of the role of monetary forces in the cycle is somewhat limited at this stage, it will be covered in more detail in Part II.
2. Although not mentioned in *SIF*, Bickerdike had also written on the Acceleration Principle in 1914 (see *EJ*, September 1914, pp. 427–29). See DHRs review of A. Aftalion (op cit.). The Principle became associated later with the work of J. M. Clark.
3. Nothing is said here of the time lags which may be present in this relation.
4. For one of the most proficient discussions of this, see G. Haberler, op cit., pp. 85ff.
5. A. Aftalion, 'Le Rhythme de la Vie Economique', *Revue de Metaphysique et de Morale*, (1921) p. 278.
6. DHR, *SIF*, p. 92.
7. Ibid, pp. 122–5; here the conventional accelerator is referred to (without price changes).
8. Ibid, p. 156.
9. Ibid, p. 157.
10. Ibid, p. 125. DHR uses the argument that the prosperity of one of the consumption trades, heralded by an increase in the exchange value of its product, will merely be at the expense of others where exchange values have fallen. There will be little net extension of aggregate effort by producers.
11. See Part II; Chap. 10, 'Saving, Investment and the Multiplier'.
12. DHR, *EC*, p. 71.
13. DHR, *EMT*, p. 179.
14. DHR, 'Is Another Slump Coming', *The Listener* (28th July 1937) pp. 174–5.
15. DHR, *LEP*, p. 426.
16. DHR, *EC*, pp. 72–4.
17. DHR, *LEP*, p. 425.
18. Ibid, p. 427. In *LEP* DHR adds that the accelerator will not operate symmetrically downwards.
19. DHR's alternative title for the construction trades.
20. DHR, *LEP*, p. 410.
21. For an excellent discussion of this see G. Haberler, op cit., Ch. 5.
22. For a summary of the under-consumption school see G. Haberler, ibid. ch. 5.
23. W. T. Foster and W. Catchings, *Money*, (Boston, 1923) and *Profits*, (Boston, 1925).

24. DHR, 'The Monetary Doctrines of Messrs. Foster and Catchings', *QJE*, Vol. 43, (1929) pp. 473–99, reprinted in *EEA*, pp. 139–162.
25. See DHR, *SIF*, pp. 235–7.
26. On the connection between over-investment and under-consumption theories see also W. Fellner, Ch. 2 in H. Ellis (ed) *A Survey of Contemporary Economics*, (American Economic Association, Blakiston 1948).
27. Modern macro-textbooks tend to associate a *deficiency in spending* as the cause of unemployment with JMK. What must be appreciated is that JMK belonged neither to the under-consumption nor over-investment schools. He emphasised that unemployment is caused by a deficiency in both consumer spending and investment; the remedy is a general stimulation of demand. (*GT*, p. 325).
28. DHR, *SIF*, (1948), preface p. xiv.
29. Ibid, pp. 205, 241.
30. See Part II, Chap. 3, 'Saving in the Cycle . . .'.
31. See Part II, Chap. 7, 'The Robertsonian Theory of Interest'.
32. DHR, *SIF*, p. 254.
33. A. C. Pigou, *Industrial Fluctuations*, (Macmillan 1927).
34. In 1924 Pigou wrote: 'we have found as a dominating cause of trade cycles, wave-like swings in the minds of the business world between errors of optimism and errors of pessimism'. *Is Unemployment Inevitable?* (London, 1924).
35. JMK, *GT*, pp. 321–2.
36. J. S. Mill, *Principles of Political Economy*, (Longman, Green & Co., 1848).
37. J. Mills, 'Credit Cycles and the Origin of Commercial Panics', *Transactions of the Manchester Society*, (1867).
38. Ibid.
39. W. H. Beveridge, *Unemployment*, (London: Longman, Green & Co., 1909 and 1930).
40. See DHR, *SIF*, pp. 8–9, pp. 38–9.
41. Ibid, pp. 92–3.
42. See DHR, *Money*, (1928), pp. 159, 170.
43. DHR, *EMT*, p. 176.
44. DHR, 'Is Another Slump Coming', *The Listener*, (28th July, 1937) p. 174.
45. See Part III.
46. R. G. Hawtrey, *Good and Bad Trade*, (London: Macmillan, 1913).
47. DHR in fact saw two types of monetary theory. (*BPPL*, p. 2). Hawtrey's theory was the most extreme type where: 'the trade cycle is a purely monetary phenomenon'. The less extreme theory DHR associated with JMK (*Tract on Monetary Reform*) where monetary forces do not cause the cycle, but monetary policy can *prevent* the cycle occurring.
48. R. G. Hawtrey, op cit., p. 272.
49. Ibid, p. 98.
50. Ibid, p. 199.
51. Ibid.
52. See Part II, Chap. 9, 'Natural and Market Rates of Interest . . .'.
53. A comment by DHR in the preface of *Money*. (1948 ed.) p. xii.

54. *Cf.* R. G. Hawtrey's theory. DHR in the *SIF* chose, in particular, to comment upon the thesis of Bilgram and Levy, *The Causes of Business Depressions* (see *SIF*, p. 211).
55. See DHR, *SIF*, pp. 213ff.
56. The implication here is that money wages will lag behind prices during the recovery.
57. An argument which DHR used extensively in later writings, see pp. 161–4.
58. See Part II, Chap. 9, 'Natural and Market Rates of Interest . . .'. (See also *SIF*, pp. 219–21).
59. This was DHR's view of monetary theories in 1915. Later he had reason to qualify this view as a result of the analysis relating to 'lacking' found in *BPPL* Ch. 5, see Part II, Chap. 4, 'Robertson on Saving (1918–40)'.
60. 'Nature does not leap'. Found in the title page of A. Marshall, *Principles of Economics*, (Macmillan, 1890).
61. A. Marshall, *Economics of Industry*, 1925 ed. (London: Macmillan).
62. A. Marshall, *Money, Credit and Commerce*, (London: Macmillan, 1923).
63. J. B. Say, op. cit. (Part I: 1 Note 22).
64. DHR, *SIF*, preface (1948) p. xii.
65. See A. Marshall *Economics of Industry*, p. 154.
66. DHR, *SIF*, preface (1948) p. xii.
67. Ibid, pp. 200–5.
68. For a discussion of this point see J. N. Wolfe, 'Marshall and the Trade Cycle', *Oxford Economic Papers*. No. 1, (February 1956) pp. 90–101.
69. W. Mitchell, *Business Cycles*, (Burt Franklin, 1913).
    G. Hull, *Industrial Depressions*, (New York, 1911).
70. Defined as construction over and above necessary construction which consists principally of replacement investment.
71. W. Mitchell, *Business Cycles*, (1927) p. 107.
72. In his 1913 book Mitchell did not mention the acceleration principle. In later work he did utilise the principle in explaining the cycle.
73. 'A slow accumulation of stresses within the balanced system of business-stresses which ultimately undermine the conditions upon which prosperity rests', taken from W. Mitchell, *Readings in Business Cycle Theory*, p. 50.
74. K. Wicksell was perhaps the best example of an economist who emphasised price movements in his theory of the cycle; but his work was not read by DHR in preparing the *Study*.
75. A. Marshall, *Principles of Economics*, pp. 163, 710–11.
76. Taken from E. Eshag, op cit., p. 6.
77. A. Marshall, *Economics of Industry*, p. 154. This quote continues: 'it begins as soon as traders think that prices will not continue to fall: and with a revival of industry prices rise'.
78. DHR, *LEP*, p. 416.
79. Quoting from A. Marshall, *Principles of Economics*, pp. 710–11.
80. DHR, *SIF*, p. 235.
81. See, for example, A. Marshall, *Principles of Economics*, pp. 710–12, and *Money, Credit and Commerce*, pp. 249ff.

PART II   SAVING AND INVESTMENT IN THE TRADE
          CYCLE

1: INTRODUCTION

1. JMK, *Treatise on Money*, (London: Macmillan, 1930).
2. JMK, *The General Theory of Employment, Interest and Money*, (London:
   Macmillan, 1936).
3. J. W. Conard, *An Introduction to the Theory of Interest*, (Los Angeles:
   University of California Press, 1959).

2: BACKGROUND TO THE ROBERTSON–KEYNES DEBATE

1. DHR, an address to a Conference of Economics Teachers, Oxford, January
   4th, 1947 titled: 'The Frontiers of Economic Thought'. The brackets
   are mine. The man of genius is, of course, J. M. Keynes.
2. See R. Harrod, *Life of Keynes*, (Macmillan, 1951) later published as
   a Pelican Biography, (Penguin books, 1972).
3. JMK in fact attempted to persuade DHR to join him in the Treasury.
4. DHR, *EF*, p. 222.
5. Keynes, *Economic Consequences of the Peace*, (London: Macmillan, 1920).
6. DHR, *EF*, p. 222. The Treaty referred to is the *Treaty of Versailles*,
   signed at the end of World War I.
7. See JMK, *Economic Consequences of Mr. Churchill*, (London: Woolf,
   1925).
8. E.g., JMK contributed to the 'Liberal Yellow Book' — *Britain's Industrial
   Future*, working alongside Lloyd George on the Liberal Committee
   (1927).
9. In 1923 DHR delivered a lecture at the Summer School entitled 'The
   Ebb and Flow of Unemployment', *New Way* series, No. 6 (Daily
   News Ltd., 1923).
10. E.g. DHR also contributed to the 'Liberal Yellow Book' — *Britain's
    Industrial Future* (1927).
11. H. Johnson, 'Keynes and British Economics', in M. Keynes (ed), *Essays
    on John Maynard Keynes*, (Cambridge Univ. Press, 1975) p. 115.
12. D. Moggridge, (ed), *The Collected Writings of John Maynard Keynes*,
    Vols. XIII and XIV, (Macmillan, for the Royal Economic Society,
    1973). These contain 28 letters from DHR to JMK beginning on the
    27th February, 1925 and ending on 7th October, 1937 and 24 letters
    from JMK to DHR beginning on 28th September, 1913 and ending
    on 28th October, 1937.
13. Harrod, op cit., p. 436, (Pelican Biography edition 1972). Robertson was
    also a member of Keynes' Political Economy Club which met every
    Monday during term to discuss a paper written by either a 'selected
    economics undergraduate, or by one of the economics dons'. But this
    was only a limited forum for discussion between the two. But Harrod,
    ibid, p. 385, comments, for example, that Keynes (in 1922) read a
    paper on the 'Malthusian Devil' arguing that it was still with us.

In the discussion which followed: 'Robertson seemed to know what he was talking about, and I had an uncomfortable feeling that it was he, and not my master (Keynes), who was right on this occasion'.

14. Keynes and Professor J. S. Nicholson were the examiners on that occasion; Cannan and Foxwell acted as examiners in 1914 when Robertson was successful. On Keynes' flattery of Robertson's work see the letter from JMK to DHR, 28th September 1913. JMK, *CW*, Vol. XIII, p. 1.

15. Ibid, p. 1, 'A most brilliant and important contribution to the subject', was Keynes' reaction to the published version of the *Study*.

16. 'How Far are Bankers Responsible for the Alterations of Crisis and Depression?' Read at the Political Economy Club meeting, Hotel Cecil, (Dec. 1913). See JMK, *CW*, Vol. XIII, pp. 2–14.

17. JMK uses the expression 'deliberate' saving, the implication being that there is also undeliberate saving created by the expansion of credit.

18. JMK, *Tract on Monetary Reform*, (London: Macmillan, 1923).

19. JMK, *Treatise on Money*, (London: Macmillan, 1930).

20. See DHR, *BPPL*, Ch. 1, (p. 2).

21. See DHR, *SIF* (1948 ed.) preface p. xii.

22. Value theory related to relative as opposed to absolute prices.

23. See Part II, Chap. 4, 'Robertson on Saving (1918–40)'. Robertson wrote to Keynes in May 1925: 'What seemed to you howlers, may be only differences of emphasis and methods of approach'; the only point of substance was Keynes contention that real hoarding and new short lacking were the same; a point which Robertson accepted. See JMK, *CW*, Vol. XIII, p. 38.

24. This followed detailed correspondence from September 1924 to November 1925 concerned entirely with Keynes' early thoughts on what was to become the *Treatise on Money* and the drafts of DHR's *BPPL*. In relation to this latter book the correspondence covered chapters V and VI.

25. DHR, *BPPL*, p. 5.

26. JMK, *CW*, Vol. XIII, p. 39.

27. Ibid, p. 40.

28. JMK, *CW*, Vol. XIII, p. 51. In 1948, in the revised edition, Robertson wrote: 'The immeasurable debt which both the original and 1928 editions of this book owe to Mr. John Maynard Keynes has not been diminished by the lapse of time'.

29. But no correspondence remains over the drafts of *Money*, 1922.

30. F. A. von Hayek, *Prices and Production*, (London: George Routledge & Son Ltd., 1931; 2nd & enl. ed. 1935).

31. JMK, *GT*, pp. 79–85, (Papermac 12).

32. See later discussion of the Forced Saving Issue in Part II: 4.

33. JMK appears to have started work on the *Treatise* in July 1924, before the publication of *BPPL*, and it was published in 1930. See JMK, *CW*, Vol. XIII, p. 15.

34. JMK, *CW*, Vol. XIII, p. 16.

35. Ibid, pp. 104–8.

36. Letter from DHR to JMK January 8th, 1930, Robertson wrote on the Treatise: 'How full of meat it is .... It will be a noble book'. See JMK, *CW*, Vol. XIII, pp. 121–22.

37. Letter from DHR to JMK 7th January 1931, ibid, p. 202.
38. See Letter from DHR to JMK, 2nd May 1931, ibid, p. 211.
39. See *BPPL* (1949 ed.) preface p. xi.
40. Definitions and concepts will be made clearer in Part II: 4. (See JMK, *CW*, Vol. XIII, pp. 122–3).
41. Letter from DHR to JMK, 4th March, 1930. JMK, *CW*, Vol. XIII, p. 123.
42. *BPPL*, Preface to 1949 edition p. xi.
43. See Part II: 14 'The Value of Money' for a fuller discussion of this point. See JMK, *CW*, Vol. XIII, p. 91.
44. See Harrod, op cit., p. 482.
45. See DHR, 'Industrial Fluctuation and the Natural Rate of Interest', *EJ*, (Dec. 1934) pp. 650–66. It was the cause of the change in productivity which was responsible for the crisis.
46. See especially: DHR, 'Mr. Keynes' Theory of Money', *EJ*, (Sept. 1931) pp. 399–411, and 'Saving and Hoarding', *EJ*, (Sept., 1933) pp. 399–413. R. G. Hawtrey, 'Mr. Robertson and "Saving and Hoarding"', *EJ*, (Dec. 1933); see also the reply to DHR, pp. 709–12.
47. F. A. Von Hayek, 'Review of JMK's "Treatise on Money"', *Economica*, (August 1931) pp. 270–95.
48. Letter from DHR to JMK, 4th October, 1931. JMK, *CW*, Vol. XIII, p. 271.
49. Letter from JMK to DHR, 6th Oct. 1931. JMK, *CW*, Vol. XIII, p. 272.
50. Letter from JMK to DHR, 6th October, 1931, JMK, *CW*, Vol. XIII, p. 273.
51. Letter from DHR to JMK, 7th January, 1931, ibid, p. 202 also see p. 220.
52. See D. Moggridge, *Keynes*, (Macmillan, 1976) pp. 100–106.
53. The Cambridge 'Circus' met during the period January–May 1931. Its principal members included R. Kahn, J. Meade, J. & E. A. G. Robinson and P. Sraffa. They originally met to discuss the *Treatise*, but out of these meetings came the ideas for the *GT*. It is thought that Robertson only attended one meeting of the Circus. See JMK, *CW*, Vol. XIII, pp. 337–343. More recently Professor E. G. Davis of Carleton University has discovered a multiplier analysis in the work of R. G. Hawtrey. This analysis may have influenced JMK long before the 'circus' met. ('The Role of R. G. Hawtrey in Keynesian Economics', E. Davis, unpublished paper.)
54. Letter from DHR to JMK February 10th, 1935, ibid, p. 506. Even Robertson remarked on his comments on chapters 18 and 19: 'I'm afraid you feel the general tenor of my comments rather hostile'.
55. Letter from JMK to DHR, January 1935. See JMK, *CW*, Vol. XIII, pp. 495–6.
56. Letter from DHR to JMK 3rd February 1935, ibid, pp. 496–7.
57. Letter from DHR to JMK, 10th February 1935, ibid, p. 506.
58. Letter from JMK to DHR, 20th February, 1935, ibid, p. 520.
59. For those readers not yet familiar with some of these terms their meaning will be fully explained in later sections.

60. A. Marshall, *Principles of Economics*, (London: Macmillan, 1890).
61. A. C. Pigou, *Industrial Fluctuations*, (London: Macmillan, 1927).
62. The full quote should read: 'I regard Mr. Hawtrey as my grandparent and Mr. Robertson as my parent in the paths of errancy'. See JMK, *CW*, Vol. XIV, p. 202 and also JMK, 'Alternative Theories of the Rate of Interest', *EJ*, (June 1937) p. 242n.
63. DHR, *EF*, p. 164. DHR describes this occasion as: 'too memorable, too exceptional, to breed true appreciation or comprehension'.
64. He regarded himself as one of the spiritual grandsons of Marshall. Ibid, p. 164.
65. A. Marshall, *Money, Credit and Commerce*, (London: Macmillan, 1923).
66. Letters from A. Marshall to DHR dated 20th September, 1921 and 14th January, 1922.
67. A. C. Pigou, *Economics of Welfare*, (London: Macmillan, 1919).
68. DHR, *LEP*, p. 12.
69. See Part I: 1 2nd para.
70. Compare *BPPL* with A. C. Pigou's *Industrial Fluctuation*, (1927) (for example on the question of forced levies).
71. But see a letter from JMK to DHR, 31st August, 1937. JMK, *CW*, Vol. XIV, p. 250.
72. M. Labordère, 'Autour de la crise américaine de 1907' reproduced as an appendix to DHR, *SIF* (1948 reprint).
73. DHR, *SIF* (1948 reprint) p. xii.
74. Letter from DHR to JMK, February 3rd, 1935. JMK, *CW*, Vol. XIII, p. 504. 'I am *very* much out of sympathy with your treatment of what you call the classical and I call the modern economists!'
75. Letter from JMK to DHR, December 13th, 1936, reply from DHR to JMK 26th December, 1936. JMK, *CW*, Vol. XIV, pp. 89ff.
76. Letter from DHR to JMK December 29th, 1936, ibid, p. 95.
77. Ibid, p. 95.
78. DHR, *LEP*, p. 326. Robertson began a lecture in Cambridge, to undergraduates, on the 25th April, 1946 by using a similar description of Keynes' treatment of the neo-classical economist.
79. See JMK, *CW*, Vol. XIII, p. 243. The reviews by Hayek appeared in *Economica*, (August 1931 and February 1932).
80. Letter from DHR to T. Wilson, 31st October, 1953.
81. J. R. Hicks, 'The Monetary Theory of D. H. Robertson', *Economica*, New Series 9–10, (February 1942) p. 54.
82. T. Wilson, 'Robertson on Effective Demand and the Trade Cycle' *EJ*, (Sept. 1953) p. 555.
83. D. E. Moggridge, *Keynes*, (Macmillan, 1976) pp. 96–7.
84. DHR uses the phrase: 'dogs wag tails as well as tails dogs'. *LEP*, p. 420, taken from *EMT*, Essay No. 9.
85. Letter from DHR to JMK, 3rd February, 1935. JMK, *CW*, Vol. XIII, p. 497.
86. See DHR, *EMT*, Essay No. 9, pp. 114–121.
87. In the form of the Quantity Theory and the Cambridge Equation.
88. See Part II: 14 'The Value of Money'.
89. See letters from JMK to DHR, and DHR to JMK in February 1935,

JMK, *CW*, Vol. XIII pp. 510–19.
90. See Part II: 7 'The Robertsonian Theory of Interest'.
91. See for example, DHR, 'Industrial Fluctuation and the Natural Rate of Interest', *EJ*, (December 1934) pp. 650–56.
92. J. R. Hicks, op cit., p. 55.
93. DHR, *UAT*, p. 76.
94. A. Hansen, *Monetary Theory and Fiscal Policy*, (New York: McGraw-Hill, 1949) p. 81n. And T. Wilson, op cit., p. 555.
95. A. C. Pigou, *Lapses from Full-Employment*, (London: Macmillan, 1945).
96. Ibid, preface.
97. Letter from JMK to DHR 31st August, 1937. JMK, *CW*, Vol. XIV, p. 250. One of the papers referred to was DHR, 'The State and Economic Fluctuation', in *EMT*, Keynes' articles appeared in *The Times* between 12–14th June, 1937.
98. Letter from DHR to JMK, 29th December, 1936, ibid, p. 95, and letter from JMK to DHR, 13th December, 1936, ibid, p. 94.
99. E. A. G. Robinson, 'A Personal View', in M. Keynes (ed.), *Essays on John Maynard Keynes*, (Cambridge Univ. Press, 1975) p. 13.
100. There are a number of personal letters between JMK and DHR which indicate that their personal relationship was still very strong after 1936. The disagreement between them was on purely *academic* grounds.
101. Letter from JMK to his mother 25th July, 1944. Hicks finds this a somewhat condescending attitude. See *EMI*, p. 19. The second quotation is taken from a letter from JMK to Sir Richard Hopkins, 22nd July, 1944. See R. Harrod, op cit., p. 685.
102. Taken from the text of an unpublished introduction to a lecture to Cambridge Undergraduates dated 25th April, 1946.
103. Ibid.

3: SAVING IN THE CYCLE: THE ROBERTSONIAN APPROACH IN THE 'STUDY'

1. See Part II: 4 'Robertson on Saving (1918–40)'.
2. See Part I: 1 'Background to a Study of Industrial Fluctuation in 1915'.
3. DHR, *SIF*, (1948 ed.) preface p. xv. See also JMK, *CW*, Vol. XIII pp. 119–21.
4. M. Labordère, op cit.
5. W. Mitchell, *Business Cycles: The Problem and Its Setting*, (New York: Burt Franklin, 1st edn. 1913).
6. See JMK, *CW*, Vol. XIII, pp. 2–14.
7. G. Cassel, op cit., A. Spiethoff, op cit., see especially also the work of E. Von Boehm-Bawerk, e.g. *Capital and Interest*, (London: Macmillan, 1922).
8. DHR, *BPPL*, Chs. VI and VII.
9. A similar example was used by DHR in *LEP* pp. 34–35; although he pointed out that he did not believe in the 1950s that the 'real saving' thesis was totally valid for a monetary economy.

10. DHR, *Money*, Ch. V, (1922).
11. Although Robertson accepted that the shortage of real saving was a possible cause of the American crisis in 1907, he did not see it as an alternative to the over-investment theory outlined earlier. Crises could occur even where the stock of consumable goods was high. DHR, *SIF*, p. 180.
12. See W. Mitchell, op cit., pp. 10–11.
13. Insofar as Robertson went some way to support this thesis, one can recognise some of his discontent with the *under-consumption theory of the cycle*; for in the 'shortage of real saving' thesis there is an implication of under-saving during the expansion phase of the cycle, not over-saving; there is over-consumption, not under-consumption. The respective theories are complete opposites in this respect. See Part II: 4 'Robertson on Saving (1918–40)'.
14. DHR, *SIF* (1948 ed.) Appendix p. 1. Robertson comments, 'He did not appear to have any acquaintance with the works of those economists whose approach has most affinity with his own'.
15. Ibid, p. 1.
16. Ibid, pp. 1–31, English translation available from the author.
17. Ibid, p. 7.
18. JMK, *CW*, Vol. XIII, p. 1.
19. DHR, *SIF*, p. 171n.
20. M. Tugan-Baranowski *Les Crises Industrielles en Angleterre*, French ed., (Paris: Giard & Brière, 1913).
21. R. G. Hawtrey, *Good and Bad Trade*, op cit.
22. See DHR, review of *Good and Bad Trade*, *Cambridge Review* Nov 27th 1913 and review of *Les Crises Industrielles en Angleterre*, *EJ*, March 1914 pp. 81–9.
23. Aggregate money savings (by all individuals and businessmen) — is termed 'free capital'.
24. Capital goods, machinery, buildings etc. are called 'real capital' in Tugan-Baranowski's analysis.
25. See especially DHR, *BPPL*, Ch. 5.

4: ROBERTSON ON SAVING (1918–1940)

1. This was Robertson's term for saving. He had great difficulty in finding an appropriate word for his view of saving. In 1926 he rejected 'waiting', he thought 'abstinence' implied some moral judgement, and 'going without' was too clumsy. Hence he settled for 'lacking'. Later on, in the 1930s debate on Saving/Investment, he was forced to return to the use of the term saving. In his *LEP*, he did not use 'lacking', but 'waiting'. (See *LEP*, pp. 214–6).
2. DHR, *BPPL*, Ch. V, 'spontaneous lacking corresponds pretty well to what is ordinarily thought of as saving, and scarcely requires further definition', (p. 47).
3. DHR, 'Saving and Hoarding', in *EMI*, pp. 46–64. A similar definition is given much later in his *LEP*, p. 215.

4. DHR, *EMI*, p. 47.
5. S_t = voluntary saving on day (t),
     Y_{t-1} = income received on day (t − 1),
     C_t = consumer spending on day (t).
6. See DHR, *BPPL*, Chs. 6 and 7.
7. And also induced lacking, see pp. 106–7.
8. DHR, *EMI*, pp. 46–64.
9. DHR, *LEP*, p. 102.
10. Ibid, p. 102.
11. DHR, *BPPL*, p. 41.
12. DHR, *LEP*, p. 102, 'working' capital is preferred in *LEP*.
13. H. Henderson, *Supply and Demand*, (Cambridge Economic Handbooks, 1921) p. 124, and also by G. Cassel, *Theory of Social Economy*, (Unwin, 1923).
14. DHR described this view as that 'countenanced by Adam Smith and Jevons', *BPPL*, p. 42.
15. Assuming that no hoarding occurs; for a fuller discussion of this see B. Corry, *Money, Saving and Investment in English Economics, 1800–1850*, (Macmillan, 1962) pp. 18–19.
16. See DHR, *BPPL*, p. 42, Cf. DHR, *Money*, 1928, p. 103.
17. DHR, *Money*, Ch. V, and *BPPL*, Ch. 5.
18. Where W = circulating or working capital required each period,
     D = the production period,
     R = real output.
If the value-added is greater during the earlier stages of production then the circulating capital required will be somewhat greater than one half of the value of production in that production period.
19. The best example of which is found in JMK's *GT*.
20. See Part II: 6 'Saving in the Cycle'.
21. DHR, *BPPL*, p. 45. The categories of lacking so far outlined are not exhaustive. Of less importance is the distinction between direct and indirect lacking, the former occurring where lacking flows directly into investment, where, for example, an individual buys a capital good with his own spontaneous saving rather than financing the purchase by using the lacking of another individual (through the banks).
22. DHR also interprets Marshall's use of the term 'capital' in this manner, although there is convincing evidence that Marshall used it to depict the *real resources* which were free to be used for investment projects (see E. Eshag, *From Marshall to Keynes*, (Oxford: Basil Blackwell, 1963) pp. 46ff).
23. For a further discussion see DHR, *LEP*, pp. 102–3.
24. A. C. Pigou, *Industrial Fluctuation*, (London: Macmillan, 1927).
25. See later pp. 108ff.
26. See Part II: 2.
27. DHR, *Money*, pp. 90–93.
28. Ibid, p. 89.
29. Ibid, p. 90.
30. Robertson saw this mechanism as redistributing income away from the rentier and salaried classes.

31. See especially Part II: 14 'The Value of Money'.
32. Some may find it surprising that DHR chose not to alter the 1928 edition of *Money* in the light of his discovery of induced lacking in *BPPL*. The explanation is to be found in correspondence between DHR and D. Patinkin (letter from DHR to Patinkin 7.8.1956). *Money* was regarded by DHR as a general textbook, not requiring the detailed analysis of *BPPL* which was directed towards fellow academics; *BPPL* was the book from which DHR wanted his contribution to the inter-war debate to be judged.
33. The opposite of Automatic Stinting was called Automatic Splashing. This could be caused by net hoarding, or by a reduction in the money supply.
34. DHR, *BPPL*, pp. 74–77. See also Part II: 14 'The Value of Money'.
35. DHR cites Cannan as holding this view. See E. Cannan, *Economica*, Vol. 1, (January 1921) pp. 28–36.
36. See DHR, *BPPL*, pp. 71–72, 88–89.
37. See Part II: 9 'Natural and Market Rates of Interest and the Trade Cycle'.
38. See Part III: 2 'Robertson and the Price Level'.
39. By the time he wrote 'Saving and Hoarding' (EMI) in 1933 his attention had been brought to this by Hayek. See F. A. von Hayek, 'A Note on the Development of the doctrine of Forced Saving', *QJE*, Vol. 47, (1932–33) pp. 123–33.
40. See D. O'Brien, op cit., pp. 162–65, and T. Wilson, *Fluctuations in Income and Employment*, (Pitman, 1942) Ch. 1.
41. See J. Viner, *Studies in International Trade*, (London: Allen & Unwin, 1955) pp. 187–8.
42. J. Bentham, *Collected Works*, (Edinburgh, published 1843) but written as early as 1804. (Published as *Manual of Political Economy*, (edited by Bowring)). p. 44.
43. See L. Robbins, op cit., p. 146.
44. See Part II: 14, 'The Value of Money'.
45. See A. Marget, *Theory of Prices*, Vol. 1, pp. 307ff.
46. Adequate reference can be found to each of these writers in the works already mentioned by Hayek, O'Brien, and Corry.
47. See Part II: 7 'The Robertsonian Theory of Interest'.
48. See T. Wilson, *Fluctuations in Income and Employment*, (London: Pitman & Sons, 1942) pp. 11–12. Also T. Joplin, *Views on the Currency*, London 1826.
49. See L. Walras, *Théorie Mathématique du Billet de Banque*, (1879) reprinted in *Études d'Economie Politique Appliqué*, (Lausanne and Paris 1898) for further comment see pp. 152ff.
50. See Part II: 9 'Natural and Market Rates of Interest and the Trade Cycle'.
51. L. Von Mises, *Theorie des Geldes und der Umlaufsmittel*, (Münchën, 1912) J. Schumpeter, *Theorie der wirtschafflichen Entwicklung*, (Leipzig, 1912). For extensive reference to Hayek's work see pp. 155ff.
52. See Part II: 9 (as above) pp. 155ff.
53. DHR, *EMT*, pp. 81–2.

54. E. Eshag, op cit., pp. 59–60.
55. See, for example, A. Marshall, *Economics of Industry*, (London: Macmillan, 1892) pp. 165ff. A. Marshall, *Money Credit and Commerce*, was first published after *Money*, in 1923, therefore the discussion of income distribution and prices in this book could not have been an influence upon Robertson.
56. J. Schumpeter, *Theory of Economic Development*, 1911, (German edition). English translation 1934.
57. H. Henderson, op cit., Ch. 9. See the preface of the 1949 edition of *Money*.
58. DHR, Review of A. Aftalion, (op cit.), *EJ*, (March 1914).
59. See Part II: 2.
60. J. M. Keynes' paper delivered to the Political Economy Club, 3rd December, 1913, Hotel Cecil, London. Reproduced in JMK, *CW*, Vol. XIII, pp. 2–14.
61. J. M. Keynes, *GT*, p. 183.
62. Ibid, pp. 183ff. See also J. Bentham, *Collected Works*, (Edinburgh, 1843).
63. Letter from JMK to DHR, 28th May, 1925. JMK, *CW*, Vol. XIII, p. 35. That Keynes was aware of this is supported by this correspondence. Keynes wrote on Robertson's draft in 1925 of his forced saving thesis: 'the fact that at present there are unused resources, and you are unconsciously regarding as an argument in your favour the admitted power of inflation in some conditions to bring unused resources into use'.
64. See Part II: 10 'Saving, Investment & the Multiplier (1936 and after)'.
65. JMK introduced a concept of 'finance' in the post-*GT* debate. See pp. 200–2.
66. See JMK, *CW*, Vol. XIII, p. 21.
67. Which followed in the period May–November 1925 and covered Chs. 5 and 6 of the final book, that is those chapters which defined 'lacking' and the nature of lacking over the cycle.
68. Letter from JMK to DHR, 28th May, 1925. JMK, *CW*, Vol. XIII, p. 34.
69. Letter from DHR to JMK dated June 1925. Ibid, p. 39.
70. Ibid, p. 32.
71. Letter from DHR to JMK June 1925, ibid, p. 39.
72. Letter from JMK to DHR, May 31st 1925, ibid, p. 36.
73. DHR, *BPPL*, pp. 75–6. Note the similarity of this argument with what is later called the Pigou, or Real Cash Balance Effect. Here increased prices can increase the desire to hoard and lead to less spending. Pigou argued that lower prices would increase the real value of cash balances and reduce the desire to hoard and hence increase spending.
74. See Part II: 14. 'The Value of Money'.
75. In a letter to T. Wilson (31.10.53) DHR writes: 'It was Keynes who *made me* introduce "Induced Lacking"'.
76. Letter from JMK to DHR, 31st May, 1925. JMK, *CW*, Vol. XIII, p. 38.
77. Letter from JMK to DHR 10th November, 1925, ibid, p. 40.

78. See Part II: 2.
79. This was a draft of chapter 23. Reproduced in JMK, *CW*, Vol. XIII, pp. 83ff.
80. It is interesting to note that Keynes had argued in this context that wherever investment and voluntary saving are equal prices must change, exactly the same theory as that of Robertson.
81. See JMK, *CW*, Vol. XIII, pp. 104–8.
82. See J. M. Keynes 'The Pure Theory of Money — A Reply to Dr. Hayek', *Economica*, (November 1931). Reproduced in JMK, *CW*, Vol. XIII, pp. 243–56.
83. F. A. von Hayek, *Prices and Production*, op cit.

5: CRITICAL COMMENT ON THE FORCED SAVING THESIS AND THE ORIGINALITY OF ROBERTSONIAN THEORY

1. In the early classical literature see J. Bentham, *Economic Writings*, (ed. W. Stark), (London: Allen & Unwin for the Royal Economic Society, 1952), see especially Vol. 1, p. 237. See also for an excellent discussion B. Corry, op cit. pp. 55–61 and D. O'Brien, *The Classical Economists*, (Oxford: Clarendon Press, 1975) pp. 162–5.
2. See, for example, F. Lavington, *The English Capital Markets*, pp. 130ff.
3. F. W. Taussig, *Principles of Economics*, 3rd Ed., (New York: Macmillan, 1939) Vol. I, p. 357. See also DHR, *BPPL*, p. 52.
4. See especially R. G. Hawtrey, *Capital and Employment*, (Longmans, 1937) Ch. VIII.
5. Although the debate between Keynes, Robertson and Hawtrey does cover this to some extent. See various issues of the *EJ* 1932–4. Letters from R. G. Hawtrey to DHR are also critical of the forced saving thesis in this period. (R. G. Hawtrey correspondence can be consulted in Churchill College Library, Cambridge).
6. R. G. Hawtrey, *Capital and Employment*, p. 252: 'If there is any net addition to wealth, it is because the recipients of this money do not spend the whole of it. But that is *voluntary* not forced saving'.
7. The following quotation from a draft of R. G. Hawtrey's comments upon Robertson's forced saving thesis is typical of this criticism: 'If the creation of new money continues for a considerable period the diminution of stocks of goods will become perceptible. Prices will begin to rise. Alongside the rise of prices due to the increase in the amount of money in circulation, a *temporary* rise is further called for to enable traders to reconstitute their stocks. Prices must be high enough to restrict sales to something less than output. It is through this temporary rise of prices above replacement value that the additional working capital is paid for. The holders of the depleted stocks of commodities are enabled, as it were, to levy a tax upon the consumer to make good the deficiency.
'Here again Mr. Robertson's analysis is vitiated in its application

to the real world by the assumption that the retail price level is always instantaneously adjusted to any variation in demand'. (in the R. G. Hawtrey Correspondence, Churchill College Library, Cambridge)
8. DHR, *Money*, Ch. V.
9. R. G. Hawtrey, *Capital and Employment*, p. 253.
10. However, some of the early expositors of forced saving were aware of this. See B. Corry, op cit., pp. 55–7 also J. Bentham op cit., p. 330.
11. See, for example, JMK, *CW*, Vol. XIV, p. 70.
12. See Part II: 10 'Saving, Investment and the Multiplier (1936 and after)'.
13. J. Robinson, *An Introduction to the Theory of Employment*, (London: Macmillan, 1937) Ch. III.
14. See Part II: 10 (as above).
15. S. Strigl, *Kapital Und Produktion*, (Vienna, 1934) p. 195.

6: SAVING IN THE CYCLE

1. See DHR, *LEP*, Part 2, p. 216.
2. It was also utilised by Lionel Robbins.
3. DHR, *SIF*, (1948 ed.) preface xvi.
4. See the preface to *BPPL*.
5. DHR, *BPPL*, p. 79n.
6. See earlier Part II, Chs. 3 and 4.
7. DHR, *BPPL*, Ch. 2.
8. DHR 'Industrial Fluctuation and the Natural Rate of Interest', *EJ*, (December 1934) pp. 650–656, see especially p. 653.
9. DHR, *EMT*, p. 173.
10. DHR, ibid, p. 175.
11. This will be demonstrated later in a comparison of the theories of DHR and Hayek see pp. 154ff.
12. DHR, *BPPL*, pp. 75–6.
13. DHR, ibid, p. 76.
14. DHR, ibid, p. 74.
15. G. Cassel, *Theory of Social Economy*, Vol. 2, (London: Fisher Unwin Ltd., 1923) p. 594.
16. Robertson attributed this argument to Hastings, *Costs and Profits*, Ch. VI.
17. DHR, *BPPL*, Ch. VII & Ch. V.
18. Ibid, p. 91.
19. On banking policy see Part II: 9 'Natural and Market Rates of Interest . . .'.
20. A. C. Pigou, *Industrial Fluctuation*, (London: Macmillan, 1927) and F. von Hayek, *Monetary Theory of the Trade Cycle* and *Prices and Production*, (London: Routledge & Sons, 1935). It would be unfair to omit the name of Lionel Robbins who recognised the Forced Saving Thesis, possibly under the influence of the work of Hayek. Also A. MacFie, *Theories of the Trade Cycle*, (London: Macmillan, 1934) followed

Robertson's views on forced and voluntary saving, see especially chapter VI.

21. A year later than *BPPL*.
22. A. C. Pigou, op cit., pp. 146ff.
23. Ibid, p. 141.
24. Ibid, p. 151. His discussion was 'an interlude in the main argument'. It represented a comment upon the mathematical appendixes of *BPPL*.
25. Ibid, pp. 253ff.
26. Pigou's theory of fluctuation is discussed elsewhere see Part I, Ch. 7. There were possible monetary causes of fluctuation in Pigou's theory, but these were less important than the real and psychological causes. See Pigou, ibid, Part I, Ch. VIII.
27. Note again the similarity to Robertson's thesis.
28. A. C. Pigou, op cit., pp. 251–2.
29. F. von Hayek, 'A Note on the Development of the Doctrine of "Forced Saving"', *QJE*, Vol. 47, (1932–3) pp. 123–133.
30. F. von Hayek, *Monetary Theory of the Trade Cycle*, (1932 ed.) pp. 218–20. One possible explanation of this is that he is assuming that productivity is increasing. If prices are stable, those members of the workforce on fixed money incomes are unable to share in the increased production by increasing their consumption; they are thus forced to save.
31. F. von Hayek, *Prices and Production*, p. 57.
32. See R. Hawtrey, *Capital and Employment*, p. 235 and G. Haberler, *Prosperity and Depression*, p. 44.
33. J. R. Hicks, *Critical Essays in Monetary Theory*, (Oxford: Clarendon Press, 1967) Ch. 5, Ch. 12.
34. Ibid, p. 208.
35. I owe a debt for this section of the book to the comments and work of Miss S. Shenoy of the Cranfield School of Management who has researched the work of F. Hayek on the trade cycle.
36. See pp. 155ff.
37. G. Haberler, op cit., Ch. 3. A theory of over-investment where over-investment is caused by monetary forces.
38. See F. von Hayek, *Monetary Theory of the Trade Cycle*, pp. 182ff.
39. F. von Hayek, ibid, p. 177. Hayek calls this theory the 'additional credit theory of the trade cycle'.
40. Ibid, p. 168.
41. Ibid, p. 226.
42. F. von Hayek, *Profit, Interest and Investment*, Collection of Essays (London: Routledge & Sons, 1939) see especially pp. 3–71.
43. See G. Haberler, op cit., Ch. 13, also R. G. Hawtrey, *Capital and Employment*, pp. 248–52.
44. See especially G. N. Halm, *Monetary Theory*, (Toronto: Blakiston Co., 1942) Ch. 20 and G. Haberler, op cit., Ch. 13. It is not within the scope of this thesis to examine the validity of the 'Ricardo effect', but in general economists have been unimpressed by its application to cycle theory.

7: THE ROBERTSONIAN THEORY OF INTEREST

1. DHR, *UAT*, p. 83. Robertson complains of the over-emphasis upon the rate of interest.
2. This is most obvious in reading JMK, *CW*, Vols. XIII and XIV.
3. See Part II: 14 'The Value of Money'.
4. See DHR, *LEP*, Part II Chs. IV, V & VI. *Cf.* DHR, 'Industrial Fluctuation and the Natural Rate of Interest', *EJ*, (December 1934) pp. 650–56.
5. See pp. 142–5.
6. See pp. 206–7.
7. F. von Hayek, op cit., and DHR, 'Industrial Fluctuation and the Natural Rate of Interest', op cit.
8. DHR, *EMI*, p. 151.
9. DHR, *LEP*, p. 376.
10. This might arise through an increase in the marginal productivity of capital brought about by, for example, a new invention; this increases the marginal productivity of using loanable funds by entrepreneurs; the rate of return on capital increases, and hence raises the demand for loanable funds and the natural rate of interest. If the banks react by increasing the money supply, increasing the supply of funds, and holding the interest rate constant, the natural rate will then exceed the actual market rate of interest. This argument disguises some of the complexities which will be discussed later. (See Part II: 9).
11. E. Boehm-Bawerk, *Recent Literature on Interest*, (London and New York: Macmillan, 1903).
12. JMK, *GT*, Ch. 13.
13. See for example, DHR, *UAT*, p. 83, and 'What has happened to the Rate of Interest', *Three Banks Review*, (March 1949) pp. 15–31. Also *UAT* p. 97, and 'Some Notes on the Theory of Interest'. *EMI*, pp. 202–22.
14. DHR, *LEP*, pp. 231ff; although DHR had made specific reference to additional supply being provided by the liberation of depreciation quotas (p. 376).
15. DHR, *BPPL*.
16. DHR, *LEP*, p. 231.
17. In terms of the Cambridge Equation, hoarding could be recognised by a change in the value of 'K', the proportion of the individual's stock of money holdings to his level of money income. If 'K' increased, the supply of loanable funds would be diminished, and vice versa.
18. See Part II: 11. 'Robertson and the Liquidity Preference Theory of Interest'.
19. The ease with which they can be transferred back into cash.
20. DHR, *LEP*, pp. 231ff; this reference represents the most sophisticated discussion of the influences on the supply of loanable funds in Robertsonian literature.
21. DHR, *EF*, p. 5.
22. A. Marshall, *Principles of Economics*, p. 235.
23. G. Cassel, *Nature and Necessity of Interest*, 1903.

24. Ibid, pp. 147, 155. Cassel writes: 'in a broad sense it might be said that capital is just as willingly supplied at 3% as at 6%!'.
25. DHR, *EF*, p. 14.
26. See especially 'Industrial Fluctuation and the Natural Rate of Interest', *EJ*, (December 1934) pp. 650–56, and *LEP*, pp. 231ff.
27. DHR, *LEP*, pp. 231ff. This represents an enlargement of DHR, 'Some Notes on the Theory of Interest' reprinted in *EMI*, pp. 202–222.
28. See also DHR, *EMI*, p. 202. This is taken from a chapter written by DHR in *Money, Trade and Economic Growth*, essays in honour of Prof. J. Williams, (New York: Macmillan, 1951).
29. DHR, *LEP*, p. 240.
30. F. Ramsey, 'A Mathematical Theory of Saving', *EJ*, (December 1928) pp. 543–59; for a fuller discussion of this model see (Conspard, *An Introduction to the Theory of Interest*, pp. 83–9.
31. The term used by DHR, see *EMI*, p. 205.
32. DHR, *BPPL*, p. 77.
33. See, for example, JMK, *CW*, Vol. XIV.
34. See Part II: 4 'Robertson on Saving (1918–40)'.
35. See especially DHR, *EMI*, pp. 150–233.
36. See DHR, *UAT*, pp. 102ff, and *LEP*, pp. 216ff.
37. F. Ramsay, op cit., A. Lerner, *The Economics of Control*, (New York: Macmillan, 1944).
38. DHR, *UAT*, p. 104.
39. DHR, *EMI*, pp. 150–87; Given as a lecture at the London School of Economics, (Summer Term, 1939).
40. Ibid, p. 152.
41. DHR, *LEP*, pp. 224ff.
42. A. Lerner, op cit., pp. 330–8. See DHR, *UAT*, p. 103.
43. Ibid, p. 103.
44. DHR, *LEP*, pp. 226ff.
45. A. Lerner, 'On the Marginal Productivity of Capital and the Marginal Efficiency of Investment', *Journal of Political Economy*, Vol. 61, (1953) pp. 1–14.
46. DHR, *LEP*, p. 228; 'its expected net quasi-rent represents a smaller and smaller rate of return on its cost of construction'.
47. Ibid, p. 229.
48. Ibid, p. 222.
49. Ibid, p. 219.
50. Ibid, p. 220. Widening is defined as 'An increase both in capital and in output, and not necessarily, an initial increase in capital per unit of time'.
51. Ibid, p. 221.
52. It may be that net hoarding rather than net dishoarding will take place, but this does not alter the conclusion of this section.
53. The elasticity of money with respect to the rate of interest will depend upon from where the change in money originates. If it is created by the monetary authority then it can be expected to be insensitive to the rate of interest. If it arises from the excess liquidity position

of commercial banks it may well be sensitive to changes in the rate of interest.
54. In which case the supply curve on the previous diagram must intersect with the positive axis. ($\Delta M = 0$)
55. DHR, *LEP*, p. 247.
56. See DHR, *EMI*, pp. 194–5.

8: ORIGINS OF THE ROBERTSONIAN APPROACH TO THE THEORY OF INTEREST

1. JMK, *GT*, p. 186.
2. See E. Eshag, *From Marshall to Keynes*, (Oxford, 1963) Ch. 3.
3. DHR, *EMI*, p. 151, and *LEP*, p. 212.
4. DHR, *LEP*, p. 213.
5. See Part II: 9 'Natural and Market Rates of Interest and the Trade Cycle'.
6. This failure is most evident in his criticism of Keynes' treatment of Marshall in which Keynes uses the Marshallian 'capital' to mean capital goods; Robertson believes that the only legitimate meaning of this term is investible funds and not *real* capital. See DHR, *UAT*, p. 102n.
7. E. Eshag, op cit., pp. 45ff.
8. See Part II: 9 (as above).
9. E. Eshag, op cit., p. 46.
10. Ibid, p. 47.
11. DHR, *UAT*, p. 102.
12. In fact DHR quoted directly from Marshall on the influence of the rate of interest (DHR, *LEP*, p. 239).
13. A. Marshall, *Principles of Economics*, p. 229 (1920 edition).
14. See E. Eshag, op cit., p. 50.
15. DHR, *UAT*, p. 102.
16. A. Marshall, *Money Credit and Commerce*, (London, 1923) p. 254.
17. Taken from DHR, *LEP*.
18. DHR, *LEP*, p. 72.
19. DHR, Alternative Theories of the Rate of Interest, *EJ*, Vol. 47, (1937) p. 428.
20. JMK, *GT*, Book IV.
21. DHR, 'Alternative Theories of the Rate of Interest', *EJ*, Vol. 47, (1937) p. 428.

9: NATURAL AND MARKET RATES OF INTEREST AND THE TRADE CYCLE

1. DHR, 'Industrial Fluctuation and the Natural Rate of Interest', *EJ*, (December 1934) pp. 650–56.
2. See T. Wilson, *Fluctuations in Income and Employment*, (London: Pitman, 1942) p. 9n.

3. A. Smith, *Wealth of Nations*, (London, 1904 ed.) Vol. 1, p. 337.
4. J. S. Mill, *The Parliamentary History and Review*, (1826) p. 646.
5. See, for example, H. Thornton, *Paper Credit*, p. 235.
6. Taken from T. Wilson, op cit., p. 9n.
7. A. Marget, op cit.
8. D. Patinkin, *Money, Interest and Prices*, (New York: Harper and Row, 1965 ed.) p. 631, Appendix J.
9. See earlier pp. 108–9.
10. K. Wicksell, *Lectures on Political Economy*, Vol. 2, pp. 209ff. See also DHR, *EMT*, p. 127.
11. K. Wicksell, ibid, Vol. 5, p. 220.
12. See G. Haberler, op cit., pp. 34ff.
13. T. Tooke, *Lectures on Political Economy*, p. 202.
14. DHR, *BPPL*, p. 99.
15. This is developed later see pp. 158–61.
16. F. von Hayek, *Monetary Theory of the Trade Cycle*, pp. 179–180. Wicksell had similarly made this very point in relation to price movements, emphasising that the longer the difference between the two rates persisted, this being determined by the elasticity of the volume of currency to changes in interest, the greater would be the effect upon prices. (K. Wicksell, *Geldzins Und Guterpreise*, p. 101).
17. F. von Hayek, *Profit and Interest and Investment*, 1939.
18. F. von Hayek, *Monetary Theory and the Trade Cycle*, p. 188.
19. Ibid, Ch. 4.
20. Ibid.
21. JMK, op cit.
22. See L. Klein, *The Keynesian Revolution*, (London: Macmillan, Papermac, 1965) p. 21.
23. See L. Klein, op cit., Ch. 1.
24. This is an observation which has been made by J. Hicks, *Critical Essays in Monetary Theory*, (Oxford University Press) p. 201.
25. DHR, 'Industrial Fluctuation and the natural rate of interest' was a comment upon the Wicksellian theory of Hayek, *Prices and Production* (1931) and J. M. Keynes, *Treatise on Money*, (1930).
26. See B. Thomas, 'The Monetary Doctrines of Professor Davidson', *EJ*, Vol. 45, (1935) pp. 36ff.
27. DHR, *EMT*, p. 149.
28. JMK, *GT*, p. 242.
29. DHR, 'Some Notes on Mr Keynes' General Theory of Employment', *QJE*, Nov. 1936, pp. 168–91.
30. See DHR, *EMT*, p. 148.
31. This was Robertson's term for those looking at monetary equilibrium by considering natural and market rates.
32. See DHR, *EMT*, pp. 148ff.
33. See Part II: 11 and 12.
34. See Part II: 12 and 13.
35. e.g. through invention. Assuming initially that natural and market rates of interest coincide at R_1.

36. See Part II: 4. 'Robertson on saving (1918–40)'.
37. An assumption which Robertson appears to make (*EMI*, p. 66).
38. It is interesting to note the contents of a letter from Robertson to T. Wilson dated 31.10.53: 'Later in my own thoughts about the trade cycle, I came to lay great stress, following Cassel, on the changes in saving due to changes in the distribution of income during a cycle'.
39. See DHR, *EMI*, p. 225, also D. Patinkin, *Money Interest and Prices*, note J, pp. 630–3. In a letter to D. Patinkin, Robertson writes: 'Even when the inflation is over, we may find that the curve of voluntary savings has been displaced to the right, owing to the distortion of contracts which has occurred'. (7th August, 1956).
40. Hayek in particular, op cit.
41. See Part II: 3 'Saving in the Cycle'.
42. DHR, *EMI*, p. 68.
43. The exception being according to Robertson the crisis of 1907.
44. DHR, *EMI*, p. 68.
45. DHR, ibid, p. 71.
46. Robertson did not return in later publications to the distinction which he had made between the quasi-natural and the natural rates of interest. It must be borne in mind however, that the Hicks-Hansen interpretation of Keynes' *GT*, which was accepted to a large degree by Keynesians, took the *GT* a good way towards the above Wicksellian analysis. As Hicks pointed out ('Mr Keynes and the "Classics"', *Econometrica*, Vol. V, No. 2, April 1937), the intersection of IS and LM curves can be regarded in special circumstances as an equating of natural and market rates of interest.

10: SAVING, INVESTMENT AND THE MULTIPLIER (1936 AND AFTER)

1. JMK, *GT*, p. 63.
2. Letter from DHR to JMK, 3rd February 1935. JMK, *CW*, XIII, p. 497. (See also *Money* 1949 edition, Ch. 10).
3. B. Ohlin, 'Some Notes on the Stockholm Theory of Savings and Investment', *EJ*, Vol. 47, (June 1937) pp. 211–240.
4. F. Lutz, 'The Outcome of the Saving–Investment Discussion', *QJE*, Vol. 52, (1937–8) pp. 588–614.
5. JMK, *GT*, Ch. 10.
6. DHR, *EMT*, p. 61. According to DHR, Keynes proceeds to 'define an elephant's trunk and its proboscis in identical terms, and then to enter upon a complicated discussion of the biological principles which ensure that the trunk is always equal to the proboscis'.
7. The value of the multiplier is equal to: $1 \div (1 - \text{marginal propensity to consume})$.
8. JMK, *GT*, p. 122. Keynes wrote: 'the logical theory of the multiplier which holds good continuously, without time lags, at all moments of time'.

9. JMK, *GT*, p. 117. JMK remains faithful to this view in 1937. See JMK, 'Alternative theories of the rate of interest', *EJ*, (June 1937) pp. 241–52. Reprinted in JMK, *CW*, Vol. XIV, p. 210.
10. See JMK, *CW*, Vol. XIV, p. 57.
11. Ibid, pp. 7ff. Correspondence between JMK and J. R. Hicks.
12. See especially letter from JMK to J. R. Hicks, 31st August, 1936, reproduced in JMK, *CW*, Vol. XIV, p. 71.
13. This is a point recognised also by Hicks. Letter from Hicks to JMK, (2nd September, 1936) ibid, p. 73.
14. See Part II: 2. 'Background to the Robertson–Keynes Debate'.
15. R. Kahn, 'The Relation of Home Investment to Unemployment', *EJ*, (June 1931).
16. See G. Shackle, *The Years of High Theory*, Ch. 14, (Cambridge University Press, 1967).
17. G. Haberler, op cit., p. 227.
18. A. Marshall, *Principles of Economics*, p. 711.
19. Ibid, p. 710.
20. DHR, *LEP*, p. 239.
21. Letter from DHR to JMK December 29th, 1936. See JMK, *CW*, Vol. XIV, p. 97.
22. Letter from DHR to JMK, 3rd February, 1935, JMK, *CW*, p. 497.
23. JMK, *GT*, p. 123.
24. J. Robinson, *An Introduction to the Theory of Employment*, (London: Macmillan, 1937) pp. 20–1.
25. DHR, *EMI*, p. 141. Also DHR, *EMT*, p. 183.
26. DHR, *LEP*, p. 423.
27. DHR, 'Some Notes on Mr. Keynes' General Theory of Employment', *QJE*, Vol. 51, (1936–7) pp. 168–191.
28. DHR, *LEP*, p. 421.
29. Ibid, p. 421.
30. Ibid, p. 422.
31. JMK, 'The ex-ante Theory of Interest', *EJ*, (December 1937) pp. 241–52, especially pp. 247–8.
32. Ibid.
33. Ibid.
34. JMK, *GT*, pp. 95–6.
35. A belief which Keynes himself might have held had he thought more in terms of a dynamic rather than a static multiplier.
36. JMK, *GT*, Ch. 8.
37. DHR, *LEP*, pp. 424–5.
38. J. S. Duesenberry, *Income, Saving and the Theory of Consumer Behaviour*, (Harvard University Press, 1949).
39. Ibid, p. 421.
40. DHR, *Money*, p. 212.
41. DHR, *LEP*, p. 424.
42. Not utilised by DHR in his comments on the *GT*, but an argument acknowledged in a letter from DHR to T. Wilson 31.10.53.
43. DHR, *EC*.

44. DHR, *EMT*, p. 120.
45. DHR, *Money*, p. 212.
46. In a letter to T. Wilson (31.10.53), DHR admits to being a 'little naughty' in relation to the multiplier, but does not feel even so that he can do more than remove 'little' before 'brick' in his assessment of the multiplier's importance.

11: ROBERTSON AND THE LIQUIDITY PREFERENCE THEORY OF INTEREST

1. See Part II: 7 'The Robertsonian Theory of Interest'.
2. See, for example, G. Ackley, *Macroeconomic Theory*, (Collier-Macmillan, 1961).
3. JMK, *GT*, p. 165.
4. Ibid, p. 167.
5. Ibid, p. 167.
6. Ibid, p. 167.
7. See Part II: 7 'The Robertsonian Theory of Interest'.
8. JMK, *GT*, p. 171. (Unless, according to Keynes, a fall in the rate of interest causes the level of income to increase and necessitates a greater transactionary demand for money, or, additionally, if the fall in the cost of holding cash in terms of the interest rate reward foregone, leads to some increase in transactionary demand.)
9. It is also a motive which economists have searched for in pre-*GT* literature. See pp. 207–9.
10. JMK, *GT*, pp. 199ff.
11. Ibid, p. 202.
12. Ibid, p. 201.
13. JMK, 'Alternative theories of the rate of interest', *EJ*, Vol. 47, (1937) pp. 241–52. See pp. 200–2.
14. See for example DHR, *EMI*, pp. 150–169 and especially DHR, 'Some notes on Mr. Keynes' General Theory of Employment', *QJE*, Vol. 51, (1937) pp. 168–191.
15. See Part II: 7 'The Robertsonian Theory of Interest'.
16. See Part II: 9 'Natural and Market Rates of Interest and the Trade Cycle'.
17. Ibid.
18. If disposable income falls, consumption will decline, giving the appearance of an increase in the propensity to save out of total income before taxation. It also yields less total saving since disposable income is reduced. DHR did not comprehend this fact (see *LEP* p. 387), failing to appreciate the paradox of thrift.
19. JMK, *GT*, p. 165. See also DHR, *EMI*, p. 167.
20. JMK, ibid, p. 185, and DHR ibid, p. 160.

21. JMK, *GT*, p. 178, see also p. 166 for an alternative view of Keynes on the desire to save and the rate of interest.
22. For example by the time Hicks', 'Keynes and the "Classics"', had been shown to him.
23. See JMK, *CW*, Vol. XIV, pp. 1–35 and JMK, *CW*, Vol. XIII, pp. 522ff.
24. JMK, *CW*, Vol. XIII, pp. 522–3. Letter from JMK to DHR 14th March, 1935.
25. JMK, *CW*, Vol. XIV, p. 12. Letter from R. G. Hawtrey to JMK, 6th March, 1936. See also pp. 15 and 16, letter from JMK to Hawtrey, 24th March, 1936.
26. JMK, *CW*, Vol. XIII, p. 515. Letter from JMK to DHR 20th February, 1935.
27. JMK, *CW*, Vol. XIV, p. 34. Letter from Joan Robinson to JMK, 29th May, 1936.
28. See Part II: 10 'Saving, Investment and the Multiplier (1936 and after)'.
29. JMK, *GT*, pp. 140, 165, 184ff.
30. DHR, 'Some Notes on Mr. Keynes' General Theory of Employment', *QJE*, (1937) pp. 182–183.
31. DHR, *LEP*, p. 388.
32. See p. 147.
33. JMK, *GT*, p. 207; 'I know of no example hitherto'.
34. DHR, *EMI*, p. 175.
35. Ibid, p. 174: 'the rate of interest is what it is because it is expected to become other than it is'.
36. See pp. 205–7.
37. See JMK, *CW*, Vol. XIV.

12: LOANABLE FUNDS VERSUS LIQUIDITY PREFERENCE — THE HICKS-HANSEN FRAMEWORK

1. See in particular JMK, 'Alternative theories of the rate of interest', *EJ*, (June 1937) pp. 241–52 (reprinted in JMK, *CW*, Vol. XIV, pp. 201–15) and JMK 'Mr. Keynes on Finance', *EJ*, (June 1938) pp. 314–322.
2. J. R. Hicks, 'Mr. Keynes and the classics', *Economica*, Vol. 5, (April 1937) pp. 147–55 and A. Hansen, *A Guide to Keynes*, Chapter 7, (New York: McGraw-Hill, 1953).
3. See A. Hansen, op cit., Ch. 7, pp. 140–141. DHR had argued that the supply curve for loanable funds was only determinate if the level of money income was assumed constant. He was therefore aware of the problem of indeterminacy (see JMK, *CW*, Vol. XIV, p. 97).
4. See Part III.
5. See JMK, *CW*, Vol. XIV, p. 79. Letter from Keynes to J. Hicks, 31st March 1937: 'I found it very interesting and really have next to nothing to say by way of criticism'.

6. As below:

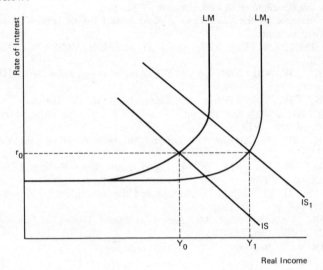

7. See JMK, *CW*, Vol. XIV, p. 80.
8. JMK, 'Alternative theories of the rate of interest', *EJ*, (June 1937). See also G. Haberler, op cit., p. 216.
9. DHR, *UAT*, p. 105, Cf. R. Harrod, *Towards a Dynamic Economics*, (London: Macmillan, 1948) p. 67.
10. DHR, 'Industrial Fluctuation and the Natural Rate of Interest', *EJ*, (December 1934) pp. 650–56. (Reprinted in DHR, *EMI*, pp. 64–74).
11. Robertson was also convinced that such an attempt would almost inevitably lead to confusion — as he suggests it did for Keynes (DHR, *UAT*, p. 105).
12. See especially DHR, *LEP*, pp. 384–9, also DHR, *EMT*, pp. 18–21. See also H. Johnson, 'Some Cambridge Controversies in Monetary Theory', *Review of Economic Studies*, Vol. 19, pp. 97–8 and DHRs comments pp. 107–8; also for a discussion of this point see A. Lerner, 'Alternative Formulations of the Theory of Interest', *EJ*, (June 1938) p. 229.
13. H. Johnson, op cit., p. 97, agreed by DHR, p. 107.
14. DHR, *LEP*, p. 386.
15. See Part I: 2 'The Nature of Industrial Fluctuation . . .'.
16. JMK, *GT*, p. 167.
17. Ibid, p. 174, see also JMK, 'Alternative theories of the rate of interest', *EJ*, (June 1937) p. 250.
18. Taken from DHR, *UAT*, p. 90, but derived by DHR from an article

by J. R. Hicks 'World Recovery after War — a theoretical analysis', *EJ*, (June 1947) pp. 151–164.
19. See Part II: 2 'Background to the Robertson–Keynes Debate'.
20. JMK, *GT*, p. 166.
21. DHR, *LEP*, p. 213.
22. DHR, 'Alternative theories of the rate of interest', *EJ*, (September 1937) p. 431.
23. As Keynes seems to imply, *GT*, p. 174 (last sentence).
24. See DHRs views on this, Part II: 7 'The Robertsonian Theory of Interest'.
25. DHR, *EMI*, pp. 165–6.
26. DHR, 'Alternative theories of the rate of interest', *EJ*, (September, 1937) p. 431. See also DHR, *EMI*, pp. 165–6.
27. DHR, *EMI*, p. 165.
28. Ibid, pp. 166–7.
29. H. Johnson, op cit., pp. 96–7.
30. This problem is commented upon at length in J. Tobin, 'Liquidity Preference as Behaviour towards Risk', *Review of Economic Studies*, Vol. 25, (February 1958) pp. 65–86. It prompted Tobin to develop the probability distribution approach.
31. DHR, *LEP*, p. 381.
32. In the first case:

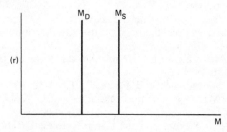

no determinant rate exists.
In the second:

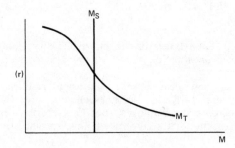

M_T is interest elastic.

33. See pp. 177ff. A kinder interpretation of the *GT* would suggest that the distinction between Bonds and Money was only an expository device: Keynes was anxious to distinguish between liquid and illiquid assets.
34. See DHR, *UAT*, pp. 78–9 also *LEP*, pp. 381ff. See also chapter by W. Fellner 'Employment Theory and Business Cycles', in *A Survey of Contemporary Economics*, (edited by H. Ellis), (Philadelphia: Blakiston Co., 1948).
35. Ibid, p. 388.
36. Ibid, p. 399.
37. Ibid, pp. 399ff.
38. See Part II: 11 'Robertson and the Liquidity Preference Theory of Interest'.
39. DHR, *UAT*, pp. 78–9.
40. DHR, *LEP*, p. 390.
41. See B. F. Haley, 'Value and Distribution', Chapter 1, in the book edited by H. Ellis, op cit., p. 44.
42. See Part III.
43. DHR, 'Comments upon Mr. Johnson's Notes', *Review of Economic Studies*, Vol. 19, (1950–1) p. 106.
44. JMK, *GT*, Book IV.
45. Ibid, p. 207.
46. DHR, *LEP*, p. 390.
47. For further details on this debate see:
    (i) DHR, 'Alternative theories of the rate of interest', *EJ*, Vol. 47, (1937) pp. 428–36.
    (ii) JMK, 'The "Ex Ante" Theory of the Rate of Interest', *EJ*, Vol. 47, (1937) pp. 663–9.
    (iii) DHR, 'Mr. Keynes and Finance', *EJ*, Vol. 48, (1938) pp. 314–8.
    (iv) JMK, 'Mr. Keynes and Finance', *EJ*, Vol. 48, (1938) pp. 318–22.
    (v) DHR, 'Mr. Keynes and the rate of interest', *EMI*, pp. 150–187.
48. JMK, (as in (ii) above).
49. See Part II: 10 'Saving, Investment and the Multiplier (1936 and after)'.
50. See JMK, *CW*, Vol. XIV, pp. 207–8.
51. JMK, *CW*, Vol. XIV, p. 209.
52. Ibid, p. 209.
53. Ibid, p. 209.
54. E. S. Shaw, 'False Issues in the Interest-Theory Controversy', *Journal of Political Economy*, Vol. 46, (1938) pp. 838–56; see also DHR, *EMI*, pp. 164–5.
55. Although a good deal of the confusion resulted from a failure by DHR and JMK to clearly spell out the different definitions (e.g. of saving) being employed. (See G. Haberler, op cit., pp. 213–4). Diagrammatically the argument of this section can be represented thus:

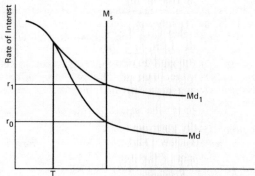

M_d = demand for cash balances/period.
T = demand for transactionary balances.
M_s = money supply.
If the demand for 'finance' increases M_d moves to M_{d1}, the rate of interest increases to r_1.
NOTE: diagram refers to *flows* of balances, and not to the demand/supply at a point in time.

56. See Part I.
57. How substantial is still a source of debate: see, for example, E. S. Shaw, op cit., p. 848.
58. See DHR, *LEP*, pp. 396ff, pp. 377ff. *EMI*, pp. 169–172. *EC*, pp. 59–64.
59. See Part II: 9 'Natural and Market Rates of Interest and the Trade Cycle'.
60. JMK, *GT*, pp. 171–2, pp. 200–1; also J. Robinson, *An Introduction to the Theory of Employment*, (London: Macmillan, 1937) pp. 76–8.
61. DHR, *EMI*, p. 169.
62. IS/LM curves are used here to analyse a dynamic situation. DHR would have been wary of such a use because of the underlying instability of the curves. We therefore need to assume '*ceteris paribus*'.
63. Note that in the liquidity-trap the rate of interest would not decline as the money supply expanded.
64. See Part II: 9 (as above).
65. DHR, *LEP*, p. 397, *EMI*, p. 170.
66. See A. Marshall, *Money, Credit and Commerce*, p. 257, also *Official Papers*, pp. 273–4, pp. 48–52.
67. In *LEP*, p. 397 DHR hints at a third possibility — that the change in M, through its influences upon prices will change 'K' bringing 'an increase in confidence which leads people to desire to devote an increased proportion of resources to real investment and so raises the demand for investible funds'. But here there is no explanation as to why this change in confidence should come about.

68. This section has particular relevance for the operation of monetary policy. Similarly, as H. Johnson argues (op cit., p. 100), the difference between DHR and JMK over the behaviour and effects of changes in 'V' in the cycle, can also be put down to a difference in assumptions. DHR develops (*LEP*, pp. 398–400) the argument linking changes in the money supply to the rate of interest, recognising that in some phases of the cycle a rise in the rate may be associated with a *fall* in prices.

69. See DHR, *LEP*, pp. 394–6. *UAT*, pp. 109–115. *EMI*, pp. 178–182.

70. See, for example, DHR, *LEP*, p. 396.

71. N. Kaldor, 'Speculation and Economic Stability', *Review of Economic Studies*, Vol. 7, (October 1939) pp. 1–27. See also J. R. Hicks, *Value and Capital*, (Clarendon Press, 1939) Ch. XI.

72. For DHR it also reflects 'the extra trouble and inconvenience to the borrower of continually renewing short loans'. DHR uses Fisher's phrase (*Theory of Interest*, (Kelley, 1930) p. 210): 'the readiness or convenience takes the place of some of the interest' (for short loans).

73. See also M. Kalecki, *Economic Fluctuations*, p. 112 and J. R. Hicks, op cit., p. 145.

74. See A. Marshall, *Principles of Economics*, (Macmillan) pp. 81–2. F. Lavington, *English Markets*, (London: Methuen & Co., 1929) esp. Ch. VI. A. C. Pigou, op cit.

75. DHR also recognised the liquidity preference theory in the writings of a Spanish Economist. See DHR, 'A Spanish Contribution to the Theory of Fluctuations'. *Economica*, (February 1940) pp. 50–65.

76. JMK, *GT*, p. 174.

77. See Part II: 14 'The Value of Money'.

78. F. Lavington, op cit., p. 30; see also A. C. Pigou, *Essays in Applied Economics*, p. 181.

79. A. Marshall, op cit. A. Pigou, op cit. F. Lavington, op cit.

80. DHR cites the following passage (A. Marshall, *Money, Credit and Commerce*, p. 254): 'it (meaning the rate of interest) may be raised to a vast height by the fears that commercial or political disturbances may soon restrict the operations of credit'.

81. See E. Eshag, op cit., pp. 65–66.

82. JMK, *CW*, Vol. XIV.

83. See, for example, E. Eshag, op cit., p. 66.

84. See especially DHR, 'Industrial Fluctuation and the Natural Rate of Interest', *EJ*, (December 1934) pp. 650–56. However the remedy may have been found with the aid of JMK. (See DHR, 'Some Notes on Mr. Keynes' General Theory of Employment', *QJE*, Nov. 1936, pp. 168–91).

85. See Part II: 7 'The Robertsonian Theory of Interest'.

86. See Part II: 9 'Natural and Market Rates of Interest and the Trade Cycle'.

87. DHR, op cit.

88. See preface to *SIF*.

89. Although it is possible to construct a loanable funds theory which

does fit into Keynesian analysis. See J. W. Conard, *The Theory of Interest*, (Univ. of California Press 1963) Ch. XII.

90. I am sure that Professor Tew would not consider himself either a businessman or speculator.

91. B. Tew, 'Interest Rates and Asset Prices', *Economica* Vol. 28, (November 1961) p. 429.

92. Letter from JMK to J. Hicks, 31st March 1937. (JMK, *CW*, Vol. XIV, pp. 79–81). For Keynes however it was the IS curve which was unstable.

93. DHR, 'The Frontiers of Economic Thought', an address to the Conference of Economics Teachers, Oxford, January 4th, 1947.

94. JMK, *GT*, pp. 96ff.

95. Letter from DHR to JMK, 10th February 1935. (JMK, *CW*, Vol. XIII, p. 506).

96. DHR, *LEP*, p. 424.

97. In *LEP*, (p. 392), there is also a further reason given: 'many kinds of capital outlay ... depend on broadly conceived estimates of the progress of whole regions' — not upon the demand for consumption goods, and these outlays are sensitive to changes in the rate of interest.

13: THE SIMILARITY OF KEYNES' AND ROBERTSON'S WORK

1. T. Wilson, 'Robertson and Effective Demand and the Trade Cycle', *EJ*, (September 1953) p. 555.

2. See Part III.

3. DHR, *SIF*, preface (1948 edition) also re-read Part I: 3 'The Robertsonian Theory of Industrial Fluctuation — An Outline'.

4. See especially Part I: 1–5.

5. See pp. 28–9.

6. JMK, *GT*, Ch. 22 is very illuminating on the similarities between DHR and JMK in their view of the trade cycle.

7. See Part III.

8. See pp. 59–63.

9. I am thinking particularly of Keynesian Growth Models associated with R. Harrod and E. Domar.

10. See pp. 170–1.

11. See Part II: 11 'Robertson and the Liquidity Preference Theory of Interest'.

12. See Part II: 4 'Robertson on Saving (1918–40)'.

13. See various articles in DHR, *EMI*. Remember J. R. Hicks' comment see pp. 85ff.

14. See pp. 85ff.

15. Letter from DHR to Professor T. Wilson 31.10.53.

14: THE VALUE OF MONEY

1. See especially D. Patinkin, *Money, Interest and Prices*, (New York: Harper & Row Ltd., 1956).
2. DHR, *Money*, 1st ed. (1922) Preface p. vii. [Note the similarity here with JMK, *Tract on Money Reform*, (London: Macmillan, 1923) see especially pp. 68ff.]
3. Ibid, p. 17, defined as the purchasing power of a unit of money.
4. Ibid, p. 28.
5. Ibid, pp. 30ff.
6. With given conditions of demand for money (and vice versa).
7. Ibid, pp. 32–33.
8. Hence Robertson viewed the quantity theory as: 'No longer either a triumphant Credo or a pestilant heresy, the "quantity theory of money" remains as a dowdy but serviceable platitude', ibid, p. 34.
9. DHR, *Money*, (1928 ed.) p. vii.
10. See Part II: 4 'Robertson on Saving (1918–40)'.
11. DHR, *Money*, (1928 ed.) p. 37.
12. Ibid, p. 39.
13. DHR, *Money*, 1st ed. p. vii.
14. E. Eshag, op cit., Ch. 1.
15. Ibid, pp. 22–3.
16. A. C. Pigou, *Essays in Applied Economics*, (London, 1917).
17. E. Eshag, op cit., p. 19.
18. Ibid, p. 19.
19. DHR, *Money*, 1st ed. pp. 89–93.
20. See Part II: 4 'Robertson on Saving (1918–40)'.
21. See Part II: 9 'Natural and Market Rates of Interest . . .'.
22. And also the constancy of R or T.
23. See Part II, Chs. 7 and 11.
24. DHR, *Money*, (1928 ed.) p. 92.
25. Ibid, p. 118.
26. Ibid, Chs. 5 and 6.
27. DHR, *BPPL*, (1926 ed.) Chs. V–VII.
28. Letter from DHR to D. Patinkin dated 7th August, 1956.
29. DHR, *BPPL*, (1926 ed.) Ch. 5, App. 2.
30. Ibid.
31. See Part II: 4 'Robertson on Saving (1918–40)'.
32. Robertson in fact hints at this in Ch. 5 where he says: 'Induced lacking occurs when, the same process that imposes Automatic Lacking on certain people having also reduced the real value of their money stocks, these people hold money off the market, and refrain from consuming the full value of their current output, in order to bring the real value of their money stocks up again to what they regard as an *appropriate* level'. (*BPPL* p. 49). The key word here appears to be *appropriate*. This seems to imply that the level of real balances need not return to its original level.

33. DHR, *BPPL* (1926 ed.) p. 60.
34. See Part II: 4 (as above).
35. DHR, *BPPL*, pp. 75–6.
36. DHR, *BPPL*, (1932 ed.) preface p. v.
37. Ibid, p. 76.
38. Ibid, p. 76.
39. See Part II: 4 'Robertson on Saving (1918–40)'.
40. An expansion phase involves both a rise in prices, because of the forced saving it generates, and a rise in production.
41. Ibid, pp. 76–7.
42. See the preface to DHR, *SIF*, (1948 ed.). Although in the Appendix to Ch. V (*BPPL*) he assumes that T is constant and in *LEP*, part 1 and 2 he assumes, in analysis not relating to industrial fluctuation, that there is a tendency to full employment. (*LEP*, p. 325).
43. See Part II: 4 (as above).
44. DHR, *Money*, 1st ed. p. 34.
45. DHR, *LEP*, p. 327.
46. Ibid, p. 333.
47. Ibid, p. 342 and also Part 3, Ch. IV.
48. Ibid, pp. 342–3.
49. Ibid, p. 345.
50. Ibid, p. 345.
51. See especially D. Patinkin, op cit., 2nd ed., (1965). Robertson's reaction is to be found in 'More Notes on the Rate of Interest', *Review of Economic Studies* Vol. 21, (1953–4) pp. 136–141. Reprinted in *EMI* p. 223. There is extensive correspondence between D. Patinkin and DHR on these issues between 1951 and 1956.
52. See the collection of articles gathered together by R. Clower in *Monetary Theory* 1st ed., (Penguin Education, 1969).
53. See Denis O'Brien *The Classical Economist*, (Oxford University Press, 1975) pp. 159–165.
54. Letter from DHR to D. Patinkin 20th May, 1951.
55. Letter from D. Patinkin to DHR 5th July, 1951.
56. G. Archibald & R. G. Lipsey, 'Monetary and Value Theory: a critique of Lange and Patinkin', *Review of Economic Studies*, Vol. 26, pp. 1–22.
57. D. Patinkin, op cit., Note G.
58. Letter from Robertson to D. Patinkin 7th August 1956. DHR continues: 'and "induced lacking" as duly recorded by me (BPPL p. 49, note) was inspired by Keynes — the pre-Keynesian Keynes who hadn't forgotten to carry real balance effects into the commodity markets'.
59. Letter from D. Patinkin to DHR 17th September 1956.
60. See pp. 194–6.
61. See Part II: 9 'Natural and Market Rates of Interest . . .'.
62. DHR, *EMT*, pp. 138–9.
63. See D. Patinkin, op cit., note (i–1) p. 622.
64. See Part II: 4 'Robertson on Saving (1918–40)'.

PART III THEORY AND POLICY — SOME CONCLUSIONS

1: ECONOMIC POLICY AND THE TRADE CYCLE

1. Letter from M. Friedman to the author, 30.11.72.
2. See especially *SIF*, and also his evidence to the Macmillan Committee.
3. An expression used by T. Wilson, op cit., p. 569.
4. In his submission to the Canadian Royal Commission on Banking and Finance (1963) he wrote: 'I do not claim to know how to hit the target or even to know how to define the target to hit'. (Essay No. 42, University of Princeton, p. 23).
5. DHR, Review of 'Purchasing Power and Trade Depression: A critique of Under-Consumption theories' (by E. Durbin), *EJ*, (1933) pp. 281–3.
6. DHR, *Money*, (1928) p. 214.
7. See Part I: 4 'The Causes of the Upturn'.
8. Part of an address given to a Liberal Summer School, 1923. Reprinted in DHR, *EF*, p. 131.
9. Part of an address 'The Frontiers of Economic Thought' to a Conference of Economics Teachers, Oxford, January 4th, 1947. (Robertson correspondence)
10. DHR, 'Wage Inflation', an unpublished paper given to the School of Central Bank Officials, Bank of England, May 27th, 1957. (Robertson correspondence)
11. P. Samuelson, 'Sir D. H. Robertson', *QJE*, No. 4, (November 1963) pp. 528–536.
12. DHR, *BPPL*, Ch. 3.
13. DHR, 'Wage Inflation'; he also called for some recorded unemployment to allow the transfer of labour between industries, arguing that the more adaptable is labour, and the greater the assistance given to it, the less the need for transitional unemployment.
14. First Report of the Cohen Council on Prices, Productivity and Incomes, (HMSO, 1957) Chapter VIII, para. 27, p. 53.
15. DHR, evidence to the Macmillan Committee, 8th and 9th May, 1930, pp. 321–47.
16. A phrase used by DHR in *SIF*.
17. See Part I: 7 'Robertson and the Alternative Theories of Industrial Fluctuation'.
18. Although DHR was aware that the existence of excess capacity would dampen the power of a change in consumer demand to stimulate more investment.
19. See Part I: 7 (as above).
20. DHR, *Money*, (1922), p. vii.
21. DHR, *SIF*, (1948), p. viii.
22. See Part II: 7 'The Robertsonian Theory of Interest'.
23. DHR, *Money*, (1928 edition).
24. e.g. DHR, *EMT*, pp. 41–2.
25. Evidence to the Macmillan Committee, para. 4898.
26. JMK was a member of the Macmillan Committee.

27. See DHR, *EMT*, pp. 60–1.
28. A phrase used by DHR in a comment upon: 'The Douglas Credit Scheme', *The Listener*, Vol. IX, (28th June, 1933) No. 233.
29. DHR, *LEP*, p. 222.
30. DHR, *UAT*, p. 87.
31. DHR, oral evidence to the Canadian Royal Commission on Banking and Finance 1962, oral evidence pp. 5125–6. (Radcliffe) Committee on the Working of the Monetary System Report. (HMSO Cmnd 827 London 1959).
32. DHR, *Memorandum submitted to the Canadian Royal Commission on Banking and Finance 1962* (Reprinted in Essays in International Finance, No. 42, May 1963, Princeton University) p. 17.
33. In particular, fiscal policy.
34. This comes out particularly in two unpublished papers by DHR, 'Credit Squeeze', and 'The Radcliffe Report'. (Robertson correspondence)
35. See Part III: 2 'Background to the Robertson–Keynes Debate'.
36. DHR, *Money*, pp. 171–2.
37. There was also a further reason suggested by DHR why this was the case (DHR, 'Credit Squeeze'). The increase in the rate of interest on loans was partially offset by a reduction in the tax burden. A marginal rate of income taxation of 50 per cent means that a 1 per cent increase in interest rates is reduced to an effective increase of $\frac{1}{2}$ per cent. Hence the interest rate rise is even less of a deterrent.
38. See Part III: 2 (as above).
39. It is a great pity that DHR never expressed a detailed opinion upon M. Friedman's policy views. He was asked by Dr. W. Mackinnon, in his oral evidence to the Canadian Commission (op cit.), to comment upon Friedman's policy recommendations, but he professed himself to be ignorant of the works of this great economist (p. 5111). He said: 'I must not claim to have studied his work properly, I can't comment on it expertly, but my hunch is that you can't get away in the last resort . . . .' Had he not been interrupted, the remainder of the text of his evidence would suggest that he would have finished the sentence by proposing that discretionary policy must be used.
40. DHR, *EMT*, p. 125.
41. See Part III: 2 'Robertson and the Price Level'.
42. See D. Moggridge, *Keynes*, (Macmillan 1976); indeed DHR himself remarked of: 'too great a disposition among the general public to believe that in the mid-1930s some revolutionary discovery was made about effective demand'. (*SIF*, p. xvii).
43. DHR, *SIF*, Part II, Ch. IV.
44. DHR, *UAT*, p. 203, see also *UAT*, p. 44.
45. Evidence given to the Macmillan Committee on May 8–9th, 1930.
46. Ibid, pp. 4873–4.
47. Ibid, p. 4883.
48. See, for example, J. L. Stein (ed.) *Monetarism*, (North Holland, 1976).
49. Evidence to the Macmillan Committee, Section 13, see especially pp. 4921ff.

50. DHR, *EF*, p. 142.
51. It is also possible to interpret this section in terms of the loanable funds theory — by shifting the demand and supply curves for loanable funds.
52. See Part II: 11 and 12.
53. DHR, *UAT*, p. 93.
54. Oral evidence to the Canadian Royal Commission on Banking and Finance, p. 5128. In fact in his evidence to the Macmillan Committee in 1930 he was aware of the time lags existing in relation to the impact of public works policies on unemployment.
55. DHR, *UAT*, p. 93.
56. Oral evidence to the Canadian Commission, p. 5184.
57. Ibid.
58. In an article entitled 'Wage Grumbles', reprinted in *EF*, pp. 42–57.
59. DHR, *LEP*, Part II, Chs. VIII to XI.
60. DHR, 'Is another slump coming?' *The Listener*, (28th July, 1937) p. 1089.
61. DHR, *LEP*, pp. 442–6.
62. A. C. Pigou, 'The Classical Stationary State', *EJ*, Vol. LIII, (1943) pp. 343–51.
63. See Part II: 4 'Robertson on Saving (1918–40)'.
64. DHR, *LEP*, p. 445.
65. Ibid, p. 446.
66. See Part I: 5 'The Theory of Crisis — From Boom to Recession'.
67. DHR, *UAT*, p. 44.
68. A phrase used by DHR in 'Mr. Lloyd's Fireworks', an address to the Marshall Society, (Cambridge, October 19th, 1961).
69. Ibid.
70. DHR, *SIF*, p. 242 and p. 246; but DHR did qualify this by pointing out that the industry with the best information service at that time (Shipbuilding) was also the most prone to fluctuation.
71. Cohen Report, op cit., pp. 38, 53.
72. Taken from 'Mr. Lloyd's Fireworks', op cit.

2: ROBERTSON AND THE PRICE LEVEL

1. DHR, *EMT*, p. 59. Reprint of a paper delivered at the London School of Economics Feb 13 1928 and published as 'Theories of Banking Policy' *Economica* June 1928.
2. First Report of the Cohen Council op cit. p. 31, para. 99.
3. See Part II: 4 'Robertson on Saving (1918–40)'.
4. DHR, *EMT*, p. 57.
5. *Cf.* JMKs view in the *Treatise on Money*.
6. DHR, *BPPL*, p. 72.
7. Letter from DHR to JMK May 1925. JMK, *CW*, Vol. XIII, p. 32.
8. DHR, *EMT*, p. 174.
9. DHR, *LEP*, p. 360.
10. Ibid, p. 361.

11. See DHRs contribution to *Monetary Policy*, a Report of a subcommittee on Currency and the Gold Standard, (King & Son Ltd., London, 1921).
12. First Report of the Cohen Council, op cit., p. 52.
13. Ibid, p. 31.
14. Ibid, p. 52.
15. DHR, *EMI*, p. 186.
16. See oral evidence to the Canadian Commission, p. 5109, p. 5150.
17. DHR, *LEP*, p. 356.
18. See DHR, *Monetary Policy*, op cit., p. 62.
19. DHR, *LEP*, p. 356, *Money*, p. 136.
20. Oral evidence to Canadian Commission, p. 5109.
21. See Part II: 4 'Robertson on Saving (1918–40)'.
22. Ibid.
23. The Cohen Report is perhaps the best illustration of this.
24. DHR, *UAT*, p. 91.
25. Ibid, p. 91: 'it was fairly evident to everybody that if an exhorbitant level of wage rates was demanded, the money would simply not be there to pay the wage bill' (writing of the pre-1914 situation in Britain).
26. DHR, 'Credit Squeeze', unpublished paper (Robertson correspondence).
27. First Report of the Cohen Council, pp. 50ff.
28. DHR, 'Wage Inflation', an address to Central Bank Officials, Bank of England, May 27th, 1957.
29. DHR, *LEP*, p. 345.
30. First Report of the Cohen Council App. VIII, p. 71.
31. Evidence to the Canadian Commission, p. 5153.
32. First Report of the Cohen Council, p. 35.
33. DHR, *UAT*, p. 94.
34. On the link between income taxes and the price level read DHR, *EF*, pp. 23–41, also 'Gold, Reparations and Tariffs', *The Listener*, (16th December, 1931) p. 1089.
35. This comes out forcibly in DHR's oral evidence to the Canadian Royal Commission pp. 5183–4.
36. Ibid, p. 5146.
37. DHR, *LEP*, p. 359. The same warning is also given in the evidence to the Canadian Commission, and in the first report of the Cohen Council.

Bibliography of the Writings of Dennis Holme Robertson

I am greatly indebted to Professor S. R. Dennison
for allowing me to use this comprehensive bibliography.

BOOKS

* denotes collection of essays and lectures mostly published previously in journals etc.

A Study of Industrial Fluctuation 1915, London: P. S. King & Son Ltd. Reprinted with a new introduction, in Reprints of Scarce Works on Political Economy (The London School of Economics and Political Science) 1948.

Money (Cambridge Economic Handbooks) 1922, London: Nisbet & Co. Ltd. Revised edition 1924: reprinted 1924, 1926, 1927. Revised edition 1928. Reprinted 1930, 1932, 1935, 1937 (with new preface), 1940, 1941, 1943, 1944, 1945, 1946. New edition (with two new chapters) 1948. Translations into Portuguese, Spanish, Japanese.

The Control of Industry (Cambridge Economic Handbooks) 1923, London: Nisbet & Co. Ltd. Reprinted 1924, 1926. Revised edition 1928. Reprinted 1930, 1933, 1936, 1941, 1943, 1945, 1946, 1947, 1948, 1949, 1954, 1955. New edition (with S. R. Dennison) 1960. Translated into Japanese.

Banking Policy and the Price Level 1926, London: P. S. King & Son Ltd. Reprinted 1926. Reprinted with revisions 1932. Reprinted in the United States of America with a new preface 1949, New York, Augustus M. Kelley.

Economic Fragments 1931, London: P. S. King & Son Ltd.

Economic Essays and Addresses (with A. C. Pigou) 1931, London: P. S. King & Son Ltd.

A Scheme for an Economic Census of India: Report by A. L. Bowley and D. H. Robertson, 1934. Government of India Press, New Delhi.

*Essays in Monetary Theory 1940 London: P. S. King & Son Ltd. Reprinted 1946, 1948, 1956. Translations into Italian and Spanish.

*Utility and All That 1952, London: George Allen & Unwin Ltd.

Britain in the World Economy (The Page-Barbour Lectures at the University of Virginia) 1953, London: George Allen & Unwin Ltd.

*Economic Commentaries 1956, London: Staples Press Ltd.

Lectures on Economic Principles 3 Volumes 1957–59, London: Staples Press Ltd. Paperback edition in one volume 1963, London: The Fontana Library. Translations into Italian, Spanish and Japanese.

Growth, Wages, Money (The Marshall Lectures at the University of Cambridge) 1960, London: Cambridge University Press.

Memorandum submitted to the Canadian Royal Commission on Banking and Finance 1962 (Reprinted in Essays in International Finance No. 42, May 1963, University of Princeton).

*Essays in Money and Interest 1966, London: Fontana Library. Selected, with a Memoir, by Sir John Hicks.

ARTICLES

Re-prints of articles, reviews etc., in the six volumes of collected essays noted under Section I above are indicated as follows:

    EF Economic Fragments

    EEA Economic Essays and Addresses

    EMT Essays in Monetary Theory

    UAT Utility and All That

    EC Economic Commentaries

    EMI Essays in Money and Interest

The essays re-printed in *Essays in Money and Interest* are all taken from the other five volumes. The five collections include the following essays not published in any other form:

Economic Fragments

'Wage Grumbles' (1930) (Reprinted in *Readings in the Theory of Income Distribution*, Blakiston, 1946, pp. 221–236)

'Family Endowment' (1924)

'Instinct and Reason' (1931)

'Chemist and Alchemist' (1914)

Economic Essays and Addresses

'The Transfer Problem' (1929) (also in *Essays in Monetary Theory*)

Essays in Monetary Theory

'Mr. Keynes and the Rate of Interest' (also in *Essays in Money and Interest*) Reprinted in *Readings in the Theory of Income Distribution*, (Blakiston, 1946) pp. 425–460.

Economic Commentaries

'Some Recent (1950–5) Writings on the Theory of Pricing Economic Verse: (1) The Marshall Plan (2) The Non-econometrician's Lament.'

EF 'A Narrative of the Coal Strike', *EJ*, (Sep. 1912) pp. 365–387.

'Philosophical Liberalism and Compulsory Military Service', *Cambridge Review*, (22nd May, 1913).

'Some Material for the Study of Trade Fluctuations', *Journal of the Royal Statistical Society*, (Jan. 1914) pp. 159–173.

EF 'What is Force and Why Resist It?', *War and Peace*, (July 1914).

'A Reminiscence', By a Territorial Officer. *War and Peace*, (Mar. 1915).

'An Open Letter to One who Wants to Stop the War', By A Territorial Officer. *War and Peace*, (May 1915).

EF 'Economic Incentive', *Economica*, (Oct. 1921) pp. 231–245.

EF 'The Slump in Shipping and Shipbuilding', *Manchester Guardian Commercial Supplement* "Reconstruction in Europe", (May 18th 1922) pp. 71–76.

'Women and Cambridge University', *Nation and Athenaeum*, (7th July 1923).

EF 'A Word for the Devil', *Economica*, (Nov. 1923) pp. 203–208.

EF 'The Ebb and Flow of Unemployment': Pamphlet published by the Daily News Ltd. *The New Way Series* No. 6, (1923).

'Those Empty Boxes', *EJ*, (Mar. 1924) pp. 16–31.

EEA, EMT 'A Note on the Real Ratio of International Exchange', *EJ*, (June 1924) pp. 286–291.

EF 'A Narrative of the General Strike', *EJ*, (Sep. 1926) pp. 375–93.

EF 'The Colwyn Committee, The Income Tax and The Price Level', *EJ*, (Dec. 1927) pp. 566–581.

EEA, EMT, EMI 'Theories of Banking Policy', *Economica*, (June 1928) pp. 131–146.

EEA 'The Monetary Doctrines of Messrs. Foster and Catchings', *QJE*, (May 1929) pp. 413–499.

'"Fair Wages" and "Net Advantages"', *EJ*, (Dec. 1929) pp. 643–645.

'Lahore and After', *The Nation and Athenaeum*, (4th Jan. 1930).

'Increasing Returns and the Representative Firm', *EJ*, (March 1930) pp. 79–89, 92–93.

EEA 'Memorandum of Evidence', Submitted to the *(Macmillan) Committee on Finance and Industry*, (Apr. 1930).

'How do we want Gold to behave?' *The International Gold Problem*, Royal Institute of International Affairs, (London 1930).

'Suspense in India', *The Nation and Athenaeum*, (10th May 1930).

'Mr. Keynes' Theory of Money', *EJ*, (Sep. 1931) pp. 395–411.

EMT 'A Visit to the Laccadive Islands', Broadcast talk, reprinted in *The Listener*, (1931).

EMT, EMI 'The 1931 Crisis', *The Cambridge Review*, (Oct. 1931).

'Why Does Poverty Continue?' Six broadcast talks, reprinted in *The Listener*, (Nov.–Dec. 1931).

'Monetary Policy and the Trade Slump', *The Highway*, (Mar. 1933). This is a comment on an article in the previous issue by E. M. F. Durbin entitled 'Do we Really Lack Purchasing Power?' See also the review of Durbin's book *Purchasing Power and Trade Depression* in *EJ* (June 1933).

EMT, EMI 'Der Stand und die nächste Zukunft der Konjunkturforschung' *Festschrift fur Arthür Speithof*, (Munich 1933) pp. 238–242.

'The Douglas Credit Scheme', *The Listener*, (28th June 1933) pp. 1005–6, 1039–40.

EMT, EMI 'A Note on the Theory of Money', *Economica*, (Aug. 1933) pp. 243–247.

EMT, EMI 'Saving and Hoarding', *EJ*, (Sep. 1933) pp. 399–413.

'A Reply to J. M. Keynes and R. G. Hawtrey on Saving and Hoarding', *EJ*, (Dec. 1933) pp. 709–712.

'Mr. Harrod and the Expansion of Credit', *Economica*, (Nov. 1934) pp. 473–475.

EMI 'Industrial Fluctuation and the Natural Rate of Interest', *EJ*, (Dec. 1934) pp. 650–56.

EMT, EMI 'The State and Economic Fluctuation', Paper delivered at the Harvard Tercentenary Conference of Arts and Sciences, (1936). In *EMT* and *EMI* entitled 'The Snake and the Worm'.

'Is Another Slump Coming?', *The Listener*, (28th July 1937) pp. 174–5.

EMT, EMI 'The Trade Cycle — An Academic View', *Lloyds Bank Review*, (Sep. 1937) pp. 502–11.

'Alternative Theories of the Rate of Interest', *EJ*, (Sep. 1937) pp. 428–436.

EMT, EMI 'A Survey of Modern Monetary Controversy', *Manchester School*, Vol. IX No. 1, (1938) pp. 1–19.

EMT 'The Future of International Trade', *EJ*, (March 1938) pp. 1–14.

'Changes in International Demand and The Terms of Trade', *QJE*, (May 1938) pp. 539–540.

'Mr. Keynes and "Finance"', *EJ*, (June 1938) pp. 314–318.

'Mr. Keynes and "Finance"', (Reply to Keynes), *EJ* (Sep. 1938) pp. 555–556.

'Indemnity Payments and Gold Movements', *QJE*, (Feb. 1939) pp. 312–314. Also Reply by J. Viner, pp. 314–317 and Rejoinder by D.H.R., p. 317.

EMT, EMI 'British Monetary Policy', *Lloyds Bank Review*, (May 1939) pp. 146–157.

'Mr. Clark and The Foreign Trade Multiplier', *EJ*, (June 1939) pp. 354–356.

'A Spanish Contribution to the Theory of Fluctuations', *Economica*, (Feb. 1940) pp. 50–65.

'The Post War Monetary Plans', *EJ*, (Dec. 1943) pp. 352–360.

'The Inter-relations of Shifts in Demand', *Review of Economic Studies*, Vol. XII(1), (1944) pp. 71–72.

UAT 'The Problem of Exports', *EJ*, (Dec. 1945) pp. 321–325.

UAT 'Is there a Future for Banking?' *The Banker*, (Nov. 1946) pp. 77–81.

'Some Notes on Mr. Keynes' General Theory of Employment', *QJE*, (Nov. 1936) pp. 168–191.

'Some Reflections on the Controlled Economy', *Amsterdam Economics Faculty Year Book*, (Dec. 1946) pp. 1–7.

UAT 'The Economic Outlook', *EJ*, (Dec. 1947) pp. 421–437. (Presidential Address to Section F of the British Association for the Advancement of Science, Dundee 1947).

UAT 'Does Britain Face Collapse?' *Melbourne Argus*, (1948).

UAT 'Western European Economic Union', *The Listener*, (2nd Sep. 1948).

UAT, EMI 'What has happened to the Rate of Interest?' *Three Banks Review*, (Mar. 1949) pp. 15–31.

UAT 'Britain and European Recovery', *Lloyds Bank Review*, (July 1949) pp. 1–13.

UAT 'On Sticking to One's Last', *EJ*, (Dec. 1949) pp. 505–509. (Presidential Address to the Royal Economic Society, 1949).

UAT 'A Revolutionist's Handbook', *QJE*, (Feb. 1950) pp. 1–14. Review article of "A Survey of Contemporary Economics", edited Howard S. Ellis.

UAT 'Utility and All That', *Manchester School*, (May 1951) pp. 111–142.

UAT 'The Terms of Trade', *International Social Science Bulletin*, (Spring 1951).

'Phillip Barrett Whale 1898–1950', *EJ*, (June 1951) pp. 439–442.

UAT 'British National Investment Policy', *Nationalekonomiska Föreningens Förhandlingar*, (Oct. 1951) pp. 63–77.

'Comments on Mr. Johnson's Notes', *Review of Economic Studies*, Vol. XIX(2), (1951–2) pp. 105–110 (Mr. Johnson's Notes are entitled 'Some Cambridge Controversies in Monetary Theory', *Review of Economic Studies*, Vol. XIX(2), (1951–52) pp. 90–104. The "order of the topics . . . follows very closely" Robertson's Essay 'Mr. Keynes and the Rate of Interest'.

UAT, EMI 'Some Notes on the Theory of Interest', In *Money, Trade and Economic Growth*, Essays in Honour of John Henry Williams, (New York, 1951) pp. 193–209.

'Die Austausch verhältnisse im Aussenhaudel', *Zeitschrift für Nationaloekonomie*, (Vienna, Jan. 1952) pp. 377–383.

'Comments on Monetary Policy and the Crisis', *Oxford Institute of Statistics Bulletin*, (Apr.–May 1952) pp. 154–56.

'Sir Hubert Henderson', *EJ*, (Dec. 1953) pp. 923–931.

EC, EMI 'More Notes on The Rate of Interest', *Review of Economic Studies*, Vol. 21 No. 2, (1954) pp. 136–141.

'The Path of Progress towards Currency Convertibility', *Optima*, (1954) pp. 1–4.

EC, EMI 'Thoughts on meeting some Important Persons', *QJE*, (May 1954) pp. 181–190.

EC 'La Convertibilidad', *Moneda y Credito*, (Madrid, Sep. 1954) pp. 15–17.

EC 'Utility and All What?' *EJ*, (Dec. 1954) pp. 665–678.

'Sir Henry Clay', *Year Book of the American Philosophical Society*, (1954) pp. 406–409.

EC 'Wages', The Stamp Memorial Lecture 1954. (University of London, Athlone Press 1955) 18 p.

EC, EMI 'The Problem of Creeping Inflation', *Times Review of Industry*, (Mar. 1955) pp. ii–iv.

'La Convertibilidad', *Revista de la Facultad de Ciencias Economicas y Administracion de Montevideo*, (June 1955) pp. 101–114.

EC 'The Role of Persuasion in Economic Affairs', *National Okonomisk Tidsskrift*, (1955) pp. 193–204.

'What All is Utility? A Rejoinder', *EJ*, (Sep. 1955) p. 410.

'Keynes and Supply Functions', *EJ*, (Sep. 1955) pp. 474–477.

EC 'The Trade Cycle in the Post-War World', *Proceedings of International Economic Association Conference*, (Oxford, 1952; Macmillan, 1955).

EC 'What does the Economist Economize?' *Proceedings of Conference on National Policy for Economic Welfare at Home and Abroad*, (Columbia University, May 1954; Doubleday & Co. New York, 1955).

'Keynes and Supply Functions', *EJ*, (Sep. 1956) pp. 485–487.

'Some Marshallian Concepts', *EJ*, (June 1959) pp. 382–384.

'A Squeak from Aunt Sally', *The Banker*, (Dec. 1959) pp. 1–5.

'A Comment on "The Erosion of Marshall's Theory of Value" by Peter Newman', *QJE*, (Nov. 1960) pp. 600–601.

'Another Comment (On Elasticity of Derived Demand)', *Oxford Economic Papers*, (Oct. 1961) p. 266.

'An American "Radcliffe" Report', *Lloyds Bank Review*, (Jan. 1962) pp. 16–26.

'Welfare Criteria', *EJ*, (Mar. 1962) pp. 226–229.

'A Note on an Ambiguity in Supply Curves', *EJ*, (Mar. 1962) pp. 250–251.

'The Variorum Edition of Marshall's "Principles"', *EJ*, (Sep. 1962) pp. 677–684.

Index